ALBERTA

A Health System Profile

Alberta: A Health System Profile provides the first detailed description of Alberta's health care system and the underpinning political and social forces that have shaped it. Drawing on significant wealth from government revenues generated through the energy sector, Alberta has been able to develop an extensive public health and health care infrastructure.

Alberta has used its financial resources to attract health professionals by offering the highest levels of financial compensation in Canada. However, although it spends more per capita than other Canadian jurisdictions, Alberta's health care system costs and health outcomes are mediocre compared to those of many other Canadian jurisdictions. This unexpected outcome is the consequence of the unique interplay of economic and political forces within Alberta's political economy.

Through an examination of Alberta's political and economic history, and using research on the structures and services provided, *Alberta: A Health Systems Profile* provides a detailed description of the programs and services that constitute Alberta's health care system.

(Provincial and Territorial Health System Profiles)

JOHN CHURCH is a professor in the Department of Political Science at the University of Alberta.

NEALE SMITH is a research coordinator at the Centre for Clinical Epidemiology and Evaluation at the University of British Columbia.

Provincial and Territorial Health System Profiles

Series Editor: Gregory P. Marchildon, Director of the North American Observatory on Health Systems and Policies

This series of provincial and territorial health system profiles is sponsored and directed by the North American Observatory on Health Systems and Policies, a collaborative partnership of academic researchers, governments, and health organizations promoting evidence-informed health policy decision-making.

ALBERTA

A HEALTH SYSTEM PROFILE

John Church and Neale Smith

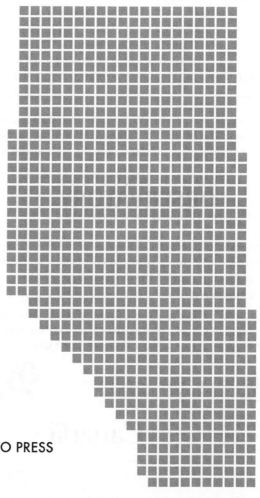

UNIVERSITY OF TORONTO PRESS
Toronto Buffalo London

© University of Toronto Press 2022
Toronto Buffalo London
utorontopress.com
Printed and bound by CPI Group (UK) Ltd, Croydon, CR0 4YY

ISBN 978-1-4875-0752-7 (cloth) ISBN 978-1-4875-3642-8 (EPUB)
ISBN 978-1-4875-2516-3 (paper) ISBN 978-1-4875-3641-1 (PDF)

Library and Archives Canada Cataloguing in Publication

Title: Alberta : a health system profile / John Church, Neale Smith.
Names: Church, John, 1961–, author. | Smith, Neale (Research coordinator),
    author.
Series: Provincial and territorial health system profiles.
Description: Series statement: Provincial and territorial health system profiles |
    Includes bibliographical references and index.
Identifiers: Canadiana (print) 20210329629 | Canadiana (ebook) 20210329718 |
    ISBN 9781487507527 (cloth) | ISBN 9781487525163 (paper) |
    ISBN 9781487536428 (EPUB) | ISBN 9781487536411 (PDF)
Subjects: LCSH: Medical care – Alberta. | LCSH: Medical policy – Alberta.
Classification: LCC RA395.C3 C58 2022 | DDC 362.1097123 – dc23

We wish to acknowledge the land on which the University of Toronto Press
operates. This land is the traditional territory of the Wendat, the Anishnaabeg,
the Haudenosaunee, the Métis, and the Mississaugas of the Credit First Nation.

This series of provincial and territorial health system profiles is sponsored and
directed by the North American Observatory on Health Systems and Policies,
a collaborative partnership of academic researchers, governments, and health
organizations promoting evidence-informed health policy decision-making.

University of Toronto Press acknowledges the financial support of the Government of Canada, the Canada Council for the Arts, and the Ontario Arts
Council, an agency of the Government of Ontario, for its publishing activities.

To our families and friends who support us in all that we do

Contents

Figures, Tables, and Box

Figures

Tables

Box

Series Editor's Foreword

There is not, and has never been, a single Canadian health system. As subnational jurisdictions in one of the most decentralized federations in the world, provincial and territorial governments are the principle stewards for publicly financed health services and coverage in Canada. This makes it very difficult to describe the "Canadian system," much less compare Canada's system to national health systems in the rest of the world. These were the key challenges I faced when I researched and wrote the two editions of the *Health Systems in Transition (HiT)* study on Canada for the European Observatory on Health Systems and Policies and the World Health Organization (Marchildon, 2006, 2013; Marchildon & Allin, 2020). The *HiT* template was prepared for the comparative review of national health systems (Rechel, Maresso, & van Ginneken, 2019). In order to generalize at the pan-Canadian level of analysis, I was forced to make a number of adjustments and compromises.

This experience convinced me that a series of provincial and territorial health system profiles would be of great utility to decision-makers, providers, scholars, and students alike. I experimented with adapting the *HiT* template to the provincial context with an initial profile of the Saskatchewan health system (Marchildon & O'Fee, 2007). This was followed a few years later by a profile of Nunavut based on a two-year study of the health system of that vast northern Canadian territory (Marchildon & Torgerson, 2013).

In 2013, I began looking for lead authors to take on the task of researching and writing individual provincial and territorial health system profiles. The University of Toronto Press agreed to publish the series on the understanding that the content would eventually be made freely available after the first year of publication through the North American

Observatory on Health Systems and Policies (NAO). The purpose of the NAO is to examine and compare health systems and policies across jurisdictions, principally at the provincial and state level, and this series delivers an important component of that work for Canada. It is our hope that, eventually, similar subnational studies will be initiated in the United States and Mexico, although the current *HiT* analyses for both countries outline the significance of the role of subnational health systems (Rice, Rosenau, Unrah, & Barnes., 2021; González Block et al., 2021).

Each volume in this series focuses on the system and policies within an individual province or territory. A subject matter template was developed requiring a diamond-hard focus on the jurisdiction in question – a single case study – with some compulsory data tables and figures putting that jurisdiction in a more pan-Canadian context. This case-study approach, relying heavily on the grey literature, is essential given the lack of any extensive secondary literature on the health systems and policies in most jurisdictions. Wherever possible, however, the authors have been encouraged to link critical health system and policy challenges in their particular province or territory to the scholarly literature that focuses on the issue. The overall intent of this series is to provide a baseline for future scholarly work and to encourage the development of a richer comparative literature on provincial and territorial health systems and policies.

Templates of the sort used in this series must also be flexible enough to allow authors the flexibility to focus on areas that may be unique to the jurisdiction in question. As a consequence, individual volume authors were encouraged to go beyond the template as long as they could keep the length of the profile reasonable. In addition, the provinces and territories vary considerably in size – both in population and geography – and both in fiscal and administrative capacity. These facts also speak to allowing some flexibility within the template. In the end, however, target lengths were set for the volumes with one principle in mind: to achieve a comfortable balance between studies that are concise enough to be of use to busy decision-makers and providers but still detailed enough to be of utility for scholars and students.

Although provincial and territorial health policies and programs are nested within a pan-Canadian system in which the federal government as well as intergovernmental venues and organizations can play an important role, authors were asked to focus on their particular provincial or territorial system. For example, the Canada Health Act and the federal hospital and medical care legislation that preceded it were instrumental in shaping provincial and territorial "Medicare" regulatory and policy approaches. However, there are important variations in provincial and territorial Medicare laws, policies, and approaches across Canada, and these have not been adequately described, much less compared. Those readers interested in a national health system study or pan-Canadian – whether federal or intergovernmental – policy initiatives and structures are encouraged to consult the existing *HiT* study on Canada, now in its third edition. In many respects, the Canada *HiT* – published by both the WHO Regional Office for Europe (on behalf of the European Observatory) and the University of Toronto Press – should be treated as a contributing volume in the series. This approach avoids repetition among individual volumes while economizing on the page length of each book.

It is important to note that the data tables required of all the provincial and territorial studies rely heavily on two very different sources. The first are the data held by the Canadian Institute for Health Information, an organization that has put considerable effort into ensuring that administrative and financial data have been defined and collected in ways that make it usefully comparable. The second are the data from provincial and territorial ministries of health. Here, we can make few guarantees of comparability across jurisdictions, although the authors have been asked to be as precise as possible about the meaning assigned to terms by individual governments.

Each volume in this series has been put through the University of Toronto Press's peer-review process. While this review has lengthened the time to publication – a significant consideration in contemporary policy studies of this type – we felt that the importance of peer review outweighed the cost of the time involved. Moreover, we felt that these volumes contain much that is of permanent value, and therefore publishing through a highly reputable academic publisher would ensure longevity in a way that cannot be matched by relying solely on web-based, electronic dissemination. Indeed, in our unique arrangement with the University of Toronto Press, we hope we have achieved the best of two worlds: the high scholarly standards that come with traditional academic publication *and* the widest possible dissemination that comes with internet-based distribution one year after paper publication.

It is my hope that these studies will form the essential foundation for future comparative health system and policy study in Canada. They should be seen as a place for researchers to begin their case study or comparative health systems and policy research. No doubt we will refine and improve the template for future editions of these provincial and territorial profiles, so we encourage your feedback as interested readers.

Building on their already extensive knowledge of the Alberta health system, John Church and Neale Smith have done a remarkable job of creating a narrative out of disparate primary and secondary sources. From the introduction of health regions to their elimination in favour of a single provincial authority, Alberta has been in the forefront of major structural health system change in Canada. Church and Smith provide us with a ringside view of these and other system and policy changes. We are grateful that they have devoted so much of their time and energy these past three years in researching, writing, and preparing this volume for publication. I would also like to thank Sara Allin, the director of operations for the NAO, for her editorial advice and efforts, as well as the anonymous peer reviewers.

Gregory P. Marchildon, Series Editor
Professor and Ontario Research Chair in Health Policy
and System Design
Institute of Health Policy, Management and Evaluation
University of Toronto

REFERENCES

González Block, M.A., Reyes, H., Cahuana Hurtado, L., Méndez, E., & Balandrán, A. (2021). *Health systems in transition: Mexico*. Toronto, ON: University of Toronto Press.

Marchildon, G.P. (2006). *Health systems in transition: Canada*. Copenhagen: WHO Regional Office for Europe on behalf of the European Observatory on Health Systems and Policies. Subsequently published by the University of Toronto Press in 2007.

Marchildon, G.P. (2013). *Health systems in transition: Canada* (2nd ed.). Copenhagen: WHO Regional Office for Europe on behalf of the European Observatory on Health Systems and Policies. Simultaneously published by the University of Toronto Press in 2013.

Marchildon, G.P., & Allin, S. (2020). *Health systems in transition: Canada* (3rd ed.). Copenhagen, DK: WHO Reginal Office for Europe on behalf of the European Observatory on Health Systems and Policies. Subsequently published by the University of Toronto Press in 2021.

Marchildon, G.P., & O'Fee, K. (2007). *Health care in Saskatchewan: An analytical profile*. Regina, SK: Canadian Plains Research Center.

Marchildon, G.P., & Torgerson, R. (2013). *Nunavut: A health system profile.* Montreal, QC: McGill-Queen's University Press.

Rechel, B., Maresso, A., & van Ginneken, E. (2019). *Health systems in transition: Template for authors.* Copenhagen, DK: WHO Regional Office for Europe on behalf of the European Observatory on Health Systems and Policies. Retrieved from https://www.euro.who.int/__data/assets/pdf_file/0009/393498/HiT-template-for-web-for-authors-2019.pdf

Rice, T., Rosenau, P., Unruh, L.Y., & Barnes, A.J. (2021). *Health systems in transition: USA.* Toronto: University of Toronto Press.

Preface and Acknowledgments

As part of a series of books on provincial and territorial health care systems in Canada, *Alberta: A Health System Profile* offers the first comprehensive overview of the health care system for the province of Alberta. While it is largely descriptive, it also contains an overall assessment of the performance of the system based on comparative empirical data and periodic evaluations conducted by governmental and non-governmental agencies. Chapter 1 provides an overview of the geographic, political, economic, and health attributes that are unique to Alberta and contribute to the shape of its health care system. Chapter 2 provides an overview of the organizational evolution of the health care system up until and including the 1990s and the current overall regulatory and benefits framework. Chapter 3 outlines the patterns of health spending and finance that have shaped Alberta's health care system. Chapter 4 outlines the physical infrastructure of the health care system. Chapter 5 provides a detailed overview of the health workforce that make the system work and the challenges associated with sustaining this workforce. Chapter 6 examines the range of services and programs that are provided. Chapter 7 examines reforms to the health care system that have taken place since the beginning of the twenty-first century. Chapter 8 provides an assessment of Alberta's health care system based on comparisons with several other Canadian jurisdictions and several authoritative external reviews completed in recent years. In Chapter 9, the major trends identified throughout the book are discussed.

While the book is structured and organized according to a standardized template developed for the series, there are some inherent limitations. For example, for the reader who wants to have an integrated historical overview of the organization and governance of the system, reading chapters 2 and 7 together might provide it. A second challenge presented by the book is the relative unevenness in the presentation of statistical information. The earlier chapters tend to be more Alberta-centric, as we are trying to describe Alberta's health system and population in detail. As the story unfolds in later chapters, we begin to shift from description to assessment and increasingly draw comparisons with other Canadian jurisdictions. This is especially the case in chapters 5 and 8.

Another limitation in the presentation of statistical information is that the time frame is not standardized. The lack of standardization reflects the fact that information on different indicators is collected on an annual basis in some cases and only periodically in others. Despite these disparities, we have attempted to provide the most up-to-date and reliable comparative information that was available while writing the book. The good news is that publicly available data is getting better in terms of both quality and the regularity of reporting!

The authors would like to thank and acknowledge the contributions of Joshua Bergman, Steve Buick, William Church, Q.C., Erwin and Dawn Friesen, David Harrigan, and Donna Smith, who provided input and feedback on various aspects of the book. We also acknowledge the generous support and guidance of Greg Marchildon (series editor) and Sara Allin. Finally, we thank Meg Patterson, Carolyn Zapf, and the other editorial staff at the University of Toronto Press for their patience and guidance in transforming our work into a finished product.

Having said this, as authors, we assume full responsibility for any errors or omissions.

Acronyms

AADAC	Alberta Alcohol and Drug Abuse Commission
ABF	activity-based funding
ACB	Alberta Cancer Board
ACH	Alberta Children's Hospital
AHFMR	Alberta Heritage Foundation for Medical Research
AHFRC	Alberta Health Facilities Review Committee
AHS	Alberta Health Services
AIHS	Alberta Innovates – Health Solutions
AISH	assured income for severely handicapped
ALC	Alternative Level of Care
AMA	Alberta Medical Association
ARP	alternate relationship plans
BLS	basic life support
BSL 4	Biological Safety Level Four
CAM	complementary and alternative medicine
CBS	Canadian Blood Services
CDR	Common Drug Review
CFIA	Canadian Food Inspection Agency
CFO	confined feeding operation
CHA	Canada Health Act
CHC	community health centre
CIHI	Canadian Institute for Health Information
CIHR	Canadian Institutes of Health Research
CLS	Calgary Laboratory Services
CPAR	Central Patient Attachment Registry
CPSA	College of Physicians and Surgeons of Alberta
CSH	Canada Health Transfer

CST	Canada Social Transfer
DIAL	diagnostic imaging and laboratory
EGM	electronic gaming machine
EHDI	early hearing intervention and detection program
EHR	electronic health record
EMR	electronic medical record
EMR	emergency medical responder
EPF	Established Programs Financing
FCC	family care clinic
FCSS	Family and Community Support Services
HACCP	Hazard Analysis Critical Control Point
HQCA	Health Quality Council of Alberta
LPN	licensed practical nurse
LTC	long-term care
LULU	local unwanted land use
MHDL	Medicine Hat Diagnostic Laboratory
MSI	Medical Services Incorporated
NML	National Microbiology Laboratory
NP	nurse practitioner
NPG	New Public Governance
NPM	New Public Management
PAR	Physician Achievement Review Program
PCBF	Patient/Care-Based Funding
pCODR	pan-Canadian Oncology Drug Review
PCN	primary care network
POSP	Physician Office System Program
P3	public-private partnership
RHA	regional health authority
RN	registered nurse
SL	supportive living
SNC	strategic clinical network
STBBI	sexually transmitted and blood-borne infection
STI	sexually transmitted infection
UCC	urgent care centre
UFA	United Farmers of Alberta
VLT	video lottery terminal
WCB	Workers' Compensation Board
WHMIS	Workplace Hazardous Materials Information System

ALBERTA

A Health System Profile

Chapter One

Introduction and Overview

Since the discovery of oil in Alberta in 1947, Alberta has leveraged significant financial resources to develop and expand infrastructure, services, and programs. Within the span of six decades, the provincial economy has been transformed from one that was based mainly on agriculture to one that has diversified but is significantly tied to the fortunes of the oil and gas industry. Prior to the pandemic of 2020, Alberta was the fastest growing economy in Canada and considered to be the economic engine of the national economy.

During this time, the population has become predominantly urban, nearly doubling in size since 1991. A more nuanced look at the provincial population reveals a population that is younger than the Canadian average (which generally implies lower needs and therefore lower health service costs) and has a significant Indigenous component (which can imply higher needs and therefore costs, given the significant health disparity gap between Indigenous and non-Indigenous residents). Both of these demographics have added to the population health complexities that define Alberta.

These economic and geographic changes have been both a blessing and a curse. While Alberta boasts some of the best health care services in Canada, the lifestyle associated with the turbulent nature of its economy has created some significant social and health challenges for Albertans. This chapter will provide an overview of the economic, social, and political contexts in Alberta as a modern petrostate and the associated health benefits and challenges (Urquhart, 2010).[1] The advantages

---

1 A petrostate is defined as a government jurisdiction that depends on oil and gas for 25 per cent or more of government revenues.

include significant taxation revenues from resource sources that can be directed to health spending, as well as a demographically young population due to in-migration from other provinces and countries during the boom times when oil and gas prices are high. The disadvantages include precipitous falls in government revenues and economic activity, with consequent cuts to health budgets when oil and gas prices collapse (Marchildon & Di Matteo, 2015; Duckett, 2015). Physicians, nurses, and other health workers also tend to be paid more in Alberta than in other provinces, generally a one-way ratchet that forces the provincial government to cut other expenses including administrative overhead during economic downturn (Leonard & Sweetman, 2015; Duckett, 2015). In these periods, successive provincial administrations have relied on an array of cost-containment strategies including setting spending caps, budgets at the provider level, and volume controls, as well as, most controversially, budget shifting from public to private household budgets. While these are strategies common to other governments (Stabile et al., 2013), they have often taken a more radical form in Alberta.

1.1 Geography and demography

Spanning 661,848 kilometres, Alberta is the fourth largest province, covering almost 7 per cent of Canada's landmass.[2] The diverse landscape embraces mountains, glaciers, foothills, lakes, rivers, forests, badlands, wetlands, and open plains (Figure 1.1). Included in this diversity are the semi-arid badlands of southern Alberta, the location of some of the world's most important paleontological finds. Dinosaur Provincial Park is a UNESCO World Heritage Site (Statistics Canada, 2011, 2016b).

Alberta (along with Saskatchewan) became a province on 1 September 1905, making it one of the newest provinces in Canada. Bounded by British Columbia on its western border, Saskatchewan on its eastern border, the Northwest Territories to the north, and the United States (Montana) to the south, it is the most populous of the three prairie provinces with an estimated population of 4,330,206 as of the end of 2018 (Statistics Canada, 2019).

Approximately 79 per cent of the province's people live in urban areas (cities and towns combined). The two major census metropolitan areas of Calgary and Edmonton are home to 69 per cent of the

---

2 For comparison purposes, France has a land mass of 650,000 square miles and a population of 67 million.

Figure 1.1 Map of Alberta, Canada

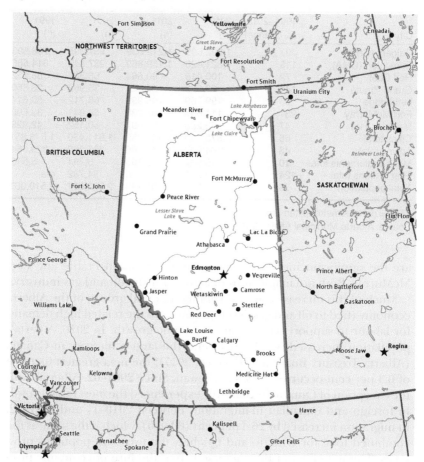

Source: Onestopmap, n.d.

province's population. Of the total population, nearly 75 per cent is concentrated in a north–south industrial corridor stretching between Edmonton and Calgary. Roughly located in the geographic centre of the province, the provincial capital of Edmonton is a major service and supply hub for the oil and gas industry and other resource development in the province (O'Brien Institute of Public Health, n.d.). Alberta also has the largest growing population in Canada. Since 1991, the total population has increased by 61 per cent (Table 1.1). Of particular note

Table 1.1 Alberta population

City	1991–2018 (% change)	2018 (n)	2011 (n)	2001 (n)	1991 (n)
Calgary (CMA)	97	1,392,609	1,214,839	951,395	708,593
Edmonton (CMA)	115	1,321,426	1,159,869	937,845	614,665
Red Deer	72	100,418	90,564	68,308	58,252
Grand Prairie	141	69,088	50,227	35,962	28,350
Lethbridge	65	99,769	105,999	68,712	60,614
Fort McMurray	231	111,687	101,238	56,841	33,698
Medicine Hat	47	63,260	61,097	50,152	42,929
Cities total	66	2,875,383	2,421,350	1,911,430	1,678,851
Towns total	43	484,977	444,906	387,230	329,654
Métis settlements total	10	5,532	8,106	5,294	5,590
First Nations total	124	128,351	65,689	54,782	n/a
Total population	73	4,330,206	3,651,143	2,962,664	2,510,001

CMA = census metropolitan area
Source: Alberta Municipal Affairs, 2019.

are the significant increases in population in Grand Prairie and Fort McMurray. Both are major hubs of activity for the oil and gas industry.

Much of this increase can be attributed to rapid growth of the Alberta economy (tied to oil and gas development) and the related high demand for labour to support accelerating economic growth. In 2016, Alberta's population increased by 11.6 per cent, the largest increase in Canada (Alberta Treasury Board and Finance, 2017); the next greatest increase of 6.3 per cent occurred in Saskatchewan. Since 2001–02, Alberta (with the exception of Ontario in 2009–10) experienced the most rapid growth in foreign and Canadian in-migration. Between 2010–11 and 2011–12, in-migration increased by 26.4 per cent (80,000), which is the same as the combined total for Ontario and Quebec, the two most populous provinces. The net effect of this increase is that the lure of economic prosperity attracts a large number of young Canadians and (increasingly) foreign workers to Alberta, making it statistically the youngest provincial population in Canada with only 11.4 per cent of the population over the age of 65 (Statistics Canada, 2012). Figure 1.2 breaks down Alberta's population by age and sex. The rapid population growth and increasing population diversity has placed significant strains on infrastructure.

In 2015, Alberta's population growth was 1.8 per cent, down from 2.8 per cent between 2012 and 2014. The population growth slowdown continued through 2017, relative to a continuing economic decline tied to the falling global price of oil.

Figure 1.2 Distribution of population by age and sex as of 31 March 2017

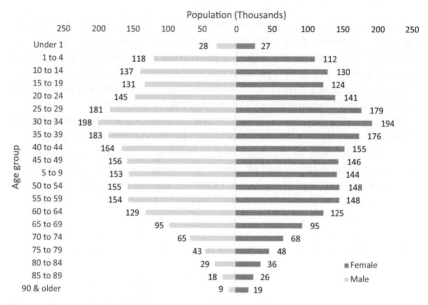

Source: Alberta Health, 2017a.

While 80 per cent of Albertans speak English, Alberta is ethnically diverse and becoming increasingly so. Aside from the typical Canadian mix of UK immigrants (England, Scotland, Wales, and Ireland) comprising approximately two-thirds of Alberta's population, there are significant German (19.2 per cent), French (11.1 per cent), and Ukrainian (9.7 per cent) populations. Other groups include Dutch, Polish, First Nations, Norwegian, Chinese, and East Indian. Alberta is the third most ethnically diverse population in Canada, after Ontario and British Columbia, and is home to the second highest proportion of francophones in western Canada. It also has an Indigenous (including Métis and Inuit) population that in recent years has been growing at a greater rate than the general population. Between 1996 and 2006, Alberta's visible minority populations grew by 58.5 per cent (Alberta Finance and Enterprise, Demography Unit, 2011). Alberta's population growth is expected to be the highest of all Canadian provinces over the next 25 years, expanding from approximately 4 million in 2013 to between 5.6 and 6.8 million by 2038. Increased ethnic and racial diversity will play a significant role in this growth (Statistics Canada, 2016a).

1.2 Political context

Alberta is unique because it has had virtual one-party rule for longer periods of time than any other Canadian jurisdiction. Moreover, Albertans have never re-elected a provincial political party once it has been defeated. While this pattern has sometimes been attributed to ideological homogeneity (politically conservative), there are several contributing factors (Macpherson, 2013; Stewart & Archer, 2001).

First, the distribution of constituencies (favouring less populated rural ridings), combined with the nature of the voting system (first-past-the-post), have tended to result in large majorities and long incumbencies. For example, in roughly half of Alberta elections, more than half the voters did not vote for the winning party. However, during the history of Alberta, only five political parties have been elected to government, with only five changes of governing party. Only three elections have resulted in anything approaching a significant Official Opposition. Colloquially referred to as having a "herd mentality," Albertans have never elected a minority government, preferring instead to either stampede towards one political party or not to show up to vote as a protest against the ruling regime.

Second, ideologically, Albertans have elected primarily right-of-centre parties since 1935 (Stefanick, 2013, p. 4; Rennie, 2004a). This pattern has led political analysts to refer to Alberta as having a one-party dominant political system. Longevity of governance has embedded a sense of inevitability and entitlement in Alberta's political culture, reinforced by institutional changes that have weakened accountability (Patten, 2015, p. 256; Stefanick, 2013). Increasingly, Albertans have also been less likely to turn out to vote. While the overall pattern of one-party dominance was briefly disrupted by the election of the New Democrats (a centre-left party) in 2015 – after four decades of rule by the Progressive Conservatives – the election of a newly configured United Conservative Party (centre-right) in 2019 seems to reaffirm the one-party dominant thesis.

Third, since the election of Ernest Manning as premier in 1944, Alberta politics have taken on a distinctly nonpartisan flavour, in the sense that politically manufactured external threats have been used successfully to galvanize Alberta voters and to mute internal dissent. Concerns with the external threat of socialism during the Cold War gave way to concerns about the external threat of eastern Canadian financial and political interests since the 1970s, particularly in relationship to the energy sector. The net result is that, over time, the prospect of developing an effective competitive party system has waxed and waned as ruling political elites periodically raise the spectre of an external threat to consolidate political support (Pal, 1992, pp. 16–22). The political executive has also demonstrated a distinctive disdain for the main institutions of parliamentary democracy, especially the legislative assembly as a source of debate and accountability (Brownsey, 2005, pp. 33–5).

Fourth, since the discovery of significant oil deposits in 1947, Alberta's economy and politics have become increasingly tied to the economic cycles of the oil and gas industry. This situation has resulted in a significant and repeating boom and bust economic cycle (Tupper, Pratt, & Urquhart, 1992, pp. 48–9).

While Peter Lougheed took a strong-state approach to natural resource development in particular, and to province building in general, successive Progressive Conservative governments (especially from the 1990s onward) adopted neoliberal rhetoric and New Public Management (NPM) principles for public sector management, including public sector privatization, low personal and corporate income taxes, and an unusually high dependence on the oil and gas industry for government revenue, although the government has maintained low royalty rates for many years (Tupper, 2004, pp. 210–20; Barrie, 2004, pp. 266–8; Stefanick, 2013, p. 4).[3]

NPM principles have had more influence in provincial health policies in Alberta compared to other provinces (Lewandowski & Sułkowski, 2018; and section 2.1.1), including policies that favour a stronger role for the private sector (e.g., continuing and home care). The recently elected United Conservative government is suggesting that the private sector will play a larger role in health care (and other policy areas) moving forward (Pike, 2019). Within this political context, entrepreneurial physicians have launched significant private business ventures that have blurred the lines between public and private interests (Taft & Steward, 2000, pp. 86–92; Church & Smith, 2006).

Connected to its close alignment with the oil and gas industry, political leadership has tended to be concentrated in Calgary,[4] with four of six *elected* premiers since 1970 representing Calgary ridings. In particular, Ralph Klein (former mayor of Calgary) preferred to conduct business as premier

---

3 Neoliberalism refers to a set of ideas and programs that emphasis laissez-faire liberalism and free-market capitalism. New Public Management (NPM) is a public sector response to neoliberalism focused on operating public agencies more like private businesses and configuring the public sector to operate more like a quasimarket. Inherent in this approach is privatization of service delivery and performance management.

4 Calgary is the corporate epicentre of the oil and gas industry in Canada.

from his political offices in Calgary because of what he referred to as the "Dome Disease" that afflicted Alberta politicians who spent too much time in their offices in the provincial legislative buildings in Edmonton (Rennie, 2004a; Barrie, 2004, p. 271). As Taft and Steward note,

> Calgary was the Klein Tories' urban power base, a strong nexus of government and corporate power that had wielded enormous influence over the entire province ever since Calgarian Peter Lougheed was elected premier almost 30 years ago. (Taft & Steward, 2000, p. 42)

Taken together, the interplay of politics and the economy has led Albertans to often vote for the party that is best connected and most accommodating to the oil and gas industry. In addition, this tendency has curtailed efforts to diversify the economy or adopt policies that might make better use of the full range of fiscal policy instruments available to provincial governments to stabilize the economy. Thus, Alberta's economy and its government have been stuck in a boom and bust cycle for decades.

1.3 Alberta's economy

Over the past several years, Alberta's economy has been the strongest in Canada. As a result of the increasing volatility of the world oil market and a decline in the traditional heavy industry economy, Alberta's energy sector has become strategically more important for Canada. This strategic significance has led to major increases in investment, jobs, and wealth. As a result, Alberta enjoys one of the highest standards of living in Canada and the developed world. Alberta's gross domestic product (GDP) per capita is the highest among Canadian provinces. Alberta's net debt to GDP ratio is 12 per cent (2020–21), making it the lowest in Canada (Royal Bank of Canada, 2021).

Although Alberta accounts for only 11 per cent of Canada's population, it accounts for a disproportionate 17 per cent of Canada's GDP. Over the past two decades, the province has experienced the highest economic growth rate in Canada, averaging 3.6 per cent per year compared to 2.7 per cent for Canada. However, a significant decline in global oil prices since 2014 has led to a recession in Alberta and consequent reduction in government revenues. Job losses in oil and gas, construction, and

Table 1.2 Health expenditures

	2000	2018
Total health expenditures in billions of dollars[1]	$6.3	$22.5
Total health expenditures as % of total government expenditures[1]	33.2	41.2
Total health expenditures as % of GDP[1]	4.3	6.1
Health expenditure per capita[1]	$2,359	$7,552
GDP per capita[2]	$57,106	$59,249

GDP = gross national product
Sources: 1. Canadian Institute for Health Information (CIHI), 2020a, Tables B.4.1, B.4.2, B. 4.4; 2. Conference Board of Canada, 2016.

manufacturing pushed the unemployment rate to 7.0 per cent by the end of 2015 (Alberta Treasury Board and Finance, 2015).

One unique economic policy instrument that Alberta has is the Alberta Heritage Trust Savings Fund (Alberta, 2021d). Created in 1976 under the Lougheed administration, the fund was designed to create a legacy fund, diversify the economy, and improve Alberta's quality of life. Although the fund could have accumulated around $190 billion by 2014 through revenues generated from the oil and gas sector, use of the fund by successive political regimes for short-term program expenditures and capital projects, and significant losses ($3 billion) in the 2008 economic downturn, left the fund at around $17 billion in 2014[5] (Giovannetti, Pereira, & Wolfe, 2017). As will be discussed in chapter 2, some of this money has been used (with relative success) to develop research capacity in the health sector.

Since 2000, health expenditures in Alberta have increased by 257 per cent. Per capita health expenditures have increased by over 220 per cent. Health expenditures as a percentage of GDP have increased by 42 per cent (Table 1.2).

While the oil and gas industry in Canada had its origins in the province of Ontario, the discovery of significant deposits in Alberta during the twentieth century, particularly after 1947, has made Alberta the centre of the oil and gas industry in Canada. Alberta is the largest producer of conventional oil, synthetic crude, natural gas, and gas in Canada and the second largest exporter of natural gas in the world. Prior to this discovery, Alberta had primarily an agricultural economy tied to the world price of wheat.

---

5 Comparisons are often made to a similar fund established by Norway during the 1970s that is now valued at around $1 trillion with an annual return of around $150 billion dollars.

Figure 1.3 Economic diversity in Alberta, 1985 and 2015 (% distribution of GDP)

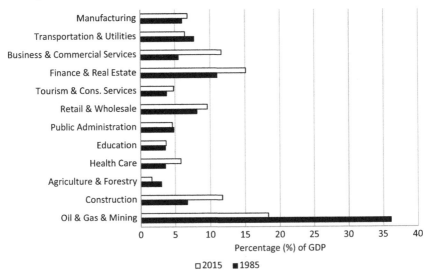

Source: AlbertaCanada.com, 2018.

As mentioned above, the combination of the relative decline of heavy industry in central Canada and the increasing strategic importance of oil as a world commodity has made Alberta and its oil and gas industry a major economic driver of the Canadian economy. While the industry only accounts for 18.3 per cent (2015) of the province's GDP, a decline from 36.1 per cent in 1986, this percentage far surpasses any other industry (see Figure 1.3).

However, the spinoffs to other segments of the economy have made oil and gas pivotal to the economic prosperity of the province.

Unfortunately, the volatility of the world oil and gas market has meant that invariably the Alberta economy has experienced booms followed by periodic busts. This cyclic pattern has made Alberta's economy highly unstable (Landon & Smith, 2013; Emery & Kneebone, 2013). In addition, Alberta's need to export oil and gas has been complicated by growing concerns with the environmental impact. Efforts to build new pipelines, both south to the United States and west to the Pacific coast, have been impeded by interjurisdictional disputes on appropriate fulfilment of regulatory processes to address concerns about the

environment and appropriate consultation with Indigenous populations (Gallichan-Lowe, 2018; Smart, 2019; Anderson, 2019).

1.4 Health status

Table 1.3 presents a selection of common measures of population health
for Alberta compared to the Canadian data.

Table 1.3 Selected health indicators

	Alberta	Canada
	2015–2017	**2015–2017**
Life expectancy at birth, total (years)	81.5	82.1
Life expectancy at birth, male (years)	79.3	80.0
Life expectancy at birth, female (years)	83.8	84.1
Life expectancy at 65, total (years)	20.9	21.0
Life expectancy at 65, male (years)	19.4	19.5
Life expectancy at 65, female (years)	22.3	22.3
	2017	**2017**
Infant mortality rate (per 1,000 total births)	4.9	4.5
Perinatal mortality rate (per 1,000 total births)	6.0	5.8
Maternal mortality (age-standardized rate per 100,000 population)	0.1	0.1
	2017	**2017**
Premature mortality (age-standardized rate per 100,000 population)	5,255.10	4,607.90
Potentially avoidable mortality (age-standardized rate per 100,000 population)	4,049.60	3,400.10
Mortality from preventable causes (age-standardized rate per 100,000 population)	2,838.30	2,244.30
Mortality from treatable causes (age-standardized rate per 100,000 population)	1,211.30	1,155.80
	2018	**2018**
Body mass index, adjusted self-reported, adult (18 years and over), overweight	35.0	36.3
Body mass index, adjusted self-reported, adult (18 years and over), obese	28.8	26.8
Arthritis, self-reported, 15 years and older	17.8	19.0
Asthma, self-reported, 12 years and older	10.4	8.3
High blood pressure, self-reported, 12 years and older	15.4	17.1
Low birth weight, less than 2,500 grams, both sexes	7.4	6.5

Sources: Statistics Canada. Table 13-10-0389-01: Life expectancy, at birth and at age
65, by sex, three-year average; Table 13-10-0714-01: Perinatal mortality (late fetal deaths
and early neonatal deaths); Table 13-10-0744-01: Premature and potentially avoidable
mortality, Canada, provinces and territories; Table 13-10-0096-01: Health characteristics,
annual estimates; Table 13-10-0422-01: Live births, by birth weight.; Statistics Canada,
2018a, 2018b, 2018c; Public Health Agency of Canada, n.d.

Table 1.4 Top 10 causes of death, 2018 (both sexes age-standardized rate per 100,000 population)

Leading causes of death	Alberta		Canada	
	Rank of leading causes of death	Age-standardized mortality rate per 100,000 population	Rank of leading causes of death	Age-standardized mortality rate per 100,000 population
Total, all causes of death	–	684.6	–	671.8
Malignant neoplasms	1	176.3	1	190.0
Heart disease	2	145.0	2	123.6
Accidents (unintentional injuries)	3	41.8	4	33.1
Chronic lower respiratory diseases	4	32.9	5	30.4
Cerebrovascular diseases	5	29.8	3	31.4
Diabetes mellitus	6	15.3	7	16.1
Intentional self-harm (suicide)	7	13.6	9	10.4
Influenza and pneumonia	8	14.8	6	19.5
Chronic liver disease and cirrhosis	9	10.5	10	8.7
Alzheimer's disease	10	8.2	8	14.6

Source: Statistics Canada. Table 13-10-0801-01: Leading causes of death, total population (age standardization using 2011 population).

When looking at the key health indicators (see Table 1.3), Alberta performs above the national average for overweight, arthritis, and high blood pressure, but below the national average for low birth weight infants, asthma, and obesity.

When looking at the top ten causes of death (Table 1.4), overall mortality rates in Alberta are higher than the Canadian average, particularly with deaths related to heart disease, accidents, respiratory conditions, and suicide. Alberta performs better than average for diabetes, cancer, cerebral vascular disease, and Alzheimer's.

Alberta's infant mortality rate is higher than the Canadian average (see Table 1.3). In part, this population trend has been attributed to the increased risks associated with delayed childbearing and the use of fertility treatments leading to increased multiple births and associated risks (Wang & Twilley, 2006). Along with low birth weight babies, the higher infant mortality may also be associated with the presence of a large Indigenous population primarily located in rural and remote areas of the province.

Higher than average rates of obesity (particular among northern residents), higher than average alcohol consumption (19.3 per cent, Alberta vs. 19.1 per cent, Canada, heavy drinking), and higher smoking rates (16.2 per cent, Alberta vs. 15.5 per cent, Canada, 12 years and older) are major contributing factors associated with heart and respiratory diseases (Statistics Canada, 2020).

However, once born, Albertans have a life expectancy comparable to that of other Canadians. When it comes to potential years of life lost, Albertans fare better than the average Canadian. However, Alberta's age-standardized mortality rate is also slightly higher than the Canadian average. With some exceptions, the health status numbers provided here suggest that Albertans are relatively healthy compared to other parts of Canada; however, this relatively positive outlook masks a more problematic population health landscape.

The combination of an economy that is subject to extreme boom and bust cycles, and a workforce that involves a significant transient, younger population operating in remote locations, living in temporary accommodations and earning significant income, has created a perfect storm for substance abuse. One newspaper headline boldly summarized the situation: "In Alberta, Cocaine Easier to Buy than Pizza" (Ferguson, 2007). According to a 2011 survey, Alberta ranked third highest among provinces for lifetime use of illicit drugs (Health Canada, 2011, Table 2). When it comes to lifetime alcohol use, Alberta is second only to Quebec (Health Canada, 2011, Table 7).

Related to substance abuse is the increasing level of addiction to gambling. A 2011 study of gambling in Alberta indicated that almost all revenues generated from gambling in Alberta come from Albertans (Williams, Belanger, & Arthur, 2011, pp. 94, 113). Nearly three-quarters of this revenue comes from electronic gaming machines (EGMs), which have come to dominate the gambling market since the mid-1990s (p. 97). Nearly three-quarters of gambling revenue (71.1 per cent) is now generated by 21 per cent of the adult population (p. 102). This population is characterized by above average income and is Indigenous or non-immigrant, male, married or common-law, over the age of 35, and living in Northern Alberta (p. 110). Within this group, problem gamblers generate 50 per cent of gambling revenues skewed towards the use of EGMs. Alberta is above the Canadian average for individuals addicted to EGMs. See chapter 6 for more detailed discussion of both illicit drug use and gambling patterns in the province.

A culture of gambling has been further reinforced by the increasing reliance of charitable organizations on gambling revenues. As a result of significant cutbacks during the 1990s in direct government funding, charitable organizations began to look to gambling activities as a means of replacing the financial shortfall. Alberta Gaming and Liquor Commission rules allow charities to work for two-day periods in gaming facilities. In exchange, charities receive a cut from the table and/or slot revenues. As one charity spokesperson characterized it, "the bottom line is this is the quickest, fastest way to get us a new playground for our children" (CBC News, 2009, 27 April). In 2010, charitable organizations received 28 per cent of net gambling revenues (Williams et al., 2011, p. 124). In recent years, it has also become a key alternative revenue stream for the provincial government (CBC News, 2009, 27 April). One additional possible result from gambling is the fact that Albertans have the highest average personal debt load in the country (Stark, 2016).

1.5 Summary

In the course of a mere 50 years, Alberta has risen from a modest, agricultural-based economy to become the economic engine of Canada. This dramatic shift is directly attributable to the discovery and development of significant deposits of oil and gas. Government revenue generated through these industrial activities has allowed for the rapid modernization of Alberta's infrastructure and a significant expansion of the programs and services provided or funded by government.

Alberta's success, however, has not been without its challenges. The social culture associated with the economically turbulent oil and gas industry has generated a number of significant adverse health consequences. While overall Alberta stacks up comparatively well to other provinces on a number of health indicators, it ranks poorly on alcohol consumption, smoking, illicit drug use, gambling, personal debt, and limiting injuries. The health problems associated with these lifestyle indicators include higher levels of heart disease, obesity, and suicide. In addition, the presence of a significant Indigenous population, based largely in rural, remote, and northern areas, contributes to higher than average low birth weights and infant mortality.

Alberta's economy has been a double-edged sword. Albertans work harder and earn more than the average Canadian, but they also play harder. In short, they drink, smoke, use illicit drugs, gamble, and spend more than the average Canadian. This population profile places unique strains on the health care system. And, despite having experienced several boom and bust cycles, successive Alberta governments have avoided employing fiscal instruments (such as a higher royalty regime and a provincial sales tax) that might buffer the effects of a turbulent economy because doing so is considered to be politically unfeasible.

Chapter Two

Organization and Regulation

Prior to the discovery of oil in 1947, Alberta's economy was mainly based on agriculture. Thus, politics was largely shaped by a concern with rural issues. In fact, the initial interest by the provincial government in health care revolved around the challenges of providing health care in rural and remote settings. The discovery of oil in 1947 led to a fundamental shift in the provincial economy, combined with a demographic shift to a much more urban society. With the creation of a new public revenue stream, the Alberta government was able to expand public infrastructure. The coinciding of this shift with the emergence of federal funding for health care made it feasible for Alberta to modernize and expand its existing health infrastructure, particularly in the province's more populated centres. This process was accelerated during the 1970s and the 1980s by a shift in the political regime from a more traditional (social and fiscal) rural-based conservatism to a more progressive and urban-based form of conservatism.

The return of fiscal conservatism under the umbrella of neoliberalism and New Public Management (NPM) during the 1990s in the Klein era, however, led to significant expenditure reductions and a major reorganization of the governance of the health care system. The major reorganizations of the health system since the early 1990s, first to a regionally organized system and eventually to a single organization – Alberta Health Services – were triggered by the desire to contain costs and limit administrative expenses.

2.1 Overview of the health system

The creation of geographically defined health regions with governance and operational authority for most health care and public health services (although not physician services or community-based pharmaceutical budgets) in tandem with the devolution from the Ministry of Health of most operational responsibilities was characteristic of the separation of the "steering" and "rowing" functions described by Osborne and Gaebler (1992) in their discussion about the restructuring of the public sector.[1] This initial restructuring was followed by further refinement of the new governance model with a reduction in the number of regions from seventeen to nine in 2004.

In 2008, the remaining nine health regions were merged into a single provincial health authority, Alberta Health Services (AHS). AHS is the largest single health authority in Canada, the largest employer in Alberta, and, with 103,000 direct employees (not including those who work in AHS subsidiaries or the 8,200 physicians who work in AHS facilities) as of 2021, one of the largest employers in Canada (Alberta Health Services [AHS], 2021). The chapter focuses on describing this evolution from the early years of the twentieth century to the contemporary time period in detail.

2.1.1 Early history

In 1905, the government of Alberta created a health branch within its Department of Agriculture. Coinciding with this initiative was the passage of the first health legislation, the Public Health Act, which became law in 1907 and led to the creation of the five-member Provincial Board of Health with the "authority and responsibility in regard to making and administering the public health regulations of the province. This Act also provided for the division of the province into health districts and for the creation of a local board of health in each district" (Bow & Cook, 1935, p. 384).

The United Farmers of Alberta (UFA) laid much of the early groundwork for Alberta's health care system. Although the UFA formed government for three consecutive terms (1921–35), the party's interest in health care emerged during the First World War as a result of a high rate of disabled soldiers. Prompted by UFA groundwork, the Liberal government passed the Municipal Hospitals Act in 1917 (revised 1918).

---

1 In the Alberta case, the ministry (Alberta Health) divested responsibility for the direct administration of continuing care, home care, and eventually mental health to the health regions and a provincial mental health advisory board.

The act allowed rural municipalities to levy a tax to build hospitals, with partial subsidization from the provincial government. Lower hospital capacity in rural areas was the result of a lack of interest from either private nonprofit or for-profit organizations in serving rural areas. Similar legislation was established in Saskatchewan. These union hospital districts in Alberta grew from one in 1919 to eleven by 1947 (Canadian Museum of History, n.d.). The provincial legislation complemented federal legislation that allowed for an increase in urban hospital capacity to deal with war-related injuries. Additional bed capacity pressures from the Spanish flu epidemic (1918–19), leading to closures of private hospitals, further fuelled growing political pressure for provincial government involvement in health care (Lampard, 2012, p. 184).

This growing pressure led Alberta to create Canada's second stand-alone health department (the first having been created by the federal government) in 1918, followed by a District Nurse Program in 1919 and travelling child welfare clinics in 1920. These latter clinics began with a focus on dentistry, but by 1924 included both physicians and nurses, and by 1927, a surgeon. Eventually a psychiatrist was added to the roster. Both of these initiatives were designed to address health needs in medically underserved rural communities. The election of the UFA in 1921 accelerated the pace of health policy development in the province (Lampard, 2012, p. 185).

Appointed in 1932, the Hoadley Commission undertook a comprehensive examination of the existing capacity to provide health care services in Alberta and the needs of the population. Filed in 1934, the commission's final report recommended the establishment of a voluntary municipal health plan. The purpose of this plan was to allow municipalities to provide hospital services and the services of physicians on salary in geographic areas where "normal insurance practices could not be expected to support a practitioner" (Naylor, 1986, p. 54). The provincial government would not take control of hospitals. In response, a municipal plan including medical, dental, hospital care, laboratory and diagnostic services, and drugs, based on fee-for-service physician payments, was established in the Camrose constituency.

The Alberta Health Care Insurance Act (1935) envisioned a contributory plan in which workers contributed five-ninths to cover the costs, employers contributed two-ninths, and the government covered two-ninths, including the costs of care for indigents. However, the electoral defeat of the UFA by the Social Credit Party in 1935 meant that the legislation was not implemented at that time. Notwithstanding this outcome, it is possibly the earliest example in Canada of a government-subsidized health care plan (Rennie, 2004b, p. 113).[2]

The new Social Credit government, which would rule the province for the next 35 years, passed the Alberta Maternity Hospital Act in 1944. The legislation was designed to provide standard ward maternity care, paid directly by the provincial government. This provision was later extended for poliomyelitis cases and social assistance recipients in the 1950s. As such, in comparison to the more extensive plan envisioned by the UFA government, this plan involved a far more limited incursion into the existing private health care market.

In the wake of the failure to achieve intergovernmental consensus around the federal government proposal for publicly funded national health insurance at the Dominion-Provincial Conference in 1945, organized medicine in Alberta launched Medical Services Incorporated (MSI) in 1948 through the College of Physicians and Surgeons of Alberta. MSI was a voluntary, contributory, nonprofit health care plan for medical, surgical, and obstetrical services.[3]

The government followed up in 1950 with a decentralized, voluntary municipal plan to allow municipalities to fund hospital services through local taxation with a subsidy from the province. Enrolment in the plan was voluntary, and it was funded through general taxation, premiums, and user fees, and administered through municipalities and multiple private insurance carriers (Marchildon 2016, p. 134). By 1953, approximately 75 per cent of Albertans were covered under this plan.[4]

In addition, some Albertans (qualifying welfare recipients) received coverage through Alberta Blue Cross (a legislated, hospital-sponsored, not-for-profit hospital insurance plan established in 1948) and the Alberta Medical Association for physician and hospital services and drug benefits. However, compared to other provinces with similar plans, the provincial government provided a much smaller subsidy (Naylor, 1986, pp. 161–3; Taylor, 1987, pp. 169–70; Canadian Museum of History, n.d.).

---

2 A similar plan was conceived in British Columbia around the same time. However, like Alberta, it was not implemented because of political opposition.

3 It is important to note here that MSI was introduced into an existing competitive market of private insurance. The difference between MSI and other insurers is that it was nonprofit and thus in a position to cover individuals who would be otherwise uninsurable.

4 Contrast this plan with the universal, publicly financed hospital insurance scheme introduced in Saskatchewan in 1946–47 by the left-of-centre Cooperative Commonwealth Federation government (Marchildon, 2016).

The introduction of a fifty-fifty cost-shared national hospital insurance plan by the federal government in 1957 prompted Alberta to replace its publicly subsidized private-municipal plan with a provincially administered hospital insurance plan with universal coverage. At the time, Alberta had approximately 102 hospitals, in which 61 per cent of the beds were funded by municipalities, 4 per cent were nonsectarian, and 36 per cent religious. Only 1 per cent was funded by the province (Boychuk, 1999, p. 46).

During the postwar economic boom of the 1950s and 1960s, Alberta also expanded funding to programs not covered by cost-shared arrangements, such as long-term care and psychiatric hospitals (Hanrahan et al., 1992, p. 145). The net result of this surge of activity was a rapid expansion of the hospital sector. Between 1954 and 1971, Alberta increased its hospital beds from 6.1 beds per 1,000 population to 9.1 beds per 1,000, bringing the number of hospitals in the province to over 200. Only Quebec matched this level of growth. In 1977, this ratio was still at 8 beds per 1,000 in Alberta, with the Canadian average only 7.1 beds per 1,000. What the Social Credit and later the Progressive Conservative governments discovered was that, once built, a hospital became politically difficult to close[5] (Taylor, 1987, pp. 234–5; Hanrahan et al., 1992, p. 145; Tupper & Doern, 1990, p. 123).

Alberta extended coverage for physician services further in 1963 (dubbed "Manningcare") with legislation to subsidize coverage of low-income earners through voluntary enrolment in either MSI or other private insurance companies. The plan was developed with the cooperation of the Alberta Medical Association. However, when it came to the growing national push for universal compulsory health insurance, Alberta continued to "loudly proclaim its opposition to a universal government plan on the grounds that it involved compulsion" (Taylor, 1987, p. 338). The province continued to favour a subsidized system for low-income earners (Bell, 2004, p. 167).

When the federal government again introduced national health legislation, "Medicare," in 1968 to provide universal compulsory coverage for physician services outside of hospitals, Alberta followed suit with its own provincial plan that was compliant with the requirements of the

---

5 Not surprisingly, the expansion of funding in health care continued during the 1970s, due to the unprecedented wealth generated by the rapid growth of the oil and gas industry, the province-building aspirations of Premier Lougheed (1971–85), and his perception of a threat from the political left.

federal legislation, specifically, universality of access, comprehensiveness of coverage, portability of benefits, and public administration.[6]

At the time that Medicare[7] was implemented in Alberta in 1969, a Hospital Services Commission and a Health Insurance Commission were accountable to the Ministry of Social Services and Community Health for the administration of hospital and medical services. In addition to the two commissions, the department also encompassed the Alberta Health Facilities Review Committee and the Alberta Cancer Board.

In 1975, both commissions were rolled into the newly created Department of Hospitals and Medical Care. At this time, these two agencies lost their semi-independent status and became divisions of a centrally administered department. In 1988, this department and the Department of Occupational Health were rolled into the new Department of Health. The department was responsible for all active treatment and auxiliary hospitals, the three medical benefits plans (health insurance, hospital insurance, and nursing homes), and after 1982, for the two provincial psychiatric hospitals and related auxiliary care centres.

When reconfigured in 1975, the department had the following divisions: Hospitals Planning and Operations, Information Systems and Evaluation, Financial Planning and Control, and the Medical Insurance Program. A further reorganization in 1979 produced the following divisional configuration: Hospital Services, Health Care Insurance, Finance and Administration, and Policy Development. In 1987, a Corporate Development Division was created to deal with corporate planning and human resources. An Information Resource Management Division was also created to consolidate all IT activities (Lesage, 2006, pp. 317–18).

Several arms-length agencies were created between 1968 and 1975. Taking on responsibilities previously vested in the Department of Health, the Alberta Cancer Board was created as the Provincial Cancer Hospitals Board in 1968. The board was responsible for the provision of cancer treatment and prevention services, including research and monitoring. The Alberta Alcohol and Drug Abuse Commission (AADAC) was created in 1970 from the previous departmental Division of Alcoholism. The AADAC reported to the Ministry of Health (and wellness) with responsibility for planning, creating, and funding programs for the prevention and treatment of alcohol, tobacco, drug, and gambling

---

6 These requirements were reiterated in the Canada Health Act, 1984.
7 "Medicare" is the unofficial term often used for the single-payer health plan initiated through federal legislation.

addictions (Lesage, 2006, pp. 297–8). The Alberta Health Facilities Review Committee (AHFRC) was created in 1972 as the Alberta Hospital Visitors Committee. Reporting to the Ministry of Health, the committee was responsible for periodic inspections, triggered by complaints, of health facilities including nursing homes[8] (p. 299).

Finally, a unique aspect of Alberta's health system has been government support of medical and population health research. Funded through revenue generated from oil and gas revenues, the Alberta Heritage Foundation for Medical Research (AHFMR) was created in 1980 through legislation to support and develop world-class health researchers through an endowment fund. During the next 30 years, a total of 8,500 researchers received approximately $800 million (Graham, Chorzempa, Valentine, & Magnan, 2012).

Table 2.1 summarizes the history of health care in Alberta with a brief chronology of significant milestones.

2.1.2   Health system restructuring, 1993–2007

During the 1990s, Alberta underwent a significant restructuring of its health care system, embedded within a broader political agenda of government reform related to the elimination of public deficit and debt. Neoliberalism, including privatization and personal choice, and the associated ideas of the NPM, with its emphasis on the role of government as "steering" rather than "rowing," informed the restructuring in health care (Osborne & Gaebler, 1992). As noted by Marchildon (2008), this restructuring was one way in which the principles of NPM were applied to the health care sector in Canada. For example, the *Rainbow Report* in 1989 called for a redistribution of power away from the Ministry of Health towards local communities and a refocusing of the ministry to

> concentrate its efforts on setting long-term goals; developing priorities and policies; establishing standards; ensuring interregional coordination and communication; and allocating funds on a global basis. Looking at the future isn't easy when you're caught up in the day-to-day administration and determination of routine programs. (Alberta Health & Premier's Commission, 1989, p. 116)

---

8 Until 1980, inspection of social care institutions was also part of the AHFRC purview.

Table 2.1 Alberta health care chronology, 1889–2008

1889	Prepaid medical care is introduced in Alberta at $5.00 per year for hospital accommodations.
1905	The Medical Profession Act is passed.
1906	The College of Physicians and Surgeons of Alberta (CPSA) and the Alberta Medical Association (AMA) are established.
1907	The Public Health Act establishes the Provincial Board of Health.
1913	The University of Alberta establishes the first Faculty of Medicine in Alberta.
1918	The Municipal Hospitals Act transfers responsibility for hospitals to municipalities while providing assistance to Albertans in need.
1924	Travelling clinics provide medical exams, small pox vaccinations, dental inspections, and treatment for children.
1928	Alberta becomes the first province to provide facilities for the treatment and care of polio victims.
1929	Mental health clinics are introduced in Edmonton and Calgary.
1936	The Tuberculosis Act provides free diagnosis and treatment for Albertans.
1938	Alberta is the first province to offer aftercare to survivors of polio.
1944	The Maternity Hospitalization Act provides free maternity care and a home care grant.
1945	Financial assistance is provided to low-income expectant mothers and free hospital services for childbirth.
1947	The Provincial-Municipal Hospitalization Plan begins providing free hospital coverage for individuals receiving old age pension and blind person pensions or mother's allowance.
1948	Medical Services (Alberta) Incorporated (MSI) is established to offer insurance coverage for medical, surgical, and obstetrical services to participants.
1950	The Municipal Hospitalization Plan provides Albertans with hospital benefits from their municipal hospital at $1 per day.
1952	The Health Unit Act allows for the division of the province into geographic health units with boards and administration.
1958	The Alberta Hospitalization Benefits Act is created in response to federal cost-sharing legislation to provide prepaid coverage for hospital insurance and care on a universal basis.
1960	The Auxiliary Hospitals Act brings auxiliary hospitals under provincial jurisdiction.
1963	The Alberta Medical Care Plan is created to provide basic health insurance through private insurance carriers.
1964	The Nursing Home Act brings nursing homes under provincial jurisdiction.

(*continued*)

Table 2.1 (*continued*)

1966	The Department of Health Act replaces the Department of Public Health Act and divides the department into two sections, hospital services and all other health services.
1969	The Alberta Health Care Insurance Act is passed to administer the new Alberta Health Care Insurance Plan.
1977	Nurses and allied health professionals unionize as the United Nurses of Alberta.
1980	The Alberta Heritage Foundation for Medical Research establishes Canada's first provincially funded medical research program.
1984	The Canada Health Act ensures full coverage of Albertans for medically necessary physician and hospital services.
1986	Extra-billing ends in Alberta.
1994	Regional health authorities replace 200 existing local health boards with 17 regional authorities (RHAs).
2008	Nine remaining RHAs are merged into a single provincial board, Alberta Health Services.

Source: Office of the Auditor General of Alberta, 2017, Appendices A, B, and C.

This view about the appropriate role of government stemmed from the larger concern at the time about increasing expenditure accountability to avoid reverting to the previous pattern of deficit spending (Church & Smith, 2013a, p. 39).

To enhance expenditure accountability, the government introduced a business planning and annual performance measurement process through legislation. The Government Accountability Act required the development of standardized accountability structures and processes, and an annual consolidated fiscal plan. Ministries were required to develop business plans and annual reports that were vetted by the provincial Treasury Board (Church & Smith, 2008).

Within this emerging policy environment, in 1994 Alberta replaced approximately 200 local hospital and public health boards with 17 regional health authorities (RHAs; Alberta, 2000g) – see Figure 2.1. As mentioned above, this reorganization reflected a desire to redistribute power both away from Alberta Health to local communities and away from local hospital boards to an intermediary regional governance structure. There was an expectation that the new authorities would facilitate greater recognition and accommodation of local needs and lead to greater equity in resource allocation. To this end, a population-based

Figure 2.1 Original seventeen health regions, 1994

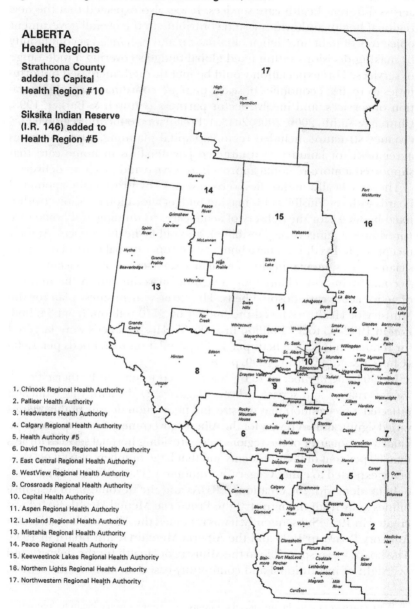

ALBERTA
Health Regions

Strathcona County
added to Capital
Health Region #10

Siksika Indian Reserve
(I.R. 146) added to
Health Region #5

1. Chinook Regional Health Authority
2. Palliser Health Authority
3. Headwaters Health Authority
4. Calgary Regional Health Authority
5. Health Authority #5
6. David Thompson Regional Health Authority
7. East Central Regional Health Authority
8. WestView Regional Health Authority
9. Crossroads Regional Health Authority
10. Capital Health Authority
11. Aspen Regional Health Authority
12. Lakeland Regional Health Authority
13. Mistahia Regional Health Authority
14. Peace Regional Health Authority
15. Keeweetinok Lakes Regional Health Authority
16. Northern Lights Regional Health Authority
17. Northwestern Regional Health Authority

Source: Alberta Health, 1997, p. 27.

funding formula was adopted, replacing a variety of funding models across different health care services. It was also expected that the new regional health authorities would contribute to the overall government objectives of debt and deficit elimination and enhanced accountability by making decisions within fixed global budgets covering a wide range of services. This expectation would be met through increased opportunities to realize economies of scale, increase coordination and integration of services, and involve sector partners (Church & Barker, 1998; Church & Smith, 2006, 2008, 2013a). Precursors to the full regional governance structure included regional capital planning, shared services agreement for laundry, and targeted partnerships in home care that supported a more regional approach to service and program delivery.

The new health authorities were governed by provincially appointed boards with responsibility for making budget allocation decisions (within fixed budgets) for the delivery of acute care, continuing and home care (previously a ministry responsibility), and public health services. At their inception, RHAs did not have budgetary or operational control over physician services, mental health, ambulance services, or pharmaceuticals. Accompanying this change was a significant reduction in the number of active acute care hospital beds. The three-year business plan for the Ministry of Health reduced the budget by $740 million, from $4.2 billion in 1992–93 to $3.4 billion in 1996–97. Hospital beds were targeted for reduction from 4.5 beds per 1,000 population to 2.4 beds per 1,000 (Church & Noseworthy, 1999, p. 188).[9]

In 2004, the number of RHAs was reduced to nine to further rationalize governance and service delivery (Figure 2.2). In part, this reduction reflected a recognition that the size and population density of the regions varied significantly. A review for the Alberta government found that approximately one-quarter of the regions were providing hospital services for less than 60 per cent of their residents and that large numbers of patients were being exported to either Calgary or Edmonton (Plain, 1995, 1997).

In tandem with the creation of RHAs and the devolution of responsibilities away from the ministry, the Provincial Mental Health Board was created in 1994. Subsequently, it was renamed the Alberta Mental Health Advisory Board in 1996 and the Alberta Mental Health Board in 1999. The board was responsible to the Ministry of Health for the delivery and oversight of institutional and community-based mental health services.

---

9 With a turnaround in the provincial economy, government would begin to "reinvest" in the health care system in 1996.

Figure 2.2 Regional health authority boundaries, post-2004

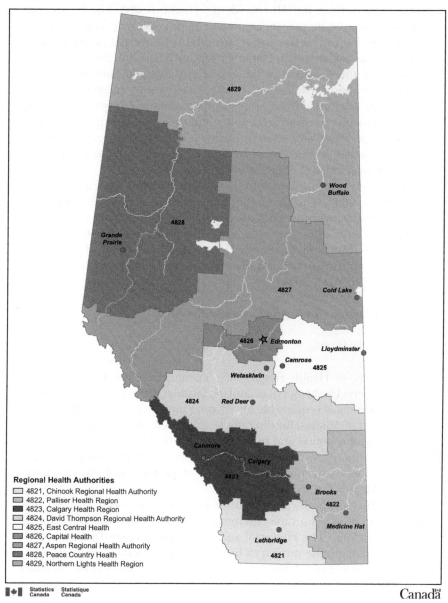

Regional Health Authorities

☐ 4821, Chinook Regional Health Authority
▦ 4822, Palliser Health Region
■ 4823, Calgary Health Region
☐ 4824, David Thompson Regional Health Authority
☐ 4825, East Central Health
▦ 4826, Capital Health
▦ 4827, Aspen Regional Health Authority
▩ 4828, Peace Country Health
▦ 4829, Northern Lights Health Region

Statistics   Statistique
Canada   Canada

Canadä

Source: Statistics Canada, 2008.

In 1999, mental health services governance and delivery were devolved to the regions from the Alberta Mental Health Board. The board continued to coordinate provincial mental health policy development and administer the provincial contract with RHAs for mental health services delivery (Church & Smith, 2008; Macfarlane & Durbin, 2005).

In 2003, the mandate of the board was changed, and responsibility for providing most mental health services was transferred to the regional health authorities. After this time, the main responsibilities of the board involved system-level policy and programmatic planning, and providing province-wide mental health services and programs such as forensic psychiatry, suicide prevention, Aboriginal mental health, and information systems (Lesage, 2006, p. 302).

AHFRC was transformed into the Health Quality Council of Alberta (HQCA) in 2004. The mandate of the new agency was expanded to include quality assurance monitoring and evaluation, including patient satisfaction and public inquiries, across the entire health care system or in response to specific incidents. However, to date, HQCA has not carried out routine inspections against standards (Health Quality Council of Alberta [HQCA], 2004).[10]

2.2 Organization of the provincial health system

2.2.1 Alberta Health

The Ministry of Health (Figure 2.3) encompasses the Department of Health, Alberta Health Services, and the Health Quality Council of Alberta. The department is responsible for advising the minister of health and the government of Alberta, funding the health system, facilitating implementation of health policy, and overall oversight of the health system. More specifically, the department manages activities related to overall design, strategic policy direction, legislation, and performance measurement (Alberta Health, 2018b, pp. 13–15).

The Office of the Deputy Minister provides leadership through policy coordination, issues management, priority setting, and operational decision-making. The Financial and Corporate Services Division develops and manages the ministry's budget, works with the provincial auditor to prepare annual financial statements, oversees health facilities

---

10 Similar agencies were set up in other jurisdictions across Canada in response to the issues of patient safety and health system errors.

Figure 2.3 Alberta Ministry of Health organizational structure as of 2018

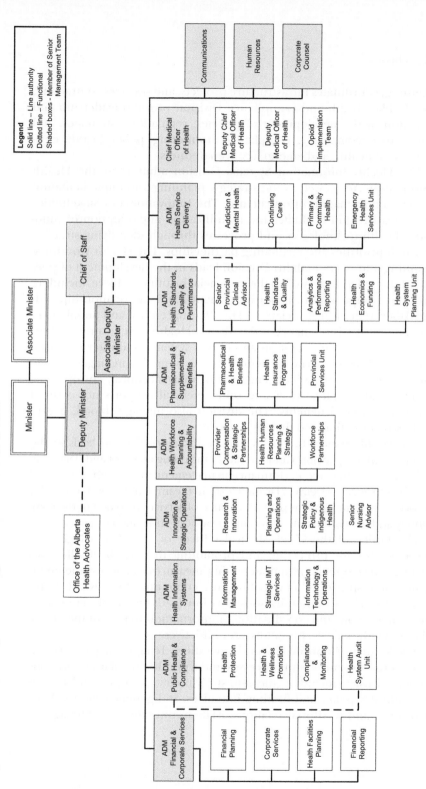

Source: Alberta Health, 2018b, p. 11.

planning, coordinates infrastructure projects, and oversees contracting. The Public Health and Compliance Division provides leadership and direction in the development of policies, regulations, strategies, and standards encompassing compliance monitoring, public health, environmental health, and emergency preparedness.

The Health Information Systems Division administers the Health Information Act as well as the strategic planning and implementation of health information infrastructure. The Innovation and Stakeholder Relations Division facilitates the identification and adoption of innovative health technologies and processes through identifying strategic research priorities and facilitating partnerships. The Health Workforce Planning and Accountability Division leads in the development of policies and regulation related to the provincial health workforce, including provider compensation, major agreements, and the relationship with the Alberta Medical Association. The Pharmaceutical and Supplementary Benefits Division manages the Alberta Health Care Insurance Plan, health provider remuneration and claims systems, and interprovincial reciprocal financial arrangements. The division also manages supplemental benefits for patients eligible for pharmaceutical, chiropractic, optical, and dental services and other medical supports not covered through universal benefits. The division also manages blood, organ, and tissue donation and dialysis services.

The Health Standards, Quality and Performance Division leads in the development of guidelines and standards, including analytics and data management, reporting and performance management, and health economics. The Health Services Delivery Division leads in the implementation of a health service delivery integration plan for a range of services provided in the community and in coordinating with other provincial and national agencies.

The Office of the Chief Medical Officer of Health has legislative responsibility for protecting and promoting the health of Albertans through developing and implementing measures to address the emergence and spread of new pathogens, communicable diseases, and infections. The Communications Division leads in the development, implementation, and coordination of information to inform the public about health policies, programs, and initiatives.

The Strategic Coordination and Operations Team manages and coordinates the structures and processes underpinning the daily operations of the ministry, including the ministry's policy, planning and reporting, ministry policy and funding initiatives, Indigenous health policy/provincial and territorial relations, AHS accountability, public agency

Figure 2.4 Alberta's health system, 2018

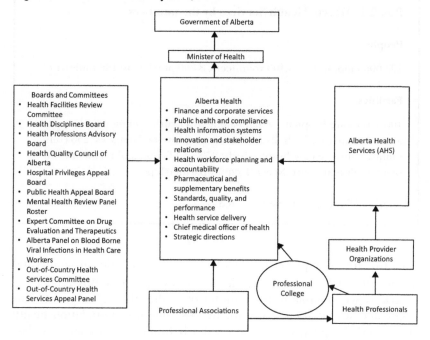

governance, human resources, legal and legislative review, ministry correspondence, and Freedom of Information applications.

Finally, the Office of the Alberta Health Advocate assists Albertans to resolve health-related issues through system navigation, providing information about Alberta's Health Charter, requesting facilities inspections, and addressing patient concerns under the Mental Health Act.

Figure 2.4 represents the Alberta health system in chart form.

2.2.2 Alberta Health Services

In 2008, the remaining nine health regions in Alberta were merged – along with the Alberta Cancer Board, the Alberta Alcohol and Drug Abuse Commission (AADAC), and the Alberta Mental Health Board – into a single provincial authority, Alberta Health Services (AHS).

Employing over 103,000 people, AHS is the largest health organization in Canada, the largest employer in the province of Alberta, and

---

Box 2.1 Alberta Health Services by the numbers

People

103,000 employees; 15,100 volunteers; 8,200 physicians; 130 midwives

Facilities

106 acute care hospitals; 5 stand-alone psychiatric facilities; 8,515 acute and subacute care beds; 27,518 continuing care beds/spaces; 256 community palliative care hospice beds; 2,785 addiction and mental health beds; 41 Primary Care Network equity partnerships

Source: Alberta Health Services, n.d.-a.

---

the fifth largest employer in Canada. Overall, it provides programs and services through over 400 facilities in the province (see Box 2.1).

AHS is accountable to the minister of health, through a provincially appointed six-member board, for the assessment of population health needs and the provision of most publicly funded health services. The board provides oversight and direction to the president and chief executive officer of AHS. Specifically, the board is responsible for the following:

a) promoting and protecting the health of the population in Alberta and working toward the prevention of disease and injury;
b) assessing on an ongoing basis the health needs of the population in Alberta;
c) determining priorities in the provision of health services and allocating resources accordingly;
d) ensuring that reasonable access to quality health services is provided to the population in Alberta; and
e) promoting the provision of integrated health services in the best possible manner. (Alberta Health Services, 2017)

In addition, the board is responsible for and accountable to the minister of health for stewardship on behalf of the public through promoting the vision, mission, and values of AHS and through good governance. Figure 2.5 outlines the organization structure of the AHS in chart form.

Figure 2.5 Alberta Health Services organizational structure, 2020

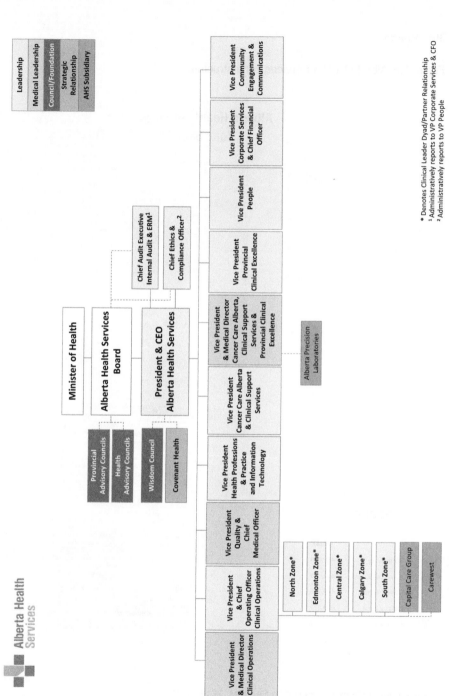

Leadership
Medical Leadership
Council/Foundation
Strategic Relationship
AHS Subsidiary

Minister of Health

Alberta Health Services Board

President & CEO Alberta Health Services

Chief Audit Executive Internal Audit & ERM[1]

Chief Ethics & Compliance Officer[2]

Provincial Advisory Councils

Health Advisory Councils

Wisdom Council

Covenant Health

Vice President Community Engagement & Communications

Vice President Corporate Services & Chief Financial Officer

Vice President People

Vice President Provincial Clinical Excellence

Vice President & Medical Director Cancer Care Alberta, Clinical Support Services & Provincial Clinical Excellence

Vice President Cancer Care Alberta & Clinical Support Services

Vice President Health Professions & Practice and Information Technology

Vice President Quality & Chief Medical Officer

Vice President & Chief Operating Officer Clinical Operations

Vice President & Medical Director Clinical Operations

Alberta Precision Laboratories

North Zone*
Edmonton Zone*
Central Zone*
Calgary Zone*
South Zone*
Capital Care Group
Carewest

* Denotes Clinical Leader Dyad/Partner Relationship
[1] Administratively reports to VP Corporate Services & CFO
[2] Administratively reports to VP People

Alberta Health Services

Source: Alberta Health Services, 2018d.

Figure 2.6 Alberta Health Services zone structure

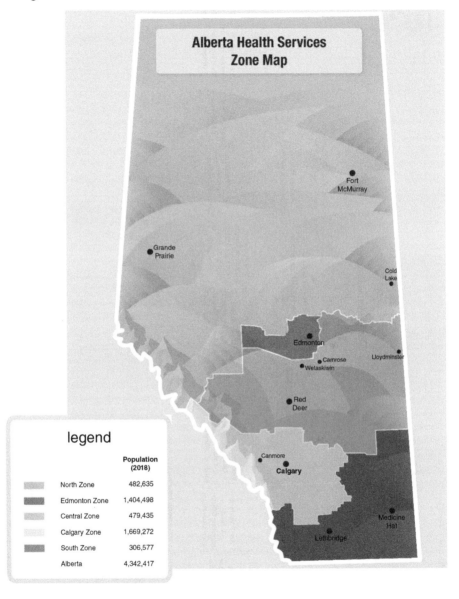

Source: Adapted from Alberta Health Services, 2019a, p. 9.

As shown in Figure 2.6, five geographic service delivery zones have replaced the previous nine geographic regions. While ambulance services (previously a municipal responsibility) were included in the scope of new responsibilities, AHS still does not control the budgets for physician services or pharmaceuticals.

In addition to the five geographic service zones, AHS also has twelve geographic health advisory councils: a provincial Advisory Council on Cancer, a provincial Advisory Council on Addiction and Mental Health, a Patient and Family Advisory Council, a Clinician Council, and a Wisdom Council (Aboriginal). Each of these councils provides AHS leadership with advice and feedback on relevant program and service issues (Alberta Health Services, n.d.-b).

2.2.3 Contractors

Alberta's health care system relies on a variety of contractual relationships. Physician services are provided through a negotiated fee schedule and master agreement between the provincial government and the Alberta Medical Association. Individual physicians bill the provincial government directly on a fee-per-service basis for services provided based on a provincially negotiated fee schedule (see chapter 3 for further details).

AHS spends approximately 65 per cent of its continuing care and 32 per cent of its home care budget on contracts with private not-for-profit and for-profit service providers (Alberta Health, 2018b, pp. 174, 217).

Laboratory services outside of acute care hospitals are provided through a contract with a single private contractor. While the previous New Democratic government had indicated that it planned to take over the delivery of all laboratory service by 2022, the current United Conservative government has announced that it will not proceed with this plan (Mertz, 2019).

2.3 Health system planning

As is the case with other provincial ministries and departments of health in Canada, the Ministry of Health – Alberta Health and Wellness – and the minister of health, to whom the ministry reports, are the health stewards of the provincial health system (Saltman & Ferroussier-Davis, 2000; Marchildon & Allin, 2012; Marchildon & Lockhart, 2012). Alberta Health and Wellness is responsible for the funding and regulation of universal health coverage services that must be provided to all residents without cost at the point of service (Marchildon, Allin, & Merkur, 2020, p. xx). In addition, the ministry regulates and subsidizes more targeted access to a number of other health services and programs, including coverage under a provincial drug plan as well as long-term care and home care services (Campbell, Manns, Soril, & Clement, 2017; Palley, 2013).

With the support of other provincial ministries (e.g., Alberta Infrastructure), Alberta Health and Wellness ensures that health services are planned and delivered based on community health needs and provincial goals. The infrastructure, services, and human resources required to meet the province's health needs are managed through Alberta Health Services, a delegated public body responsible for the administration and delivery of most health services in the province.

Planning occurs at the local AHS zone and at provincial levels. Zone-level internal planning focuses on the longer term (5–15 years), meant to inform more immediate operational planning (1–3 years). In 2017–18, draft internal plans were developed for the Central and Calgary zones. The plans describe the current state of health care, what change is needed, and what the system might look like over the longer term. AHS and Alberta Health have agreed to plan with a focus on "care closer to home" (Alberta Health, 2018b, p. 62).

2.4 Coverage and benefits

2.4.1. Eligibility for benefits

In accordance with the Canada Health Act, the Alberta Health Care Insurance Plan covers all "medically necessary"[11] hospital and physician services, and specific dental and oral surgical health services (Alberta, 2021c). In addition, Alberta provides supplemental coverage for certain categories of individuals for services not normally covered through the plan. These include drug, dental, and optical benefits for seniors and individuals on social assistance. Albertans are responsible for prescription drugs provided outside of hospital and other institutional settings.

The government of Alberta offers supplementary drug coverage for eligible Albertans through eighteen drug and supplementary

---

11 Medical necessity is determined through the professional judgment of individual physicians. However, the funding of services is specified in a provincial fee schedule determined through periodic negotiation of a master agreement between the provincial government and the provincial professional medical association.

Table 2.2 Government-sponsored supplementary health benefits plans

Benefit	Eligibility
Non-group coverage	Premium-based, under 65 and dependents
Seniors	Premium-free, 65 years or older and dependents
Palliative	Palliative and receiving treatment at home
Diabetic	Insulin for diabetes
Specialized prescription drug coverage	
Outpatient cancer drug benefit program	Select medications used in the direct treatment of cancer
Specialized high-cost drug program	Drugs used in highly specialized procedures
Disease control and prevention	Treatment of TB and STIs
Acid reflux medication	Drugs used for treating acid-related disorders
Seniors benefits and programs	
Alberta seniors benefits program	Income-based monthly benefit for eligible seniors, including support in addition to federal benefits (OAS, GIS, Federal Allowance, and GST credit)
Special needs assistance for seniors program	Funding assistance for appliances, minor home repairs, and some medical costs
Dental and optical assistance for seniors program	Funding assistance for basic dental and optical services
Property tax deferral program	Defer all or part of property taxes through low-interest home equity loan
Assured income for severely handicapped (AISH)	Adults with a permanent disability affecting ability to earn a livelihood
Income support	Albertans who do not have the resources to meet their basic needs
Alberta adult health benefit	Albertans who leave income support
Alberta child health benefit	Children of low-income families

GIS = Guaranteed Income Supplement; GST = goods and services tax; OAS = Old Age Security; STI = sexually transmitted infection; TB = tuberculosis
Source: Alberta, 2021b.

health benefits programs (see Table 2.2) involving several government ministries, including benefits for individuals with long-term disability for the purchase of medical equipment and supplies (Alberta, 2021b).

A government-sponsored supplemental health benefits program provides coverage for a range of health services: prescription drugs, diabetic supplies, ambulance services, chiropractic care, clinical psychology, dental optical, and hospital accommodation (Alberta, 2021b).

For low to moderate income seniors who are Canadian residents and have lived in Alberta for at least three months, dental and optical benefits are income tested. A maximum of $5,000 of coverage for eligible dental procedures is available every 5 years. Up to $230 is available for prescription eyeglasses every 3 years.

2.5 Regulation

Alberta Health and Wellness is responsible for the monitoring and updating of over 30 laws, and 100 schedules of regulations, rules, standards, and by-laws govern health care in Alberta. Among the most important of these are the two laws (the Hospitals Act and the Alberta Health Care Insurance Act) relating to the provision of Medicare services in Alberta, laws that were originally designed to be consistent with the five criteria under the federal Canada Health Act. However, there have been disputes between the two orders of government about the interpretation of some of these five criteria, as well as about the Canada Health Act's other provisions on user charges and physician extra-billing; as a result, the federal health transfer to the province has been reduced by the amount of the user fees. Indeed, the Alberta government has often been perceived as a champion of more private financing and private provision of medically necessary hospital, surgical, and physician care services (Church & Smith, 2006; Boychuk, 2008; Blomqvist & Busby, 2015).

2.5.1 Providers

Most health providers[12] in Alberta are regulated through self-governing colleges established in 1999 under the authority of the Health Professions Act[13] (Alberta, 2018d). These colleges exercise self-governance through delegated power and authority in the following ways:

---

12 See chapter 5 for further discussion of the health professions.

13 The Health Professions Advisory Board replaced the Health Disciplines Board in 2002. The board is responsible to the minister of health for investigating and making recommendations about the regulation or self-regulation of health occupations. It is also responsible for recommending regulations related to qualifications, scope of practice, and standards of conduct (Lesage, 2006, pp. 305–6).

- establishing entry requirements (educational and practical);
- identifying services to be provided;
- setting standards for professional practice;
- setting continuing competency requirements; and
- undertaking quality assurance activities, including taking disciplinary action.

The Health Professions Act allows for nonexclusive overlapping scopes of practice (e.g., physicians, dentists, optometrists, and midwives). For example, as discussed further in chapter 5, several health professionals can prescribe drugs within their scopes of practice. Certain activities such as vaccinations and diagnostic imaging are restricted to certain professions with the requisite competencies to ensure safety and effectiveness (e.g., physicians, dentists, dental hygienists, denturists, nurse practitioners, registered nurses, licensed practical nurses, pharmacists, and chiropractors; Alberta, 2021b). Several health professions (e.g., acupuncturists, midwives, and emergency medical responders, emergency medical technicians–ambulance, and emergency medical technicians–paramedics) are regulated under the Health Disciplines Act (Alberta, 2000a). The intention of the government is to eventually bring these professions under the umbrella of the Health Professions Act.

2.5.2 Hospitals

All facilities designed as hospitals are regulated under the Hospitals Act and the Operation of Approved Hospitals Regulation (Alberta, 2000d, 1990). Both the act and the regulation encompass the planning, construction, governance, management, and operation of all acute care facilities in the province. Facilities providing mental health services are regulated under the Mental Health Act and the Mental Health Regulation (Alberta, 2000e, 2004b).

2.5.3 Continuing care

In Alberta, the continuing care system includes the following: the coordinated home care program, publicly funded supportive living facilities, and long-term care facilities. Continuing care, which is largely privately delivered, is regulated through the following legislation: the Nursing Homes Act; the Continuing Care Standards Regulation; the Public

Health Act; and the Coordinated Home Care Program Regulation. Through this legislation, the government sets standards of care and reporting requirements for all public and private operators (Alberta Health, 2016a; Alberta, 2003b). At the same time, the personal support workers who form a significant number of the staff in long-term care homes are unregulated in Alberta and the rest of Canada (Estabrooks et al., 2015).

2.5.4 Public health

Public health policy and practices are regulated though the Public Health Act and the Public Health Food Regulation. AHS administers the legislation. The chief medical officer of health provides expertise on public health policy, including health surveillance, disease control and prevention, and population health. Local public health inspectors do periodic inspections of restaurants and other venues in which food is prepared, sold, and provided.

2.5.5 Diagnostic imaging

Diagnostic imaging is regulated through the Alberta Health Care Insurance Act, the Alberta Insurance Act, and the Diagnostic Treatment and Protocols Regulation. Accreditation occurs through the College of Physicians and Surgeons (Alberta, 2006a, 2014; Alberta, 2018l; College of Physicians and Surgeons of Alberta, n.d.-a).

2.5.6 Prescription drugs

Prescription drugs are regulated under the Pharmacy and Drug Act and the Pharmacy and Drug Regulation. This legislation also regulates and licenses pharmacies, and provides for the inspection of licensed pharmacies by field officers. The Alberta College of Pharmacy is responsible for developing and enforcing pharmacy standards and practice guidelines, and the licensure of pharmacists (Alberta, 2018o, 2000f; Alberta College of Pharmacy, 2016, 2020).

Alberta also participates in the Common Drug Review (CDR). The CDR, administered by the Canadian Agency for Drugs and Technologies in Health (CADTH), provides evidence-based recommendations as to whether or not new drugs should be covered by provincial drug benefit plans. Provinces take account of the views of the expert committees, as well as other factors such as local priorities and budget impact, when deciding whether or not to follow the CDR recommendations. Research evidence suggests that, since the implementation of the CDR, the proportion of pharmaceutical products included in Alberta's plan has declined, and the length of time before new drugs are listed has increased (Gamble, Eurich, & Johnson, 2010). Cancer drugs are assessed separately through the similar pan-Canadian Oncology Drug Review (pCODR) process. Cost pressures are also increasingly compelling private plans to follow public payers in adopting measures such as mandatory substitution or drug formularies (Welds, 2017).

2.5.7 Patient health information

The collection, storage, use, and disclosure of patient health information are regulated through the Health Information Act. The act defines who may collect and use health information, and requires that they do so in a limited and discrete manner with an emphasis on anonymity whenever possible. The Office of the Information and Privacy Commissioner is responsible for oversight of how patient health information is collected, stored, and used across the health care system (Alberta Netcare, 2018; Alberta, 2000b; Office of the Information Privacy Commissioner of Alberta, 2018).

2.6 Patients

According to Flood and May (2012), to be effective, a patient charter of rights must include a clearly articulated set of rights, an "economical, easily accessible and independent complaints process," and a "patient ombudsman or commissioner empowered to hear and resolve patient concerns and complaints" and to reduce "litigation and formal disciplinary proceedings against health care professionals" (p. 1583). In 2010, the Alberta Health Act legislated the establishment of a Health Charter to outline the expectations of patients and obligations of service providers and the creation of the Office of the Health Advocate to address patient complaints. Under the charter, a patient has the following rights:

- have my health status, social and economic circumstances, and personal beliefs and values acknowledged;
- be treated with respect and dignity;

- have access to team-based primary care services;
- have the confidentiality and privacy of my health information respected;
- be informed in ways that I understand so that I may make informed decisions about my health, health care and treatment;
- be able to participate fully in my health and health care;
- be supported through my care journey and helped to find and access the health services and care that I require;
- receive information on the health system and education about healthy living and wellness;
- have timely and reasonable access to safe, high quality health services and care;
- have timely and reasonable access to my personal health information;
- have the opportunity to raise concerns and receive a timely response to my concerns, without fear of retribution or an impact on my health services and care. (Alberta Health Advocate, 2021a)

Responsibilities include the following:

- respect the rights of other patients and health providers;
- ask questions and work with providers to understand the information I am being provided;
- demonstrate that I, or my guardian and/or caregivers, understand the care plan we have developed together and that steps are being taken to follow the plan;
- treat health services as a valuable public resource;
- learn how to better access health services;
- make healthy choices in my life. (Alberta Health Advocate, 2021a)

Finally, a general expectation of government is that, "when economic, fiscal and social policies are being developed by the Alberta government, the impact of those policies on public health, wellness and prevention will be considered and steps taken to ensure that public policy is healthy policy" (Alberta Health Advocate, 2021a).

The impact of the charter is discussed in further detail in chapter 7.

2.7 Health research

Created through legislation in 1980, the Alberta Heritage Foundation for Medical Research received an endowment of $300 million to support students and research fellows in medical research. Over time, the mandate of the foundation was expanded to include technology assessment and support for scholarly excellence in medical and population health research. In 2010, AHFMR was transitioned into Alberta Innovates – Health Solutions (AIHS) as part of a larger government initiative to better align investment in research with innovation (Graham et al., 2012); health research is discussed further in chapter 7.

2.8 Summary

Although Alberta is one of the younger provinces in Canada and also the most ideologically conservative jurisdiction, the unprecedented wealth created through government revenues generated from the oil and gas industry has enticed Alberta to develop a publicly funded health care system that is comparable to other jurisdictions in the country (see chapter 3). Alberta created the first provincial health department and was one of the first provinces to provide financing for health care services. As a direct result of oil and gas revenues, it was also the first province to fund medical research.

During the 1990s, Alberta was an early adopter of a regionalized health care system that created a separation between the policy and performance measurement functions of government and the service delivery functions of the health care sector. And, despite the continuing use of neoliberal, pro-market rhetoric, Alberta was also the first province in Canada to introduce the largest public health bureaucracy in Canada in 2008, Alberta Health Services, instead of moving to a more competitive, market-based approach to hospital services.

As will be further discussed in chapters 7 and 8, there have been significant challenges in the implementation of these more recent changes, including the lack of an integrated information system and the continuing exclusion of the physician and pharmaceutical budgets from the control of Alberta Health Services. Effective accountability of physicians also continues to be a challenge.

Chapter Three

Health Expenditures and Financing

Health spending accounts for the single largest share of government expenditures in Alberta and every other Canadian province. Like Canada as a whole, Alberta exhibits a historical pattern of rising health sector expenditures, measured in constant dollars (the value of a dollar adjusted for inflation over time) and in health spending as a percentage of gross domestic product (GDP; a measure of the ability of the economy to sustain high levels of government spending). There has also been a relatively consistent split since the 1970s between public (government) and private sources of total provincial health spending, at approximately 70 per cent to 30 per cent, respectively. The 1984 Canada Health Act sets out broad conditions under which provinces will receive federal transfer payments for in-hospital and physician-provided health care services. The incentives of the act have encouraged provinces to invest in hospitals and physicians rather than in other areas such as health promotion, home support, pharmaceuticals, and so on. This focus is reflected in the data presented in this chapter, although prescription drugs as a means of treating or preventing illness have been an increasingly large component of spending over time, as the same data reflect.

Despite having a right-leaning Conservative government from 1971–2015, supposedly ideologically oriented to small government and low taxes, Alberta has long been among the top provincial spenders on health care in Canada. This expenditure may perhaps be attributed to a strong economy driven by oil resources in which public spending, including health spending, increases during booms, in part because of the more dramatic volatility of the business cycle on tax revenues in Alberta. Of course, the opposite occurs during periods of rapidly declining oil prices, when government revenues shrink (Ferede, 2013). As mentioned in chapter 1, Alberta has the highest median family income of all provinces, providing the government in good times with an abundance of revenues to spend (Duckett, 2015, p. 297). This high level of spending persists despite having a population relatively younger than that of many other provinces (p. 297), which would rather be expected to result in lower costs. However, while several analyses have ranked Alberta as fifth among all provinces in terms of population health outcomes and health system performance, it is second to last (above only Newfoundland and Labrador) in the efficiency of its per capita health spending (Institute of Fiscal Studies and Democracy, 2017).

3.1 Health system financing flows

Figure 3.1 shows (in a simplified form) how money is raised to pay the total expenditures that flow through the health system.

The figure illustrates the point that every dollar of health spending is a dollar of providers' incomes (Evans, 2016, p. 142), with all the policy challenges that this entails. It speaks to the economic importance of the health sector in terms of its contribution to jobs and government tax revenues; 12 per cent of all jobs in Alberta are in the "health care and social assistance" sector (Alberta, 2018b), making it the second largest employment generator in the province. Since health care is largely tax-funded, provincial spending depends on the state of the economy and the willingness of citizens to pay taxes at the level needed to support desired quantities of care (or the willingness of the government to borrow from the future to pay for services today). In the larger picture, we should remember that Canada is a social welfare state and that government spending and policy actions related to social conditions that determine health, such as education, employment, or housing affordability, are also substantially important for achieving population health outcomes.

3.2 Health expenditures and trends

In this section of the chapter, we describe Alberta's expenditures on health and recent trends. To allow for comparisons, we have tried to use data from the same time period throughout. In many cases, these data are the most recent available at the time of writing.

Alberta's total government expenditures on health were approximately $22 billion in 2018. This figure reflects a growth of 257 per cent over figures from the year 2000, though only about half such a rate of

Figure 3.1 Fiscal flows for health

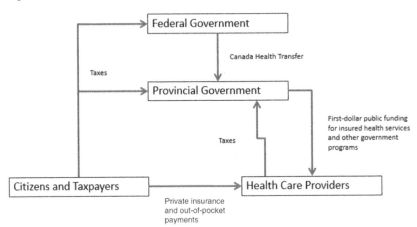

growth (117 per cent) once the numbers are adjusted to constant dollars, which account for the rate of inflation over this same time period. The provincial public sector portion of all health expenditures has been relatively consistent over time (see Table 3.1). The relatively short-lived fiscal constraint of the mid-1990s was followed by a financial rebound that fed into price and wage level increases far in excess of other provinces.

In 2010, the province's total health expenditures amounted to $4,386 per capita in current dollars, while expenditures grew to $5,164 per person by 2018 (Canadian Institute for Health Information [CIHI], 2020a). The three larger provinces (British Columbia, Ontario, and Quebec) spent between 15 to 20 per cent less per person in 2018 (CIHI, 2020a). Per capita government spending in Alberta, when adjusted for age and sex, exceeded that of other provinces throughout the decade of the 2000s (Duckett, 2015, p. 299).

Over time, the province's health expenditures (all public and private sources) as a percentage of the GDP gradually increased from 4.8 per cent in 1981 to 7.6 per cent in 1990; spending fluctuated over the following years, and by 2015 it had settled at about 9.0 to 10.0 per cent of the provincial GDP, a range where it has stayed since (CIHI, 2020a). Alberta's rate of expenditures in 2018 (9.7 per cent) was relatively less than that of other large or economically strong provinces (Quebec, 12.5 per cent; Ontario, 11.2 per cent; British Columbia, 10.8 per cent),

Table 3.1 Total health expenditures, Alberta, 2000–2018, and public-private split

Year	Total provincial government health expenditures in current dollars (millions)	Total provincial government health expenditures in constant dollars (millions), 1997 base	Public share of total provincial government health expenses (%)
2000	6,215	5,722	64.7
2001	7,034	6,243	64.2
2002	7,731	6,565	65.6
2003	8,287	6,831	65.6
2004	9,110	7,286	65.8
2005	10,198	7,833	66.6
2006	11,259	8,287	65.2
2007	12,704	9,187	66.4
2008	13,739	9,378	67.2
2009	14,587	9,665	67.6
2010	16,367	10,663	69.0
2011	16,918	10,690	68.7
2012	17,727	10,907	68.7
2013	18,461	11,138	68.8
2014	19,138	11,194	67.2
2015	19,943	11,421	66.5
2016	20,710	11,798	66.2
2017	21,506	12,180	66.7
2018	22,208	12,430	66.5
2019*	22,574	12,049	65.7

* = forecast value
Source: CIHI, 2020a, Data tables, Series B.

and since the mid-2000s, it has been consistently below the Canada-wide average (see Figure 3.2).

Figure 3.3 shows annual expenditures by different types of health activity. Across all categories, between 2000 and 2018, Alberta's share of resources devoted to each sector has been relatively stable. Hospitals account for about one-third of spending, and the province's per capita spending on hospital services greatly exceeds the national average (Duckett, 2015, p. 299). Duckett suggests that the reasons for Alberta's higher per capita hospital spending include the collapse of the oil and gas sector in the 2008 recession, which provided a pool of labour to fill long-vacant positions in the health sector, as well as weak expenditure control by AHS (Duckett, 2015, p. 301). Physician services and drugs each account for around 15 per cent of total spending.

The Canada Health Act created a system that privileges incentives for hospital-based and physician-provided services, both of which are almost

Figure 3.2 Total health expenditures as percentage of GDP, Alberta and
Canada, 2000–2018

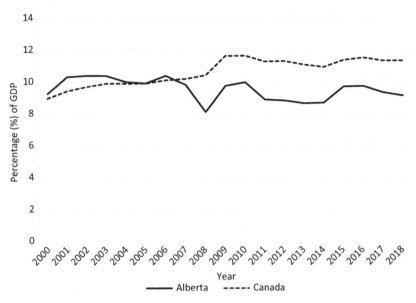

Source: CIHI, 2020a, Data tables, Series B.

100 per cent paid for by government. Drugs are covered if provided during
a hospital stay; if dispensed outside of a hospital, they are outside the act's
framework. Many Canadians can obtain prescribed pharmaceuticals through
employer-based or other forms of private insurance. In 2012, prescribed drugs
accounted for 82 per cent of all drug spending in Alberta. The remaining
18 per cent of drug spending was accounted for by out-of-pocket purchases
for over-the-counter products (CIHI, 2013). Coverage for prescribed drugs
is about equally divided between public and private sector insurance plans.

3.2.1 Payment methods

The way in which health care providers receive their payments affects
their behaviour; therefore, it is important to look at this aspect of health
financing as well.

In the 2019–20 fiscal year, the Alberta Department of Health was allocated $22.1 billion, which accounted for 41 per cent of all government

Figure 3.3 Alberta government health expenditure by use of operating funds,*
2000–2001 to 2018–2019, as a proportion of total spending

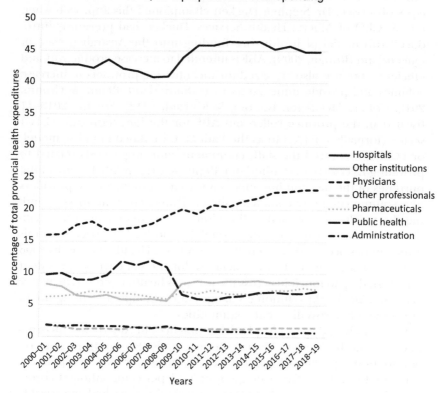

* Capital and other health spending (approx. 6 per cent of total) excluded.
Source: CIHI, 2020a, Data tables, Series F.

expenditures on programs and debt servicing (Alberta, 2020a). The department allocated $15.5 billion to Alberta Health Services (Alberta Health, 2019). Historically, both pre- and post-regionalization, individual institutions were funded with global budgets, leaving discretion over spending in the hands of local managers who were closest to care delivery and could allocate money in a way that best addressed community needs.

However, like some other provinces and countries, Alberta has begun to experiment with devoting a portion of this funding to an alternative model, activity-based funding (ABF) – where providers are compensated using a formula that incorporates both the volume and mix of services, with increased income achieved from delivering more of the desired types of service. Dr. Stephen Duckett championed this approach when he was CEO of Alberta Health Services; Duckett had previously introduced this model of health care funding into the Australian state of Queensland (Ruttan, 2009). ABF is intended to increase productivity and efficiency, but it is also criticized for incentivizing providers to increase volumes and provide unnecessary care (Sutherland, Repin, & Crump, 2012; Cohen, McGregor, Ivanova, & Kinkaid, 2012). For the 2010–11 fiscal year, the province rolled out ABF for the long-term care (LTC) sector (formally referred to as the Patient/Care-Based Funding model, or PCBF); it covered the staff, equipment, and supply costs related to providing LTC services (Sutherland, Repin, & Crump, 2013). One of the purposes of the new funding model was to incentivize service providers to accommodate more complex patients. Plans were announced, pending the results, to also make allocations to inpatient acute care facilities on the basis of this funding model, but no further progress in this direction has occurred. The creation of Alberta Health Services in 2008 revealed that payments to LTC facilities, for the same types of resident care, varied up to fourfold across the previous health regions (Duckett & Peetoom, 2013); thus, funding changes also attempted to bring about greater equity across different communities.

Most family and specialist physician practices in Alberta are incorporated private businesses. Alberta, in fact, leads the nation in this corporatization; in 1996, 61 per cent of practices were so incorporated, compared to a Canadian average of only 21 per cent, although corporatization rates in many other provinces have since reached comparable rates to those of Alberta (Nielsen & Sweetman, 2018). Physicians receive payment for services from the Alberta Health Care Insurance Plan. While it is possible for physicians to opt out of the plan and bill patients directly, they cannot work in both modes simultaneously. As a result, as of March 2020, there were only two physicians in Alberta working wholly outside the public plan (Canada, 2021, p. 177).

Doctors have historically been paid by the province on a fee-for-service basis, with fees negotiated by the province and the doctors through their bargaining association, the Alberta Medical Association (AMA), as part of the process of reaching a Physician Master Agreement. The presumed strength of the fee-for-service payment model is that physicians are rewarded for delivering more services to patients in need. A drawback to fee-for-service is that the additional services, which are incentivized, may not be needed (Stoddart & Barer, 1992). In addition, fee-for-service does not encourage the most productive use of physicians' time and skills, does not promote continuous care, and has few incentives to organize care efficiently or to practise in areas of need, such as rural areas (Birch, Goldsmith, & Mäkelä, 1994). The fee schedule can grow increasingly complex with each new contract negotiated, and both patients and taxpayers have little overall sense of how health spending is being allocated among different services.

There has been some growth over time in the interest of both physicians and governments in other payment models, or alternative payment plans – referred to in Alberta as alternative relationship plans (ARP). However, as of 2017–18, both the number of physicians who received any payment from ARP and the total proportion of physician payments delivered through ARP were the lowest among all Canadian provinces (CIHI, 2019).

3.2.2 Private and out-of-pocket spending

Government legislation/regulation in Alberta, as in many other provinces, restricts or prohibits private insurers from covering "medically necessary" care, that is, services funded under the Canada Health Act umbrella (Flood & Archibald, 2001). Thus the proportion of private spending in these sectors is small relative to other health areas (Table 3.2).

Outside of the hospital and physician service areas, individuals can and do pay significant amounts using private funding sources, either directly from their own pockets (e.g., for over-the-counter medicines or specialized services, such as nutritional counselling) or through purchase of insurance.

Table 3.2 Percentage of private spending by sector,* Alberta, 2018

Sector	Total health expenditures accounted for by private spending (%)
Hospitals	7.4
Other institutions	42.6
Physicians	0.6
Other professionals	87.8
Drugs	62.0
Public health	–

*Capital, administration, and other health spending (approximately 6 per cent of total health expenditure) excluded.
Source: Calculated from CIHI, 2020a, Data tables, Series D2 & D3.

While insurance can be individually purchased, it is more commonly made available as an employment perquisite; for instance, many employers offer health benefits for such things as dental, eye, or chiropractic services or massage therapies, usually referred to as extended or supplemental health benefits. The health insurance market consists of a mix of private, often multinational, firms and not-for-profit agencies such as Blue Cross. As of 2020, the Alberta marketplace for health insurance included operations from fifty-five private for-profit life and health insurers; only three of these firms had their head offices in the province (Canadian Life and Health Insurance Association, 2020). These data exclude a tiny number of property and casualty insurers, who may offer some health-related services but account for only a small proportion of the total private insurance products sold (Hurley & Guindon, 2008).

3.3 Public revenues

Both the federal and provincial governments contribute money towards Alberta's annual health sector spending. The province devotes its own revenues, mostly raised through the tax system, and the federal government provides a lump sum payment through the Canada Health Transfer, the value of which it calculates as a combination of cash and tax points (see more below).

3.3.1 Provincial own-source revenues

In the 2019–20 fiscal year, federal government transfers made up 21.6 per cent of funds expended by the Department of Health; the rest of the money was supplied through the province's own resources (Alberta Health, 2020a). Money from taxes goes into general government revenues and is distributed to different government departments in amounts determined by the provincial cabinet, led by the premier and minister of finance. The proposed spending, in the form of estimates, is debated each year in the Alberta Legislature and approved by that body – this control over spending is a fundamental principle of parliamentary democracy as practised in Canada and other countries with government traditions derived from the UK (or "Westminster") model. Of course, a majority government always has enough votes in the Legislature to assure that its proposals are passed (Franks, 1987).

   From 1969 to 1 January 2009, the province also raised a portion of its revenues for health spending through Health Care Premiums, which were a monthly charge to individuals and families (often covered by employers as a job benefit). While this money was notionally meant to pay for some health care costs, in practice it was simply added to the general revenues and so might best be considered as simply a tax under another name. In any event, premiums never came close to funding the total health spending. In their last year, they raised the government about $1 billion, which was less than 10 per cent of that year's more than $14.6 billion health allocation (see Table 3.1 above). PC Premier Jim Prentice announced his intention to reestablish health care premiums in the province's 2015 budget, but after his government fell to the New Democratic Party (NDP) in the May election of that year, Prentice's proposal was rescinded by the new administration (Wood, 2015).

3.3.2 Federal transfers

Federal contributions to provincial health care spending really began in 1948 with the introduction of federal health grants for hospital construction, health system planning, and public health, among other areas (Vayda & Deber, 1992). The initial elements of Medicare were agreed to by federal-provincial negotiations, with the federal government committing to pay approximately 50 per cent of provinces' costs incurred for insured hospital services (1957) and physician fees (1966). Although initially Alberta objected to a compulsory, publicly funded health insurance scheme, it was one of the first five provinces to comply with conditions needed to become eligible for federal cost-sharing for hospital care (as of 1 July 1958) and was the sixth province to join the physician cost-sharing scheme (as of 1 July 1969; Marchildon, 2016).

In 1977, the federal government consolidated most of its conditional health and other social program transfers into a single block transfer, Established Programs Financing (EPF), available to provinces subject only to the requirement that they organize a health care delivery system that met the principles of universality, comprehensiveness, accessibility, portability, and public administration. The federal government had grown uneasy over its open-ended obligation to fund a system over whose growth it had no control. It was felt that making provinces bear responsibility for rising costs that exceeded federal willingness to pay might encourage them to focus more on efficiency and effective use of spending (Vayda & Deber, 1992). For the largest provinces (with the largest GDPs), such as Alberta, the federal contributions under hospital and medical care constituted a smaller share of total provincial expenditures than in the smaller provinces, and so Alberta (like British Columbia and Ontario) had less to lose from this change. The greater freedom to reallocate resources that this method provided also appealed to Alberta, a province that had long resisted supposed federal encroachments upon its constitutional jurisdiction and prerogatives.

EPF consisted of a cash component and a transfer of "tax points." The transfer of tax points is essentially accomplished when the federal government reduces the income taxes that it levies upon taxpayers so that provinces can increase their own rates. The net tax paid by individuals remains the same, but a larger portion of it is paid to provincial governments and a smaller share to Ottawa. As a province with relatively large capacity to raise its own tax revenues, Alberta could readily live with this new EPF model (Booth & Johnson, 1993).

Since 1977, the federal government has continued to count the amount of tax money it would have raised if it had left its tax rates at the same level as part of its contribution to provinces for financing the health care system. The rising relative value of tax points has meant that the federal government can claim its contribution is steady or even increasing, even though the total amount of cash changing hands has actually shrunk (Provincial and Territorial Ministers of Health, 2000). Thus, unsurprisingly, the provinces argue that current amounts of federal support should be calculated by only looking at the cash component.

In 1996–97, federal grants were further consolidated into a renamed Canada Health and Social Transfer. Critics complained that this consolidation obscured how much money the federal government was contributing to health care and how much to other programs (e.g., income assistance, postsecondary education). In response, the grant was redivided into a separate Canada Social Transfer (CST) and Canada Health Transfer (CHT) for the 2003–04 fiscal year.

In current dollars, Ottawa reports that its CHT payments to Alberta have grown from $2.4 billion in 2012–13 to $4.3 billion in 2017–18 (a 79 per cent increase), further rising to $4.9 billion in 2020–21 (Canada, Department of Finance, 2021). Compared to the 2016–17 provincial health spending of approximately $21 billion (Alberta Health, 2018b), this figure amounts to 20 per cent of the total.

3.4 Summary

This chapter's primary purpose has been to describe the historical and current patterns of health spending in Alberta. We have eschewed any effort at normative judgment; that is, we do not presume to suggest that there is a best or most appropriate level of spending or balance between private and public sources of finance. However, certain facts are clear. Health care spending in Alberta, in both absolute and relative terms, has grown over time. Public and private shares of spending, within different health sectors, remain largely consistent. Public sector spending is concentrated on hospitals and physicians (see chapters 5 and 8 for more on this topic). Yet, technological change has become increasingly significant in transforming the health service landscape and eroding the historical balance that has guided Medicare policy in Canada during the post–Second World War years.

Alberta is a relatively high spender on health care among Canadian provinces, with potential opportunities to achieve greater efficiency. Along with other provinces, efforts are being made to better control costs, for instance, through changes to the systems by which institutions and providers are paid; evidence for the impact of these changes cannot yet be fully seen. The federal government has relatively little leverage over health care decision-making, given the small proportion of funds that are directly contributed through the existing Canada Health Transfer. And, importantly, population health outcomes depend on more than health care spending; appropriate investment by all levels of government into social determinants of health such as poverty reduction and good jobs are also essential.

Chapter Four

Physical Infrastructure

Patients can be cared for in their own homes: for instance, physicians, home care nurses, and other professionals can visit to provide services; health promotion messages can be delivered to people via the media; and people can tend to themselves or their family members through the use of over-the-counter medications and home remedies. However, most health care delivery in Alberta occurs in custombuilt and specialized facilities. This chapter summarizes the physical infrastructure of the health system in Alberta, that is, the stock of buildings and equipment through which services are delivered. See chapter 5 for information about the "human capital" side, health care providers; chapter 6 describes the quantity and quality of the services provided.

This chapter is divided into six main parts. First, we consider acute care hospitals; second, residential facilities; third, diagnostic imaging and laboratory services; fourth, community and public health centres; fifth, e-health services; and sixth, health research funding.

4.1 Hospitals and other treatment facilities

Alberta's Hospitals Act defines a general hospital as "a hospital providing diagnostic services and facilities for medical or surgical treatment in the acute phase for adults and children and obstetrical care" (Alberta, 2000d, p. 3). Additionally, we define it here as a facility that includes at least some beds to which patients are admitted for stays of one or more continuous 24-hour periods. This definition excludes some ambulatory care facilities like urgent care centres (UCCs), which provide more intensive care but without inpatient accommodation. In addition,

Table 4.1 Acute care hospital beds and beds per capita, Alberta, 1954–2017

Year	Beds (n)	Beds per capita (n)
1954	6,361	6.1
1960	9,390	7.3
1971	14,810	9.1
1986–87	17,990	7.4
1994–95	8,372	3.1
2017	8,430	5.0

Sources: 1954 and 1971 data from Crichton, Hsu, & Tsang, 1990; 1960 data from Hall, 1964; 1986–87 and 1994–95 data from Tully & Saint-Pierre, 1997; 2017 data calculated from Alberta Health, 2018b.

a range of surgical day-patient procedures continue to be contracted out to privately owned and operated centres.

Alberta's first hospital was opened in 1863 at the Catholic mission in St. Albert. Early hospitals were charitable institutions for those without other means of care or support.

> They served chiefly the poorer groups in society and were regarded as a place of last resort because of the high mortality among those who entered them. Surgery was extremely hazardous at best; in hospital there was an added risk of post-operative infection. Skilled nursing was non-existent. People who could do so arranged for care at home. (Hastings & Mosley, 1980, p. 147)

It was not until the organizational and scientific medical advances of the late 1800s (such as trained nursing, infection control, and diagnostic methods such as the X-ray) that hospitals became a service people really trusted to do them good rather than harm (Starr, 1982, p. 156).

The 1948 National Health grants, a cost-shared program to support new hospital construction, alluded to in chapter 3, led to rapid growth in the number of hospital beds and beds per capita in all provinces (Marchildon, 2013, p. 82). In Alberta, the boom continued through the 1970s as part of the Lougheed government's province-building agenda. A great retrenchment occurred in the mid-1990s, however, following Ralph Klein's election as premier on an austerity platform in 1993. During Klein's first term in office, bed numbers were almost halved, shrinking from 4.5 beds per 1,000 population to 2.4 (Church & Smith, 2013a) – or from about 13,000 to around 6,500 beds (Pratt, 2015; Table 4.1).

There are a number of ways by which to describe the extant infrastructure. Here, we describe hospitals in terms of size and geographic location, ownership, specialization, and age/structural condition.

4.1.1 Size and geography

Hospitals range from small community facilities to urban tertiary care teaching hospitals. The larger facilities have capacity for procedures that are highly complex and/or infrequently occurring, such as trauma care. Some services requiring very specialized expertise are not available in Alberta, and patients must obtain them elsewhere; for instance, only a single clinic in Canada performs sex reassignment surgery (CTV News, 2015).

As of 2018, there were 100 acute care facilities with inpatient beds in the province. These were classified as urban (10), regional (5), and community (85). Together these facilities had 8,448 acute care beds (Alberta Health Services [AHS], 2018b) – a 5 per cent growth over the 5 years from 2010–11 (AHS, 2015b, p. 156). Table 4.2 shows the distribution of these facilities and beds to the five AHS geographic zones.

Alberta's largest hospital is the Foothills Medical Centre in Calgary, with 1,081 acute care beds. Community hospitals range in size from 4 to 351 beds, but 92 per cent have fewer than 40 beds. Alberta has more people per acute care bed (447) than the Canadian average (390) or an average of internationally comparable developed nations (344; Pratt, 2015). These figures might suggest that access is relatively more difficult. However, compared to other provinces, Alberta has an atypically large number of small, rural acute care facilities, a legacy of the Lougheed-era building boom described below, though many of these facilities are not full-service hospitals.

Table 4.2 Acute care beds in Alberta, by type and zone, as of 31 March 2018

Zone	Urban hospitals		Regional hospitals		Community hospitals	
	N	Total beds	N	Total beds	N	Total beds
South	0	0	2	498	10	147
Calgary	5	2,631	0	0	8	148
Central	0	0	1	370	29	728
Edmonton	5	2,031	0	0	7	972
North	0	0	2	266	31	657
TOTAL	10	4,662	5	1,134	85	2,652

Source: Alberta Health Services, 2018b.

4.1.2 Ownership

Hospital ownership can be categorized as public, private, or not-for-profit (including religious groups). Most Alberta facilities fall under Alberta Health Services (AHS) auspices and so can be considered as public institutions, though religious-based care continues to be provided through Covenant Health in affiliation with the public provider. No privately owned, for-profit hospital facilities exist in Alberta today, though day surgeries are performed in privately owned clinics. During the 1990s, the definition of a hospital became politically controversial in Alberta when the Klein government encouraged the contracting out of various surgeries performed in public hospitals (eye and joint replacement) to private surgical clinics (Church & Smith, 2006).

Many of the earliest health care facilities in Alberta were established by religious orders. The Catholic Grey Nuns, for instance, opened Holy Cross Hospital in Calgary in 1891 and Edmonton General Hospital in 1896 (Humbert, 2004). Their individual facilities were eventually consolidated into the Caritas Health Group (now Covenant Health), which operates seventeen facilities across the province (including eight hospitals with acute care beds, the largest of which is Edmonton's Grey Nuns Community Hospital). Ten per cent of the province's emergency room visits and 20 per cent of child deliveries occur in Covenant Health facilities; 12 per cent of all acute care beds are located there (Hoskins, 2017).

Covenant facilities are integrated with AHS, yet also maintain some degree of independence; a master agreement governs relations between AHS and Covenant Health wherein the organization acknowledges both responsibilities to AHS and to its Catholic sponsors. In short, religious hospitals have a strong historical legacy in the province; they provide communal benefits such as pastoral care. However, their refusal to offer access to doctrinally offensive services such as abortion, birth control, or assisted dying has made it harder for some Albertans to receive services that are available to others in regular course (Simons, 2016).

4.1.3 Specialization

Though most Alberta hospitals are general purpose and cater to a wide range of health needs, several have a particular mandate to serve either a designated population group or type of illness.

There are two dedicated children's hospitals in Alberta: the Alberta Children's Hospital in Calgary (141 beds) and the Stollery Children's Hospital at the University of Alberta in Edmonton (159 beds). The Lois Hole Hospital for Women at the Royal Alexandra Hospital in Edmonton specializes in women's health care.

There are also some historical categories of specialty hospitals that no longer exist in Alberta. For instance, the Charles Camsell Hospital in Edmonton served for some years as an Indian Hospital offering segregated care (Drees, 2010; Lux, 2016; Geddes, 2017); today this practice can be thought of as a health sector equivalent to the infamous residential schools. The federal government ran veterans' facilities in Alberta, such as the Colonel Belcher Hospital in Calgary; these were disappearing by the 1980s, as the number of Second World War and Korean War veterans declined (Sutherland & Fulton, 1992, p. 239), and were transitioned to local authorities with the advent of regionalization. Some illness-specific hospitals, such as those designated for the treatment of tuberculosis (the Central Alberta, later Baker Memorial Sanitorium, Calgary; the William Aberhart Memorial Sanitorium, Edmonton) became obsolete due to changes in standards of care and were also closed or repurposed.

Edmonton is the location of certain specialized facilities such as the Glenrose Rehabilitation Hospital (244 beds) and the Cross Cancer Institute (55 beds). Five free-standing hospitals in the province are dedicated to the inpatient treatment of mental health and/or substance use issues: Alberta Hospital Edmonton (295 beds); the Centennial Centre for Mental Health and Brain Injury (formerly Alberta Hospital Ponoka; 330 beds); the Southern Alberta Forensic Psychiatric Centre in Calgary (33 beds); the Claresholm Centre for Mental Health and Addictions (120 beds); and Villa Caritas, at the Misericordia Community Hospital in Edmonton, which operates 150 psychiatric beds. From the 1970s, institutionalized mental health care fell out of philosophical favour among many patient advocates, who preferred greater use of community-based treatment and rehabilitation (LaJeunesse, 2002; Boschma, 2011), which were also enabled by advances in psychotropic pharmacology beginning in the 1960s. Over that decade, inpatient mental health bed numbers in Alberta fell dramatically, from 3.1 beds per 1,000 population in 1970 to only 0.8 per 1,000 in 1978–79 (Sutherland & Fulton, 1992, p. 192). Continuing pressures have been exerted to reduce or close facilities such as Alberta Hospital Edmonton, although these pressures have been countered by the opposition of some critics, families, and health care unions

(Gillespie, 2010); to date, further deinstitutionalization has gained limited traction among provincial policy-makers (Duckett, 2015, p. 321), and increased services in communities have not been provided to an extent that replaces what patients could have been offered through the closed facilities.

4.1.4 Structural condition

Canada as a whole experienced a hospital building boom between the 1940s and the 1960s, with facilities increasing in both number and size due to federal grants to the provinces for new construction (Marchildon, 2013, p. 82). In Alberta, infrastructure expansion continued on through the 1970s and 1980s: "the last great hospital-building era ... when the Tory government led by Peter Lougheed constructed facilities in dozens of small towns" (Gerein, 2014). This project of state-building, economic development, and securing rural political support left a legacy of "over-building" in rural communities (Gerein, 2015b).

About three in five hospitals date from this 1970s and 1980s period. As a consequence, much of Alberta's infrastructure is reaching its designed lifespan, and renewal or replacement is needed for many facilities. A series of articles in the *Edmonton Journal* in late 2014 described the deteriorating state of this infrastructure. At that time, two-thirds of the province's hospitals were at least 30 years old, while a third were more than 40 years old (Figure 4.1).

Alberta's capital spending in the health sector exceeds that of other provinces as a share of spending and per capita expenditure (Duckett, 2015, p. 302). Figure 4.2 shows capital spending, which includes all facilities and construction, grew annually until the 2008 recession, at which time it was curtailed before finally levelling off again about 2014. Yet, the bill for deferred maintenance across existing facilities is estimated by different sources as between $637 million and $1.02 billion (Gerein, 2014), which is equivalent to almost an entire year's worth of capital spending or more (see Figure 4.2). The bulk of capital spending goes to hospital projects, and new hospitals in particular are hugely expensive. As of 2018, the *Canadian Construction Cost Guide* projected that acute care hospital construction in Calgary would top out at $675 per square foot; by contrast, school construction would average $346 per square foot; police, fire, and library facilities, $359; and recreation and cultural facilities, $421 (Altus Group, 2018).

Figure 4.1 Decades in which Alberta hospitals were built

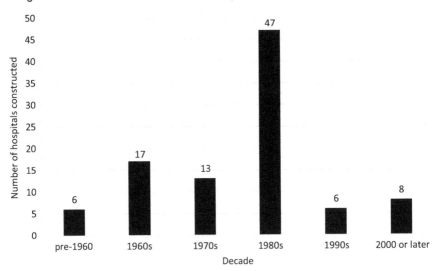

Source: Gerein, 2014.

Figure 4.2 Total provincial government health expenditures, capital, Alberta, 2000–2001 to 2017–2018 (current dollar)

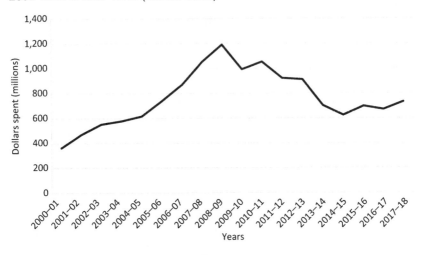

Source: CIHI, 2020a, Data tables, Series F.

This capital cost is part of the rationale for why public-private partnerships (or P3s) have been used as a mechanism for major health care construction projects in countries like the United Kingdom and in Canadian provinces such as Ontario and British Columbia (Whiteside, 2015), although they are a controversial development model. Ideally, P3s harness the efficiencies of the private sector, its expertise in project management, and the incentive given to developers to seek the lowest costs in construction and operation to maximize profits. However, such approaches also demand that the public sector develop skills in contract management; administrative expenses can be higher; decision-making authority may become muddled; and ultimately, the public sector may have to step in if a private contractor fails (Whiteside, 2015). While the Progressive Conservative Prentice government originally proposed the Calgary Cancer Centre project as a P3, the subsequent New Democratic Party (NDP) government, in power between 2015 and 2019, was ideologically opposed to the concept of P3s and employed traditional public financing mechanisms instead (Bakx, 2016).

Architectural design theories related to hospitals have changed substantially in recent years, so new facilities differ from older buildings in relation to such things as carefully considered external views and intended room occupancy. For instance, evidence shows that patients facing a green or natural view outside their window heal better; the $253 million Alberta Children's Hospital (ACH) in Calgary, which opened in 2006, was built with this principle in mind (Picard, 2006). In line with contemporary design theories, ACH also embraced the idea of family sleeping rooms, allowing parents or other family members to remain close by (Adams & Theodore, 2005; Picard, 2006). Multipatient wards and shared rooms, such as those predominant in some of Alberta's older urban hospitals like Edmonton's Royal Alexandra, have fallen out of favour, again based on evidence showing that private rooms are better at preventing the spread of disease and increasing patient satisfaction (Givetash, 2015).

Providing care on these principles tends to make retrofitting older facilities exceedingly costly; a drawback of these imperatives is that health organizations are often poor custodians of built heritage.

4.2 Long-term (continuing care) facilities

According to Alberta Health, continuing care includes long-term care (LTC), supportive living (SL), and community hospice/palliative care. We use the term "continuing care" here, consequently, to include all these

Table 4.3 Long-term care, supported living, and palliative facilities in Alberta, by zone, as of 31 March 2018

Zone	LTC, SL, and palliative facilities (n)	Total beds (n)
South	50	2,803
Calgary	76	8,206
Central	79	4,015
Edmonton	91	8,724
North	60	2,148
TOTAL	356	25,896

LTC = long-term care; SL = supported living
Source: Alberta Health Services, 2018b.

forms of care housing. These facilities provide residential accommodation for individuals who are unable to live independently and must have daily medical monitoring and attention. Most, though not all, of these residents are elderly. Additional facilities that provide solely nonmedical assistance such as meals and housekeeping are classified separately (e.g., seniors' lodges). These facilities are funded by the health sector and governed by policies and legislation under the responsibility of both the Ministry of Health (e.g., Accommodation Standards) as well as other departments such as Alberta Housing. Prior to the 1990s, the public system consisted of auxiliary hospitals (est. 1959) and nursing homes (est. 1964), along with seniors' lodges in the housing sector (est. 1959). Some private operators existed in both rural and urban areas (Armstrong, 2002).

4.2.1 Size and geography

Overall, Alberta has (as of 2018) 336 LTC and/or SL facilities, with a total of 25,653 beds. Twenty stand-alone palliative care facilities provide an additional 243 beds for those who are in the final stages of life. Table 4.3 shows their geographic distribution. Larger facilities are typically found in the major cities. In the Edmonton and Calgary zones, 38 per cent and 50 per cent of facilities, respectively, have 100 or more beds, while the proportion in the other three zones ranges from only 7 per cent to 25 per cent.

4.2.2 Ownership

Compared to acute care hospitals, there is greater for-profit involvement in ownership of continuing care facilities, with for-profit facilities

Table 4.4 Distribution of long-term care beds, by type of ownership, Alberta, 1984–2018

Year	Public beds	Not-for-profit beds	Private beds	Total beds
1984–85[1]	2,875 (33%)	2,192 (25%)	3,606 (42%)	8,673
	43 facilities	24 facilities	36 facilities	
2009–10[1]	6,147 (33%)	5,819 (31%)	6,831 (36%)	18,797
	58 facilities	63 facilities	78 facilities	
2017–18[2]	4,246 (32%)	4,260 (32%)	4,720 (36%)	13,226
	80 facilities	35 facilities	37 facilities	

Sources: 1. Daly, 2015; 2. Alberta Health Services, 2020.

responsible for about one-third of total beds since the turn of the century (Table 4.4). Although not specific to Alberta, there is more general research (and COVID-19 experience) suggesting that for-profit ownership in the LTC sector can lead to worse health outcomes for residents, attributable to such factors as lower average staff-patient ratios (McGregor & Ronald, 2011; Ontario Health Coalition, 2020). Alberta's first publicly owned long-term care facility was opened in 1963, with the public sector assuming a greater role in LTC provision in Alberta in recent years than in some other provinces (Berta et al., 2006; Daly, 2015). For instance, according to Daly, in 2009–10, 39 per cent of facilities in Alberta's LTC sector were privately owned, compared to 44 per cent in British Columbia, 65 per cent in Ontario, and a national average of 56 per cent (Daly, 2015).

Publicly operated LTC facilities go by the brand names Carewest in Calgary (10 sites) and CapitalCare in Edmonton (8 sites). Major not-for-profit, voluntary, and faith-based operators include Calgary's Bethany Care Society (Lutheran), the Good Samaritan Society (Lutheran), and Shepherd's Care Foundation (Pentecostal). As of 2013, Alberta's private LTC sector consisted of 13 corporations, the two largest being Extendicare and Revera, both headquartered in Ontario (Graff-McRae, 2021). In the supportive housing sector, Points West Living exemplifies a privately owned provider that is contracted by Alberta Health Services to provide care to residents in twelve small rural communities (Points West Living, n.d.).

4.2.3 Specialization

In smaller communities, LTC and hospitals often share the same building, while there are more stand-alone facilities in the larger towns and cities. Similarly, the palliative care system includes both designated beds in existing hospital or LTC facilities, as well as a small number of stand-alone hospice facilities. The first such stand-alone facility was established in Calgary in 1992 (Alberta Health Services, 2014).

While the federal government formerly owned and operated its own network of care homes for veterans, they have been replaced by service contracts placing veterans within the provincial network (Canadian Healthcare Association, 2009, p. 74; see also Burke, 2016). There remain two facilities in Alberta with dedicated veterans' wings and priority placement (Colonel Belcher in Calgary and Kipnes Centre for Veterans in Edmonton), but the expectation is that all post-Korea veterans will be accommodated along with the general public.

Michener Centre in Red Deer is the province's main residential care centre for persons with developmental disabilities; there are also a number of small group homes that serve the housing needs of this population.

4.2.4 Age and design

Similar to the situation in the acute care sector, Alberta's continuing care infrastructure is aging. "Some 50 percent of the long-term care facilities in Alberta are 30 years old or older" (Smith, 2010). Certain structures are approaching a half century or more; "many facilities in Alberta, including 12 Extendicare facilities, were built in the 1960's and require major renovations to bring them in line with current structural and core design standards" (Citizen Watch, n.d.). Such proposed renovations can be quite costly; as with hospitals, modern architecture suggests new design principles for LTC facilities, such as the creation of a homelike atmosphere and application of universal design principles (Wang & Kuo, 2006; Schwartz & Brent, 1999).

4.3 Diagnostic imaging and laboratory services

Diagnostic imaging and laboratory services (DIAL) are key components of the health care system; they provide clinicians with information necessary to identify, understand, and treat patient illnesses. As such, and especially when provided inside hospitals or on referral by physicians, diagnostic services are considered as medically necessary and are 100 per cent publicly funded. The Ralph Klein government attempted to privatize hospital laboratory services in the mid-1990s, but these efforts – a P3 in Calgary and a private sector contract in Edmonton – were controversial and largely unwound by 2005–06. Sutherland (2012) contends that "over the 15 years since all laboratory services were integrated under the control of the regional governments, the role of for-profit laboratories in Alberta has been significantly diminished" (p. e167).

4.3.1 Laboratory services

Local and community-based laboratory testing services include such things as blood and body fluid sample collection, urinalysis, hematology and other chemical and toxicological analyses, microbiology, and pathology. Laboratory tests for insured services are provided by Alberta Health Services, either directly or through contracts with private providers. Historically, the organization of laboratory services differs somewhat across geographic zones (Table 4.5). One impact of the privatization pressures in the 1990s was to centralize lab services away from smaller rural communities into larger urban centres (McIntosh, 2020).

Table 4.5 Historical organization of laboratory services, by zone

Zone	Organization of laboratory services
Calgary	All inpatient and outpatient services provided through Calgary Laboratory Services (CLS), a wholly owned subsidiary of AHS. The labs became publicly owned when the majority private owner was bought out in 2006 (McIntosh, 2020).
Edmonton	Most inpatient and hospital-based outpatient testing performed by public laboratories located within the hospitals; a single private provider, DynaLifeDX, exclusively contracted to provide all community outpatient testing. DynaLifeDX served the Edmonton area with 26 patient-care centres and a central laboratory.
North	Public laboratories provided all inpatient and most outpatient testing. DynaLifeDX had a small number of collection sites for a limited amount of outpatient testing work.
Central	Public laboratories provided all inpatient and most outpatient testing. DynaLifeDX had a small number of collection sites for a limited amount of outpatient testing work.
South	Public laboratories provided all inpatient and most outpatient testing. One private provider, Medicine Hat Diagnostic Laboratory (MHDL), operated in the zone, with 4 collection sites and a central laboratory; the MHDL contract expired in 2017.

Source: Lawson, 2012.

In terms of funding, AHS separately provided public laboratories with global budgets. Private laboratories received public funds in the form of fixed term, fee-for-service contracts, with payments capped once a certain threshold had been passed (Lawson, 2012; Sutherland, 2012).

A 2016 review by the Health Quality Council of Alberta recommended a restructuring of this patchwork system, and the Notley NDP government responded to it by announcing the creation of Alberta Public Laboratories, planned to be a wholly owned subsidiary of Alberta Health Services. The new system was expected to be fully integrated by 2022 with the expiration of DynaLife's government contract (Health Quality Council of Alberta, 2017). However, the United Conservative government, elected in 2019, announced that it would not proceed with this plan (Mertz, 2019).

The Provincial Laboratory for Public Health, with locations in Calgary and Edmonton, provides for many of the most complex laboratory services needed in the province as well as public health surveillance and research. Very virulent pathogens, such as Ebola, can only be handled with extreme caution in highly secured facilities. The National Microbiology Laboratory (NML) in Winnipeg is the only site in Canada equipped to do this type of work because it possesses Biological Safety Level Four (BSL 4) containment, one of only fifteen such laboratories world-wide.

4.3.2 Diagnostic imaging

According to the World Health Organization (WHO), as cited by the Canadian Institute for Health Information (CIHI), diagnostic imaging is "a means to take pictures of the structure and processes of the body and make them visible or 'accessible' to the human eye. It encompasses the use of ionizing radiation (e.g., basic X-ray, computed tomography, nuclear medicine or scintigraphy), ultrasound, magnetic resonance and a few other highly sophisticated procedures" (CIHI, 2007, p. 1).

In Alberta, public imaging services are provided at a range of sites. AHS performs about three million exams of a variety of imaging types each year (Figure 4.3). There are also private for-profit clinics that provide many of these services. As of September 2019, the College of Physicians and Surgeons of Alberta lists 312 approved imaging facilities in the province; approximately 60 per cent of these are independent (which may or may not be for-profit), and 40 per cent are in the public

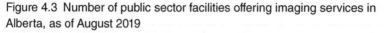

Figure 4.3 Number of public sector facilities offering imaging services in Alberta, as of August 2019

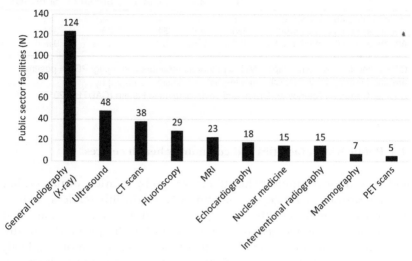

CT = computerized tomography; MRI = magnetic resonance imaging; PET = positron emission tomography
Source: Calculated from information available on the Alberta Health Services website (https://www.albertahealthservices.ca/info/page9911.aspx).

sector. Independent clinics outnumber public ones in the Edmonton and Calgary zones, with the reverse being the case in the more rural zones. Imaging done in public hospitals and/or ordered by family physicians in the community is covered under the terms of the Canada Health Act and free to patients.

Many of these tests require highly expensive equipment. Thus, their availability in the public sector has been strictly controlled by governments, which are committed to managing costs (Marchildon, 2013). For most machines, Alberta's proportion of the Canadian total is roughly comparable to its share of the population as a whole (Table 4.6).

Testing is physician-driven (Marchildon 2013, p. 85), and many of the largest operators today were initially established by doctors (Sutherland, 2011). This situation raises the possibility of conflict of interest, self-referral, and overuse (Marchildon, 2013, p. 86). In addition to public facilities, a range of private providers has emerged who offer such tests to the public, with payment out-of-pocket or by private insurance often required.

Table 4.6 Diagnostic imaging machines in Alberta and Canada, 2012

	CT	MRI	PET-CT	SPECT	SPECT-CT
Recorded number (Alberta)	56	41	4	42	32
Recorded number (Canada)	561	366	51	330	361
Alberta as % of Canadian total	10%	11%	8%	13%	9%

CT = computerized tomography; MRI = magnetic resonance imaging; PET = positron
emission tomography; SPECT = single-photon emission tomography
Source: Canadian Agency for Drugs and Technologies in Health (CADTH), 2017.

4.4 Public health facilities and community health centres

Public and/or community health centres go by a variety of names, but
overall provide a range of community-based health services such as
home care, public health nursing and immunization, restaurant and
other forms of public health inspections, and health promotion or disease prevention initiatives (the nature of these services is more explicitly
considered in chapter 6). As of 2018, AHS operated 139 such sites in
the province, distributed across the five geographic zones as indicated
in Table 4.7.

Many community health centres (CHCs) are simply buildings from
which AHS delivers its programming, but some are inspired by the
principles of the community health centre movement. Such CHCs
are distinguished by their community orientation, commitment to
health equity, emphasis on team-based primary care and health promotion, community development, and initiatives to address social
determinants of health. There are four such sites in Alberta that are
members of the Canadian Association of Community Health Centres:
Boyle McCauley Health Centre (Edmonton), CUPS Calgary, the Alex
CHC (Calgary), and L'Association canadienne-française de l'Alberta
(ACFA)-Clinique francophone de Calgary. A closer look at the Boyle
McCauley Health Centre illustrates the services offered and role
played by such facilities.

Boyle McCauley opened in Edmonton's inner city area in 1979. It
continues to be community owned and operated as a not-for-profit
society, with a board of directors elected annually for two-year terms
(Boyle McCauley Health Centre, 2018). The organization serves many
clients with multiple health and social issues, such as mental illness,
addictions, poverty, and social isolation. It provides more than 100,000

Table 4.7 Public health centres in Alberta, by zone, as of 31 March 2018

Zone	Public health centres (n)
South	17
Calgary	22
Central	34
Edmonton	21
North	45
TOTAL	139

Source: Alberta Health Services, 2018b.

annual on-site visits, and 25,000 additional services are provided through off-site programming. Services include traditional medical and dental care (publicly funded), as well as complementary/alternative care such as chiropractic and acupuncture. It is the site of a needle exchange program that operates from a harm reduction philosophy. It also provides specialized services for HIV+ clients and women/ transgendered persons involved in the sex trade. A recent addition to services is the Pathways to Housing program, based on "housing first" principles, or the idea that homelessness is best addressed through providing stable housing from which people can then access health and other social supports.

4.5 Information and communications technology infrastructure

Medical diagnosis and treatment have become increasingly high tech over time. However, technology is also increasingly key to the effective management and coordination of patient care through information and communications technology systems that support clinical service delivery – often referred to as e-health. E-health applications are best enabled when they can build upon an electronic health record, which allows patient histories to be readily shared among health care providers and institutions.

4.5.1 Electronic health records and electronic medical records

Electronic health records (EHRs) and electronic medical records (EMRs) are distinct concepts, although they are often confused in common usage. An EHR is "a patient-oriented, aggregated, longitudinal system that assembles health information about a patient," while an EMR is "a computerized health information system that is used in clinical offices to record detailed encounter information" (Ludwick & Doucette, 2009). Canada's implementation of electronic records lags behind many countries; Mossialos, Wenzel, Osborne, and Anderson (2015) reported that in 2012 the uptake of EMR by primary care physicians was 56 per cent in Canada, in contrast to rates in the range of 95 per cent for several European and Australasian countries, though by 2017 Canadian primary care physician rates had grown to 85 per cent (Canada Health Infoway, 2017). In terms of the connectivity and integration that EHRs promise, Doty, Tikkanen, Shah, and Schneider (2020) report that Canada ranks tenth out of eleven developed countries in the ability of primary care physicians to electronically exchange information about patients' medications and laboratory test results with clinicians outside their own practice, with only one-third or fewer able to do so.

Nonetheless, within Canada, Alberta is often seen as a leader in e-health and has managed to avoid the scandals and out-of-control costs that have been observed in other provinces. The province began enrolling physicians into EMR programs in 2003, before any other province, and in 2017 had the highest rate of uptake, at 91 per cent (Canada Health Infoway, 2017). Alberta's main electronic health record initiative was Wellnet, later known as Netcare, which links over fifty provincially held databases. It is mainly used by physicians, laboratories, and pharmacies and includes the following types of information: personal demographic information, hospital visits, surgeries, immunizations, laboratory test results, diagnostic images, medication information, and allergies. In spring 2016, the province announced plans to connect primary care networks and emergency room physicians to the system (Sinnema, 2016). The number of providers with access to the Netcare system has grown steadily, from 37,324 in 2014–15 to 50,477 in 2017–18 (an increase of 35 per cent over a 3-year period), with nurses, then physicians, being the most connected professions (Alberta Health, 2018b). The Connect Care project – an integrated clinical information system scheduled to be implemented in nine waves between 2019 and 2023 (Alberta Health Services, n.d.-d) – will create a single point of access for all AHS patient information in hospitals and continuing care facilities, community health centres, and laboratories. It will replace more than 1,300 individual systems currently in place, and will increase the amount of information available to populate Netcare (Gerein, 2017b).

The encouragement of EMRs in physician offices was spearheaded by the Physician Office System Program (POSP), a tripartite initiative of the province, the Alberta Medical Association, and the regional health authorities (RHAs). POSP ran in several phases, beginning in 2001, and was credited with bringing Alberta physicians to the forefront in Canada for the use of EMRs (OECD, 2010, p. 106).

The picture is not entirely rosy, however. Despite extensive early spending in the development of electronic health records (over $800 million by 2014), doctors continued to use at least one dozen different medical record systems that could not communicate with one another; one in five physicians, in fact, had not yet converted their practices to use electronic records keeping at all (Sinnema, 2016). In part, this mishmash is attributable to a decision-making process that allowed physicians significant autonomy in choosing which electronic record system they wanted to adopt.

4.5.2 Telehealth

Telehealth is a means by which diagnosis, consultation, and monitoring can be provided at a distance. Telehealth in Alberta is provided through Alberta Health Services with 37 clinical programs able to operate out of over 1,600 sites (McIntosh, 2020). Between 2002 and 2012, the number of clinical sessions conducted using telehealth grew by more than 1,000 per cent (COACH, 2013, p. 14). Many different kinds of clinical consultations and educational sessions can be carried out this way. Alberta also uses the telehealth network much more than other provinces to replace face-to-face meetings for administrative and management purposes (COACH, 2013).

4.6 Health research infrastructure

Alberta has two universities with medical schools: the University of Alberta (U of A) in Edmonton and the University of Calgary (U of C). Both have extensive research programs. The Cummings School of Medicine at the U of C reports $168 million annually in research grants and contracts received as of 2015 (University of Calgary, 2015). The U of A Faculty of Medicine and Dentistry reported $197.6 million in research funding received in 2017 (University of Alberta, n.d.-a). In addition to these universities, the University of Lethbridge, Athabasca University, and Mount Royal University also conduct a more limited range of health research projects using internal and external funds.

The Canadian Institutes of Health Research (CIHR) is Canada's major national grant council for health and medical research. It funds four streams of research: biomedical, clinical, health systems, and population health. Between 2000–01 and 2017–18, Alberta-based researchers and institutions received a total of $1.227 billion dollars in CIHR spending (about $68 million on an annualized basis), amounting to 9.6 per cent of total CIHR research investment over this time period (Canadian Institutes of Health Research, 2018). As discussed in chapter 2, Alberta Innovates is the major provincially based research grant organization. Innovation in health care is a particular funding priority, in line with general trends towards greater funder attention on applied health research and technology commercialization. It was created in 2016 from an amalgamation of four previously separate corporations, including Alberta Innovates – Health Solutions (AIHS), which had been created in 2010. AIHS itself had replaced the long-standing Alberta Heritage Foundation for Medical Research (AHFMR). In 2016–17, the Health Innovation sector of the agency was funding 1,884 investigators and 264 student trainees. This section of the funding organization spent slightly less than $93 million in that fiscal year (Alberta Innovates, 2017).

Alberta was an early Canadian leader in funding medical and health research; the AHFMR was established in 1979, while no other province had its own granting body until twenty years later. These efforts can partly be attributed to Progressive Conservative Premier Peter Lougheed's province-building and economic diversification objectives; the results were that "by 1995 Alberta was a leader among Canadian provinces for provincial funding of medical research and was identified as one of the top 10 medical research centers in North America" (Zwicker & Emery, 2015, pp. 4–5).

4.7 Summary

Historically, health care institutions such as hospitals, continuing care facilities, and public health centres were planned by separate entities, with few means to connect them into a coherent and integrated system of services. The advent of regionalization, in theory, allows for better coordination across these areas (Church & Smith, 2008). There have been changes; for example, ambulatory care has increasingly been successfully substituted for inpatient treatment. Yet, problems like stranded patients persist. Weak integration across other policy areas – community mental health, for instance – is also evident.

The physical infrastructure of Alberta's health system is aging, and replacement or repair has not kept pace. Deferred maintenance costs are accumulating and competing with demands from the education, transportation, environment, and other sectors where infrastructure investment has also fallen greatly in arrears (Federation of Canadian Municipalities, 2016).

Alberta's political leaders have historically been vocal proponents for the role of private delivery in health care. The province's reputation as a haven of privatization owes much to Klein-era policies. Yet, the evidence in this chapter suggests that this reputation may be overblown; the public sector role in areas like LTC and laboratory services in Alberta exceeds that of many other provinces, for instance, and is larger and stronger than often assumed. Alberta's regulation of publicly funded for-profit facilities, such as day surgery clinics, is relatively transparent and arguably more restrictive than that in place in many other provinces. However, many average Albertans may be challenged to distinguish between purely public facilities and those that are privately owned but funded by public contracts, as the nature of services experienced by patients varies little.

Hospitals and other care facilities are community institutions: employers, social hubs, custodians of heritage, and carriers of moral/religious values. So we need to think of them in a larger way than simply as a place to deliver health care services; their actions can be important ways to address social determinants of health within Alberta communities.

Chapter Five

Health Workforce

Like other jurisdictions, Alberta faces significant health workforce challenges. At the heart of these challenges is the number and mix of health providers required to optimize the efficient and effective delivery of health care services. Health workforce planning is a tricky business. The disconnect between the national nature of health human resources and how these resources are actually utilized (provincial and territorial jurisdictions), involvement of multiple vested interests, fiscal realities, worker moral, and an aging population are all factors that place significant constraints on thoughtful and effective planning. Given these constraints, achieving the correct balance between cost and quality is not an easy task (Rowand, 2002).

Alberta's close connection to the oil and gas sector has been a double-edged sword when it comes to its health workforce. On the one hand, during periods of economic boom, Alberta has access to significant revenues. These funds allow Alberta to pay premium wages to attract health providers from other jurisdictions. On the other hand, when the oil and gas sector is in an economic slump, the government must rely on supply-side (wage) restrictions that significantly heighten labour strife and ultimately affect the quality of patient care. Of particular note in this context is the success of health providers in minimizing the impact of wage reductions during economic downturn and realizing significant gains during economic boom periods.

For its part, the provincial government must deal with the combination of a rapidly expanding population and revenue volatility associated with an oil-based economy (see chapter 1). This situation creates significant challenges to providing stable and predictable funding for health services and therefore the health workforce. To walk this policy tightrope, the province and the major service providers have pursued various approaches assumed to be beneficial in stabilizing and optimizing the use of the available health workforce.

In this chapter, the function, number, and mix of health care providers in the province are discussed within the context of constant structural change and fluctuating finances. Specifically, the chapter notes the continuing dominance of physicians and their collective preferences, the increasing use of licensed practical nurses, and the dominance of institutional settings for nursing practice.

Table 5.1 provides a snapshot of the range of health providers per 100,000 population in Alberta compared to Canada.

5.1 Main workforce challenges

As with other Canadian jurisdictions during the 1990s, Alberta pursued policies to reduce the supply of physicians as a means of saving money. This decision resulted in a perceived shortage of physicians by the end of the 1990s (Evans & McGrail, 2008; Walker, 1993; Borsellino, 1993).

To address this challenge, physicians began formally reviewing human resource planning in the late 1990s, establishing resource targets and identifying an existing/emerging physician resource deficit through a report in 2000. This study was followed up with a report in 2006 outlining developments between 2000 and 2006. Table 5.2 summarizes these developments.

Despite these efforts, a shortage of 1,100 full-time physicians (FTEs) was identified in 2005 (Physician Resource Planning Committee, 2006, p. 4). And yet, the physician per 100,000 population ratio was higher than the Canadian average between 2008 and 2017 (Canadian Institute for Health Information [CIHI], 2018b).

Within a larger historical context that has been anti-union (Bright, 2000), registered nurses have experienced a challenging relationship with government, including legal strikes in 1977 and 1982 and an illegal strike in 1988. With the creation of health regions in early 1994, nurses saw their wages rolled back by 5 per cent (also experienced by physicians). Although the true extent of the resulting layoffs remains unknown, the United Nurses of Alberta, the union representing nurses, estimates that between 2,000 and 3,000 FTEs were lost through layoffs. The resulting workforce deficit created and the workplace culture built around part-time employment (casualization of the labour force) left a policy legacy that has been difficult to overcome, even with subsequent

Table 5.1 Alberta health care providers

Type of provider	Year	Count Alberta	Per 100,000 population Alberta	Selected provinces/ territories per 100,000 population	Female % Alberta
Audiologists	2008	130	4	4	77.7
	2017	170	4	5	78.2
Chiropractors	2008	912	25	23	24.0
	2017	1,060	25	25	30.8
Dental assistants	2008	–	–	–	–
	2017	5,898	139	65	99.1
Dental hygienists	2008	2,209	61	67	97.5
	2017	3,176	75	82	95.8
Dentists	2008	1,946	54	59	–
	2017	2,518	59	65	30.9
Dietitians	2008	929	26	27	97.7
	2017	1,288	30	33	96.9
Environmental public health professionals	2008	177	5	4	–
	2017	397	9	5	–
Genetic counsellors	2008	–	–	–	–
	2017	28	1	1	96.4
Health information management professionals	2008	641	18	13	98.7
	2017	749	18	13	94.8
Medical laboratory technologists	2008	2,341	65	60	89.3
	2017	2,567	60	56	–
Medical physicists	2008	36	1	1	–
	2017	42	1	1	28.6
Medical radiation technologists	2008	1,790	50	52	82.5
	2017	2,303	54	58	81.5
Midwives	2008	39	1	2	–
	2017	120	3	4	100.0
Occupational therapists	2008	1,485	41	39	90.6
	2017	2,145	50	49	90.4
Opticians	2008	–	–	–	–
	2016	1,054	25	–	–
Optometrists	2008	468	13	13	38.7
	2017	794	19	17	50.4
Paramedics	2008	–	–	–	–
	2017	8,286	195	96	–

(continued)

Table 5.1 (*continued*)

Type of provider	Year	Count Alberta	Per 100,000 population Alberta	Selected provinces/ territories per 100,000 population	Female % Alberta
Pharmacists	2008	3,727	104	93	62.7
	2017	5,276	124	115	60.9
Pharmacy technicians	2008	–	–	–	–
	2017	1,456	34	31	–
Physician assistants	2008	–	–	–	–
	2017	40	1	2	–
Physicians (excluding residents)	2008	7,193	203	197	32.9
	2016	10,294	242	–	38.1
Family medicine	2008	4,016	112	101	37.1
	2016	5,320	125	–	41.9
Specialists	2008	3,277	91	95	27.8
	2016	4,974	117	–	34.0
Physiotherapists	2008	2,021	56	52	77.4
	2017	2,846	67	64	73.0
Psychologists	2008	2,393	67	48	69.4
	2017	3,587	84	51	77.8
Regulated nurses	2008	37,035	1,030	1,100	95.0
	2017	51,204	1,204	1,174	92.5
Licensed practical nurses	2008	6,760	188	244	95.5
	2017	13,958	328	328	92.1
Nurse practitioners (NPs)	2008	216	6	5	91.7
	2017	481	11	15	90.4
Registered nurses (including NPs)	2008	29,091	800	840	95.6
	2017	35,929	845	830	93.2
Registered psychiatric nurses	2008	1,184	33	52	74.7
	2017	1,317	31	52	78.4
Respiratory therapists	2008	1,221	34	27	70.0
	2017	1.,823	43	33	73.4
Social workers	2008	5,684	158	101	85.1
	2017	7,035	165	143	86.4
Speech-language pathologists	2008	1,058	29	22	97.1
	2017	1,368	32	27	96.9

Source: Canadian Institute for Health Information (CIHI), 2018b.

Table 5.2 Alberta physician human resource initiatives

Initiative	Date	Impact
Creation of the Alberta Rural Physician Medicine Network	16 August 2000	Commitment to fund 40 ongoing postgraduate training positions
Increase in postgraduate training resources	14 February 2000	Annual medical school entry positions have increased by 50 per cent between 2000 and 2006–07; postgraduate positions have increased by 45 per cent
Increased physician numbers	1999–2004	Between 1999 and 2004, physician numbers increased by 20.3 per cent
Alberta Physician Resource Planning Database	2000	Allows for the collection and storage of data on RHA medical services needs
Changes to the Alberta Special Medical Register	October 2000	To provide recognition to Physician Extenders
New non-CaRMS training opportunities announced	2001	Between 2001 and 2006–07 the number of positions grew from 8 to 42

CaRMS = Canadian resident matching service; RHA = regional health authority
Source: Physician Resource Planning Committee, 2006.

efforts to increase the complement of nurses in the province (Finkel, 2012; Gereluk, 2012; Schiebelbein, 2012; United Nurses of Alberta, 2002, pp. 10–16, 24; Findlay, Eastabrooks, Cohn, & Pollock, 2002; CIHI, 2016b).

As Figure 5.1 demonstrates, this legacy of casualization has been sustained into the present context. Between 2006 and 2015, less than 50 per cent of Alberta registered nurses were employed full time. More recently, there has been a concerted effort to increase the number of full-time nurses. However, Alberta has remained below the Canadian average for full-time employment of nurses and has a higher utilization ratio of nurses to licensed practical nurses (LPNs).

5.2 Physicians

To practise medicine in the province of Alberta, physicians must be registered with the College of Physicians and Surgeons and have a practice permit. In order to be registered, applicants must provide proof of completion of the Medical Council of Canada Evaluating Exam, undergo

Figure 5.1 Percentage of registered nurses by employment status, Alberta and Canada

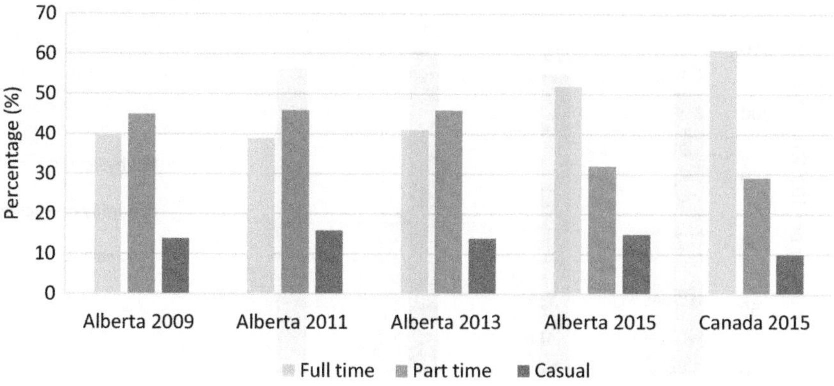

Source: CIHI, 2016b.

a practice readiness assessment, and demonstrate good character and reputation (Alberta, 2016b).

General practitioners and family physicians are the "gatekeepers" to publicly insured health care services. Operating in a variety of settings (hospitals, clinics, offices, and other community settings), they diagnose and treat a broad range of health-related issues, including making referrals for diagnostic and specialist services (Alberta, 2016b).

Medical specialists are physicians who have completed advanced medical training in a specialized area of medicine (e.g., cardiology, gerontology, oncology, psychiatry). Normally they provide diagnosis and treatment through referral from other health providers, especially general practitioners and family physicians (Alberta, 2018c).

In 2019, Alberta had a total of 10,408 physicians, approximately 6 per cent of the health workforce. Of these, approximately 55.3 per cent were family physicians and 44.7 per cent were specialists. In 2016, Alberta Health Services employed over 8,200 physicians and had an indirect relationship with an additional 1,800 physicians. Of particular note is the shift to a needs-based approach to planning indicated through the amended Master Agreement between the Government and the Alberta Medical Association ratified in the spring of 2017, as discussed further in section 5.5.2. (Canadian Medical Association, 2019; CIHI, 2018b; Alberta Health & Alberta Medical Association, 2016).

Figure 5.2 Physicians per 100,000 population, Alberta and Canada

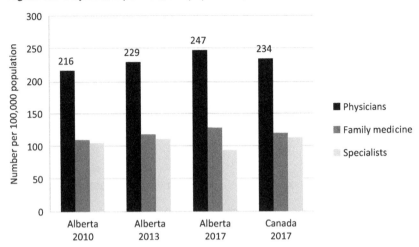

Sources: CIHI, 2018a, 2018b.

As Figure 5.2 indicates, between 2010 and 2017 the physician to patient ratio increased from 216 per 100,000 population to 247 per 100,000 population. This ratio was above the average for Canada (234 per 100,000) in 2017. Between 2013 and 2017, there was a 19.3 per cent change for family medicine and a 17.3 per cent change for specialists, which was greater than any other jurisdiction in Canada.

As Figure 5.3 indicates, there has been some movement in the overall gender distribution, although Alberta is below the Canadian average for percentage of female physicians.

Disaggregating the data further, Figure 5.4 shows that there was no major change in gender distribution within family medicine between 2011 and 2017; however, there has been a slow shift towards more women in the medical specialties (Figure 5.5).

As Figure 5.6 indicates, Alberta's physician population is younger than the Canadian average.

As noted in chapter 3, physicians are reimbursed through a variety of models, although most receive payment for services on a fee-for-service basis. As demonstrated in Figure 5.7, Alberta physicians are historically among the best paid in the country and consistently rank above the Canadian average. In 2016, they were the best paid in Canada (Gerein, 2016c). As discussed further in chapter 8, Alberta has been slower than

Figure 5.3 Physician gender distribution trends, Alberta and Canada

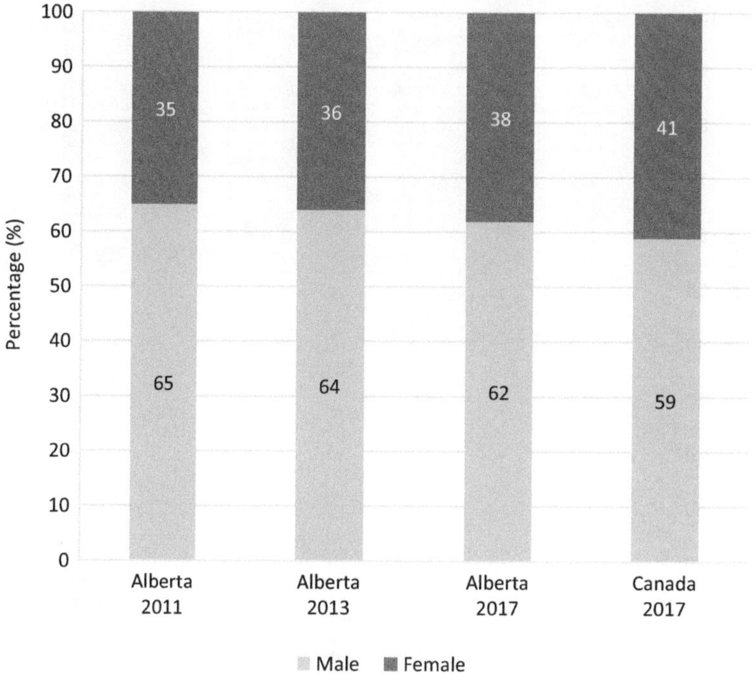

Sources: CIHI, 2018a, 2018b.

other jurisdictions to shift physicians into alternative payment mechanisms from fee-for-service.

5.3 Regulated nurses

Regulated nurses (n = 51,204) represented the largest portion of the Alberta health workforce (28 per cent) in 2013, a decline from 32 per cent in 2009. The largest portion of this group, registered nurses, represents 21 per cent of the health workforce. Between 2009 and 2013, the nursing workforce increased by 13.5 per cent, compared to 19.4 per cent for physicians and 27.6 per cent for the overall health workforce.

Registered nurses (RNs) are the most commonly recognized form of nurse in Alberta's health care system (n = 35,929). RNs are self-regulating

Figure 5.4 Family medicine gender distribution, Alberta and Canada

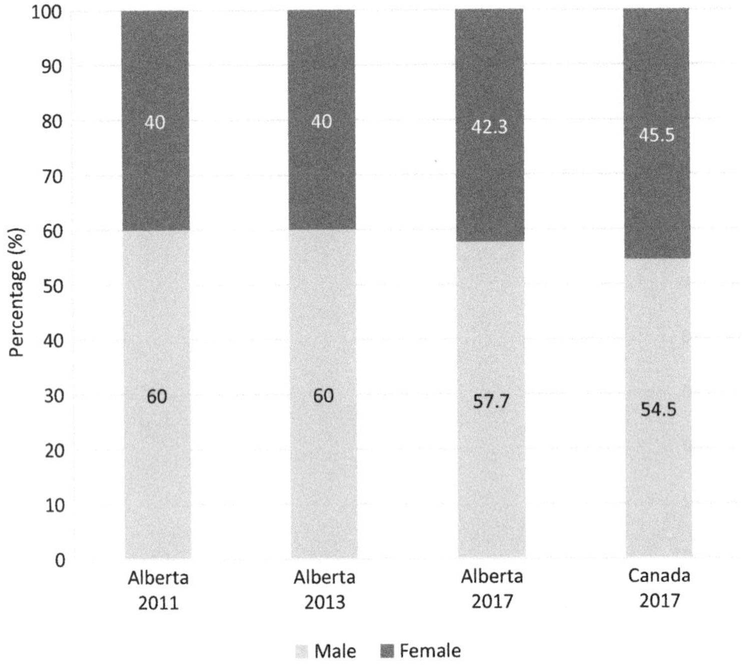

Sources: CIHI, 2018a, 2018b.

and are trained through a standardized, university-based degree. Under the terms of the Registered Nurses Profession Regulation, they are regulated by the College and Association of Registered Nurses of Alberta. They must successfully complete a national competency exam. Four years of a specialized undergraduate degree is required.

RNs provide a range of services within a defined scope of practice. These services include observing, assessing, monitoring, and documenting patient conditions; administering medications and injections; and assisting physicians with patient care. They work collaboratively with other health providers, patients, and their families in acute care, long-term care, and community settings (Alberta Health Services, n.d.-r; Alberta, 2005; College and Association of Registered Nurses of Alberta, 2020).

Figure 5.5 Medical specialists gender distribution, Alberta and Canada

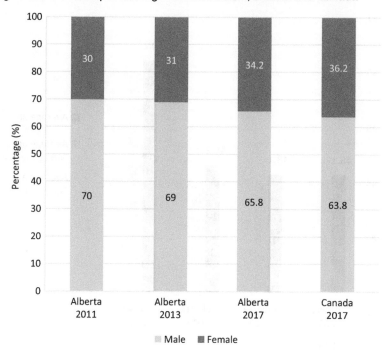

Sources: CIHI, 2018a, 2018b.

In May 2019, new regulations came into force to allow RNs with additional training to prescribe and order tests in specific clinical areas where the employer supports such activities. Additionally, nurse practitioners can now set bone (College and Association of Registered Nurses of Alberta, 2020).

Registered psychiatric nurses (RPNs) are self-regulated nurses who specialize in the provision of care for patients with mental and physical disabilities and addictions (n = 1,317). A minimum of 2 years of specialized postsecondary education is required. They must demonstrate a set of national core competencies but do not complete a standardized national exam. The College of Registered Psychiatric Nurses of Alberta is the regulatory body (Alberta Health Services, n.d.-s; College of Registered Psychiatric Nurses of Alberta, 2018; Alberta, 2018n).

Figure 5.6 Physician average age, Alberta and Canada

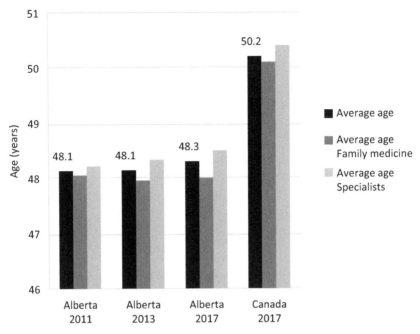

Sources: CIHI, 2018a, 2018b.

Licensed practical nurses (LPNs; n = 13,958) are increasingly seen as a substitute for RNs in the delivery of certain less skilled tasks. While they draw from the same body of knowledge as RNs, they receive their training through a 2-year college diploma rather than a 4-year university degree, as is the case with RNs. They are also more limited in their scope of practice, including assessment, planning, implementing, and evaluating patient care. They must successfully complete a national competency exam and are regulated by the College of Licensed Practical Nurses of Alberta (CLPNA) under the Health Professions Act LPN Regulation, 2003 (CIHI, 2018d; College of Licensed Practical Nurses of Alberta, 2018; Alberta, 2003a).

Nurse practitioners (NPs; n = 481) are RNs with advanced training. They complete an additional 2 years of postgraduate training beyond the standard undergraduate nursing degree and must successfully complete a national competency exam. NPs are able to diagnose, order, and interpret diagnostic tests and treat and prescribe drugs for patients within their scope of practice and provincial regulations. They are

Figure 5.7 Average gross clinical payment per physician by province, 2010–2011 to 2016–2017

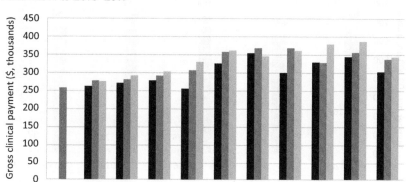

AB = Alberta; BC = British Columbia; CAN = Canada; MB = Manitoba; NB = New Brunswick; NL = Newfoundland and Labrador; NS = Nova Scotia; ON = Ontario; PEI = Prince Edward Island; QC = Quebec; SK = Saskatchewan
Source: CIHI, 2020a.

regulated in the same way as RNs (University of Alberta, n.d.-b; Alberta Health Services, n.d.-j; Alberta, 2018h).

The next paragraphs explore the relative distribution among different types of nurses in Alberta over time. As Figure 5.8 illustrates, while registered nurses have seen uneven growth since 2007, licensed practical nurses have seen a steady increase, reflecting an emerging strategy of labour substitution. Currently, Alberta is above the Canadian average for RNs (707 per 100,000) and slightly below the average for LPNs (283 per 100,000).

Figure 5.9 clearly indicates that the annual growth rate of the RN workforce since 2007 has averaged around 2 per cent, while the growth rate for LPNs has averaged around 7 per cent.

As Figure 5.10 illustrates, Alberta RNs practice primarily in the hospital setting. If we eliminated 2011–13 because of underreporting in these major categories, nurses in the hospital setting averaged 64 per cent; nurses in the community setting averaged 16 per cent; and nurses in the nursing home setting averaged 8 per cent.

As Figure 5.11 illustrates, LPNs practice primarily in the hospital setting, although over time their numbers in the community setting have

Figure 5.8 Regulated nurses per 100,000 population, Alberta and Canada

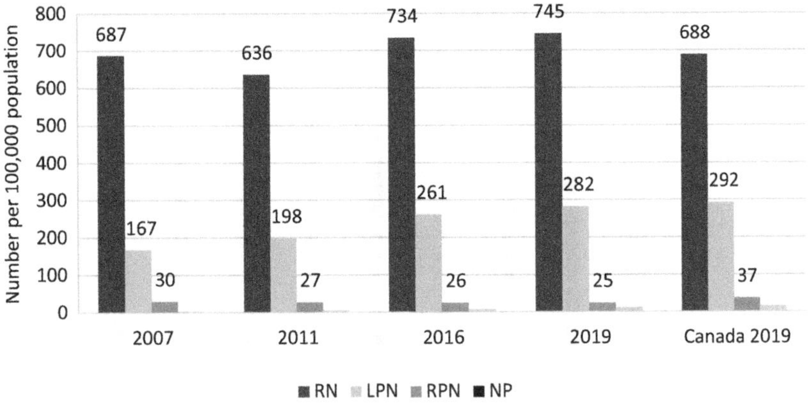

LPN = licensed practical nurse; NP = nurse practitioner; RN = registered nurse; RPN = registered psychiatric nurse
Source: CIHI, 2020c, Data tables, Table 4.

been increasing. While the annual average percentage increase in the hospital setting has been a little over 7 per cent, the increase in the community setting has been 12 per cent. Of particular note is a 112 per cent (1,099 to 2,339) annual increase in 2010 in the community setting. As Alberta Health Services (AHS) has rolled out its human resources strategy, LPNs have been increasingly employed in areas where traditionally RNs have dominated. They are employed largely in settings that are under the control of AHS (Sinnema, 2011; Mertz, 2013; Decilia, 2014).

While pursuing a policy of substituting less expensive workers for registered nurses, the government was less strident in its efforts to expand employment opportunities for nurse practitioners.

As Figure 5.12 illustrates, between 2009 and 2019, an average of 55 per cent of nurse practitioners were employed in the hospital setting. The average annual growth rate during this time period was around 8 per cent. Unlike LPNs, NPs overlap heavily with the scope of practice of physicians. Traditionally, in the academic literature, they have been viewed as a possible labour substitute for physicians. However, physicians have tended to view NPs in a negative light (Chen, 2013). Thus, while there has been some experimentation with NPs in community settings normally dominated by family physicians, they have tended to be concentrated in settings that are controlled by AHS (acute and public health) and have realized limited growth.

Figure 5.9 Annual percentage growth rate, Alberta registered nurses and
licensed practical nurses

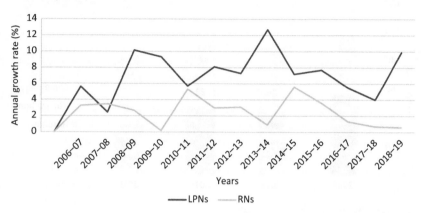

LPN = licensed practical nurse; RN = registered nurse
Source: CIHI, 2020c, Data tables, Table 4.

Figure 5.10 Percentage of nurses by practice setting, Alberta and Canada*

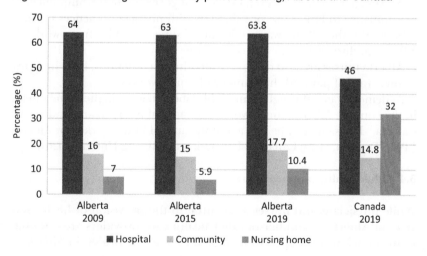

*Numbers reflect only nurses practising in these three workplace settings.
Sources: CIHI, 2020c, Data tables, Table 4; CIHI, 2017c, Data tables, Table 17.

Figure 5.11 Percentage of Alberta licensed practical nurses by practice setting

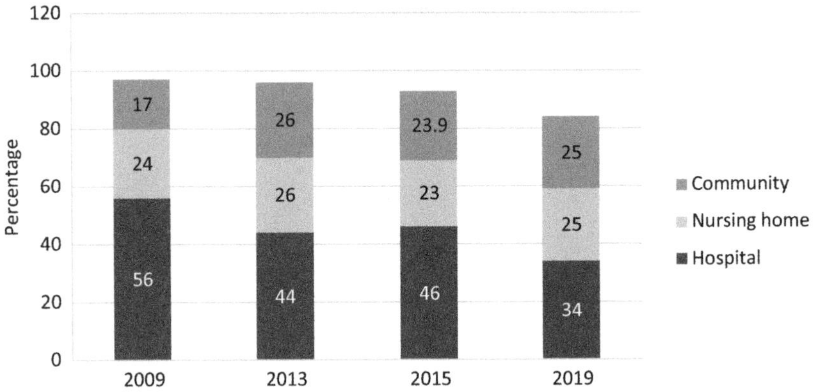

Sources: CIHI, 2020c, Data tables, Table 4.

Although traditionally, NPs have been used as a substitute for physicians in rural and remote areas, Figure 5.13 suggests that it does not appear to be the case in Alberta.

Figures 5.12 and 5.13 illustrate that, on average, over 90 per cent of NPs are located in urban institutional settings, which was above the Canadian average in 2015. However, the current government has announced a new initiative to link nurse practitioners with physician practices in rural Alberta. But there is no way within the existing legislative framework for NPs to bill directly for the services that they provide (French, 2019).

Alberta nurses are also distinct from other jurisdictions, both in terms of their rate of pay and the number of hours worked.

As demonstrated through Figure 5.14, Alberta has the highest paid nurses in the country. Alberta nurses work fewer annual hours than elsewhere in Canada.[1] The same can be said about the annual hours worked by Alberta LPNs (Duckett, 2015; Canadian Federation of Nursing Unions, 2020).

5.4 Other health care providers

While physicians and nurses are central to the provision of health services in Alberta, a number of other health care providers are essential to the delivery of the spectrum of health services provided in Alberta.

---

[1] As mentioned in chapter 1, Alberta has the highest per capita income in Canada. Thus, nurses' wages need to be considered within this larger context.

Figure 5.12 Percentage of Alberta nurse practitioners by practice setting*

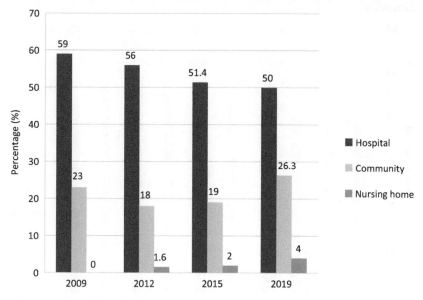

* Numbers are only for NPs employed in the three workplace settings.
Sources: CIHI, 2020c, Data tables, Table 4.

Figure 5.13 Nurse practitioners geographic distribution, Alberta and Canada

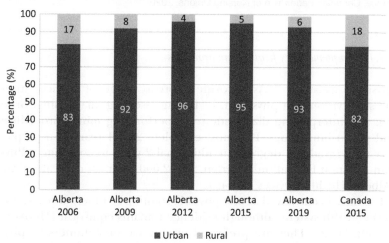

Sources: CIHI, 2020c, Data tables, Table 4; CIHI, 2017c, Data tables, Table 34.

Figure 5.14 Registered nurse hourly wages in Alberta compared to other provinces

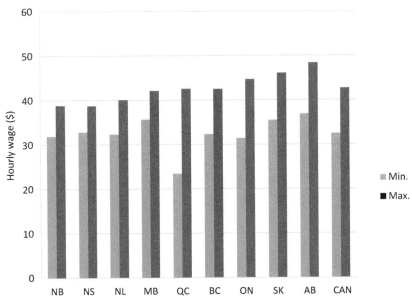

AB = Alberta; BC = British Columbia; CAN = Canada; MB = Manitoba; NB = New Brunswick; NL = Newfoundland and Labrador; NS = Nova Scotia; ON = Ontario; PEI = Prince Edward Island; QC = Quebec; SK = Saskatchewan
Source: Canadian Federation of Nursing Unions, 2020.

5.4.1 Complementary health care providers

Physician assistants (PAs) provide a broad range of services under the supervision of a physician, including assessing, diagnosing, ordering, and interpreting diagnostic tests; performing minor procedures; and prescribing drugs. PAs must complete 2 of 4 years of a preparatory undergraduate degree, an additional 2 years to complete a Physician Assistant Education Program, and 2,000 hours of clinical training (Alberta Health Services, n.d.-m).

PAs have been viewed as one possible solution to timely access to care in the health system, although evidence remains equivocal (Hooker & Everett, 2012). They are preferred over nurse practitioners by physicians because they are trained and regulated through the structures and processes of medicine. To this end, Alberta Health Services launched a demonstration project in 2013 involving ten PAs (Alberta Health Services, n.d.-m). In May 2016, the government passed legislation, the Health Professions Amendment Act, to regulate PAs under the College of Physicians and Surgeons (Alberta, 2016a).

Midwives (n = 120) are health care specialists who provide primary care to low-risk birth patients during pregnancy, birth, and six weeks postpartum. Their scope of practice allows them to diagnose, order, and interpret diagnostic tests (e.g., ultrasound), prescribe and possess a range of medications, and consult with other medical specialists. Normally, patients who choose a midwife to assist with their pregnancy do not also see an obstetrician, although a midwife may choose to consult an obstetrician if needed (Alberta Association of Midwives, n.d.).

Since the early 1990s, the increased use of midwifery services has occurred because of the changing practice patterns of family physicians and obstetricians, and the changing preferences of expectant mothers. A study of midwifery in Alberta indicates that women who choose midwives as their maternal care provider experience less medical intervention during childbirth and have similar costs and health outcomes to women who choose family physicians or obstetricians (Zelmer & Leeb, 2004; O'Brien et al., 2010).

Midwifery in Alberta was first designated as a health profession under the Health Disciplines Act in 1994. Midwives continue to be regulated through this legislation and the Midwifery Regulation. As of 2013, registered midwives gained the right of self-regulation through their own College of Alberta Midwives. In order to practise as a midwife in Alberta, individuals must complete an undergraduate degree in midwifery, pass a standardized competency exam, maintain registration to practise with the college, and follow the standards of practice prescribed in the Midwifery Regulation (Alberta Association of Midwives, n.d.).

Midwifery became publicly funded in Alberta in 2009 and was incorporated into AHS staff by-laws in 2013. As a result, midwives are now funded by AHS through a course of care funding model in which a set amount of money ($4,600) is paid for each patient. Individual midwives are funded up to a maximum of forty courses of care per year. Since this time, the number of registered midwives has nearly tripled, from twenty-five in 2008 to seventy in 2017 (Alberta Health Services, n.d.-i; Gerein, 2015a).

5.4.2 Pharmaceutical workforce

Pharmacists can prescribe, compound, or dispense listed Schedule 1 and 2 drugs. Prescriptions can be written or blood products administered where the patient cannot access a physician. The dosage of a prescription may be renewed, altered, or a generic drug substituted if the clinical benefit is similar or improved. Pharmacists require 5 years of postsecondary training. They must maintain registration with the Alberta College of Pharmacy.

Through the expansion of scope of practice in 2007, pharmacists assumed several new roles. These included renewal of prescriptions without physician approval, except for opiates, anabolic steroids, benzodiazepines, and barbiturates; administering injections; tobacco cessation counselling; and development of medication management plans. Alberta's scope of practice for pharmacists is the most extensive in Canada and internationally. Agreement between pharmacists, Alberta Blue Cross, and the Alberta government on the implementation of the expanded scope was reached in 2014. There are currently over 5,000 registered pharmacists in the province (Alberta College of Pharmacy, 2016, p. 29; Alberta, 2018o). However, the viability of independent pharmacist practice in rural settings remains a key challenge, despite a variety of support programs.

Pharmacy technicians assist pharmacists in compounding, preparing, and dispensing prescriptions and pharmaceutical products and providing services that promote health and wellness (Alberta, 2018k). They require 1 year of postsecondary training. They are regulated by the Alberta College of Pharmacy through the Pharmacists and Pharmacy Technicians Profession Regulation (Alberta, 2011). There are over 1,400 registered pharmacy technicians in Alberta (Alberta, 2018o).

5.4.3 Emergency medical workforce

With the proclamation of paramedics under the Health Professions Act in 2015, the scope of practice for paramedics was broadened to allow them to administer a range of diagnostic tests, portable blood testing, and ultrasound. The changes will allow paramedics to conduct medical tests and provide medication, and to work directly with nurse practitioners. All levels of paramedics are expected to successfully complete an approved education program, pass a provincial registration exam, and maintain registration with the Alberta College of

Paramedics. Paramedics are regulated under the Health Professions Act and the Emergency Medical Technicians Regulation. As of September 2020, there are 8,885 registered paramedics in Alberta (Alberta, 2007a; Alberta College of Paramedics, 2020, p. 15).

An emergency medical responder (EMR) is an entry-level ambulance position to provide basic life support care (BLS). It includes emergency childbirth, vital sign evaluation, oral suctioning, cardiopulmonary resuscitation and support, automated defibrillation, ventilation, oxygen, and airway management (Alberta, 2018f; Alberta College of Paramedics, n.d.; Paramedic Association of Canada, 2011).

Primary care paramedics (PCPs) provide a high level of BLS, including the scope of the EMR plus administering IV, nitrous oxide, electrocardiogram placement, monitoring and interpretation, and administering certain drugs (Alberta College of Paramedics, n.d.; Paramedic Association of Canada, 2011).

Advanced care paramedics (ACPs) provide advanced life support, including advanced air management, advanced suctioning, advanced resuscitation, needle decompression, administration of over forty medications, blood sample collection, insertion of tubes for stomach lavage, and urinary catheterization (Alberta College of Paramedics, n.d.; Paramedic Association of Canada, 2011).

Since February 2018, the number of paramedics providing care to patients in the community to avoid unnecessary trips to the emergency has been expanded.

5.4.4 Diagnostic workforce

Approximately 2,303 medical radiation technologists administer a variety of imaging technologies involving the application of ionizing radiation. These include X-ray, fluoroscopy, CT scanning, intervention radiology, and mammography. They are regulated through the Alberta College of Medical Diagnostic and Therapeutic Technologists through the Profession Regulation. A specialized 2-year postsecondary degree and completion of a standardized competency exam is required (Alberta, 2018g; Alberta, 2009).

Medical laboratory technologists (n = 2,567) support diagnosis, prevention, and public health surveillance through the systematic collection, analysis, and reporting on blood, body fluids, and body tissues. They are regulated by the College of Medical Laboratory Technologists of Alberta through the Medical Laboratory Technologists Profession

Regulation. A 2-year specialized postsecondary degree and successful completion of a national certification exam is required (Alberta Health Services, n.d.-h; Alberta, 2007b).

5.4.5 Rehabilitation workforce

Physiotherapists focus on techniques that alleviate pain and discomfort, improve fitness, and prevent injury through maximizing physical movement. They assess, diagnose, and treat conditions related to movement. There are over 2,800 physiotherapists in Alberta, of which 1,000 are directly employed by AHS. In order to practise in Alberta, they must complete a minimum of 4 years in a postsecondary degree and pass a national standardized competency exam. They must also maintain registration with Physiotherapy Alberta – College and Association (Physiotherapy Alberta – College and Association, n.d.; Alberta, 2018l; Alberta Health Services, n.d.-n; CIHI, 2018c).

Speech-language pathologists assess and treat individuals who have difficulty speaking, swallowing, or eating. In order to practise in Alberta, individuals must possess a master's degree in speech-language pathology and maintain registration with the Alberta College of Speech-Language Pathologists and Audiologists, which in turn is governed by the Health Professions Act and the Speech-Language Pathologists and Audiologist Profession Regulation. There are currently over 1,300 speech-language pathologists in Alberta (Alberta Health Services, n.d.-w; Alberta College of Speech-Language Pathologists and Audiologists, 2018).

Audiologists (n = 170) are hearing specialists who diagnose and treat individuals with hearing or balance disorders. To practise, individuals must have completed a master's degree or PhD in audiology and be registered with the Alberta College of Speech-Language Pathologists and Audiologists. There are over 150 audiologists in Alberta (Alberta College of Speech-Language Pathologists and Audiologists, 2018; Alberta Health Services, n.d.-c; CIHI, 2018b).

Respiratory therapists (RTs; n = 1,823) manage patients who have issues with breathing. They must complete a 3-year diploma in respiratory therapy and be registered, pass a national standardized certification exam, and maintain registration with the College and Association of Respiratory Therapists of Alberta. (Alberta Health Services, n.d.-t; CIHI, 2018b).

Occupational therapists (OTs) assist individuals who have experienced developmental delays or suffered an illness or injury (e.g., brain injuries, strokes, heart disorders, or serious injuries) that has impaired their ability to participate in daily activities. To practise, an OT must complete a master's degree in occupational therapy, pass a national certification exam, and maintain registration with the Alberta College of Occupational Therapists. There are over 2,100 OTs in Alberta, of which over 1,100 are employed by AHS (Alberta Health Services, n.d.-k; CIHI 2018b).

Doctors of chiropractic (DCs) diagnose, treat, and offer preventive strategies for musculoskeletal conditions through spinal manipulation and other noninvasive techniques such as massage, heat, laser, and ultrasound. Their scope of practice allows them to make referrals to medical specialists, such as an orthopedic surgeon or a physiotherapist. Recently however, the government has removed chiropractors' authority to order diagnostic imaging, so patients must now see their physician in order to have tests such as X-rays and MRIs performed. Aside from public coverage for qualifying patients, chiropractic services are not publicly funded.[2] To practise as a DC in Alberta, individuals must complete 7 years of postsecondary education, including 4 years in an accredited chiropractic program, and pass a national competency exam. They must maintain registration with the Alberta College and Association of Chiropractors and are regulated through the Health Professions Act and the Chiropractors Profession Regulation (Alberta, 2006b; Alberta College and Association of Chiropractors, 2020).

Like physicians, DCs operate independent professional corporations and charge patients on a fee-for-service basis. While the government of Alberta provides some coverage for seniors, it does not cover DC services provided to the general public. As independent private practitioners, DCs also provide assessment and treatment services for workplace-related injuries through the Alberta Workers Compensation Board and for injuries related to motor vehicle accidents through private insurance companies. There are over 1,000 chiropractors in Alberta (CIHI, 2018b; Alberta College and Association of Chiropractors, 2020).

5.4.6 Dental workforce

Dentists are medical specialists with a focus on the oral cavity (mouth) and are responsible for diagnosing, treating, preventing, and controlling

---

2 The College and Association of Chiropractors is currently discussing an expansion of the scope of practice to allow DCs to prescribe a limited range of medications related to treatment.

oral and dental disorders. They require 6 years of postsecondary education to become a doctor of dental surgery. They may administer or prescribe drugs and anaesthesia (nitrous oxide) and perform diagnostic tests (X-ray), dispense or administer a vaccine, and administer invasive procedures associated with dental treatment. Like physicians and chiropractors, they operate as independent business corporations and bill patients on a fee-per-service basis. Aside from coverage for qualifying lower income patients, their services are not publicly funded. There are over 2,500 registered dentists in Alberta, and they are regulated under the Health Professions Act (Alberta, 2018e, 2012a; Alberta Dental Association and College, 2021).

Dental hygienists assist the dentist by providing oral hygiene through cleaning, polishing, and applying fluoride to teeth. They also take X-rays and discuss dental health with patients. They may administer or prescribe drugs and anaesthesia (nitrous oxide), perform diagnostic tests (X-ray), and administer nonpermanent invasive procedures and permanent invasive procedures (under the supervision of a dentist) associated with dental treatment. They require 3 years of specialized postsecondary training. There are over 3,100 dental hygienists in Alberta (Alberta, 2018d, 2006c; Alberta Dental Association and College, 2021).

5.4.7 Eye care workforce

Optometrists diagnose and treat disorders and diseases related to human visual systems. To become an optometrist, individuals must complete 7 years of postsecondary education, including a 4-year doctor of optometry. There are currently over 700 optometrists registered to practise in Alberta (Alberta, 2018j, 2015; Alberta College of Optometrists, n.d.).

Opticians fit and adapt a variety of optical appliances (e.g., eyeglasses and contact lenses) based on a prescription provided by an optometrist or other qualified practitioner. Individuals must have 2 years of specialized postsecondary training and maintain registration with the Alberta College and Association of Opticians (formerly College of Opticians of Alberta). They are regulated through the Alberta College and Association of Opticians, the Health Professions Act, and the Opticians Regulation. There are currently over 1,000 opticians practising in Alberta (Alberta, 2018i, 2015; College of Opticians of Alberta, 2016, 2018).

In 2015, the government of Alberta approved the expansion of the scope of practice for optometrists. With the expanded scope, optometrists can now prescribe, dispense, or sell drugs related to their practice; manage and treat glaucoma; order and analyse laboratory tests; and provide ultrasound (Canadian Association of Optometrists, 2015).

5.4.8 Public health workforce

Environmental health officers (n = 397) are empowered through the Public Health Act to inspect public places (e.g., restaurants, public housing, drinking water, public pools), identify violations of the Public Health Act and its regulations, and prosecute offenders for noncompliance. A minimum of 4 years of postsecondary education is required. While they may be certified nationally, they are not currently regulated in Alberta (Alberta, 2018m; Alberta Health Services, n.d.-p).

Registered dieticians (n = 1,288) assess the nutritional needs of clients, provide counselling and education, and develop nutritional care plans. They are regulated by the College of Dieticians of Alberta through the Registered Dieticians and Registered Nutritionists Profession Regulation. A bachelor of science with specialization in foods and nutrition, and successful completion of a national competency exam is required (College of Dieticians of Alberta, 2020; Alberta, 2004a; Alberta Health Services, n.d.-f).

Social workers (n = 7,035) provide counselling and support for patients to solve issues related to human relationships and social well-being in hospitals, community clinics, and patients' homes. They are regulated by the Alberta College of Social Workers through the Social Workers Profession Regulation. Clinical social workers require 6 years of postsecondary education. Other social workers require varying levels of postsecondary training (Alberta Health Services, n.d.-u; Alberta, 2012b; Alberta College of Social Workers, 2021).

5.5 Health human resource planning and collective bargaining

5.5.1 HHR planning

As discussed in section 5.1, Alberta is facing a health labour shortage, especially for nurses. A number of factors have contributed to the lack of effective health workforce planning in the province. One result of the health care regionalization during the 1990s was that it became unclear who was responsible for health workforce planning. In addition, while decision-makers eventually became aware that a shortage of nurses was looming, they used this issue as an opportunity to begin a process of substituting less expensive workers for registered nurses in the hope that it would contain labour costs.

The profession of registered nurses was unsuccessful in getting the issue of a looming shortage on the political agenda. Many senior nursing positions throughout the health care system were eliminated, resulting in a loss of institutional memory and visibility for the nursing profession within the larger health regions. Government cutbacks during the early 1990s reduced the capacity[3] of Alberta Health to assume a province-wide leadership role, and while human resource planning continued in Edmonton and Calgary, most health regions did not have the staff or skills to do so (Findlay et al., 2002, p. 350).

Within this context, the government and other policy stakeholders made significant efforts to develop an improved capacity for health workforce planning. In spite of these efforts, in 2008, Alberta Health reported:

> There is a critical shortage of health providers. As just one example, Alberta currently has a shortage of more than 1,500 nurses. By 2020, if care patterns do not change and training is not expanded, the province may be short by more than 6,000 nurses. Adding to this shortage is the fact that only 40% of Alberta's registered nurses work full-time, the lowest rate in the country and well below the Canadian average of 56 percent. Alberta also has a growing shortage of allied health providers, including pharmacists, physical therapists, medical technologists, and especially health care aides. (Alberta Health, 2008)

Due to the financial collapse of 2008, AHS was required by the provincial government to reduce expenditures by 10 per cent. In response to this cutback and in spite of the warning about a significant impending nursing shortage, AHS began hiring increasing numbers of LPNs and decreasing the number of RNs (CBC News, 2009, 7 October). In tandem with this action, AHS embarked on a workforce planning exercise, which it claimed would better match workforce planning priorities with

---

3   Capacity was diminished by the reduction in the number of department staff and also by the gradual and selective loss of corporate memory to the health regions and other organizations like the Alberta Medical Association; legitimacy was reduced by the devolution of responsibilities from the ministry to the health regions.

population health needs.[4] As part of this process, AHS issued a discussion paper in which six potential scenarios were outlined. The scenarios allowed for the exploration of different combinations of skill mix for RNs, LPNs, and health care aides (HCAs), size of graduating class, and the relative ratio of full versus part-time employment. However, the connection between population health needs and the skill mix of the nursing workforce was unclear (Duckett, Bloom, & Robertson, 2012, p. e187).[5]

According to then AHS CEO Stephen Duckett, "the discussion paper was issued in the context of debates about the role of RNs in Alberta, stimulated by AHS leadership that challenged conventional approaches to staffing ... to advance an agenda of workplace reform" (Duckett et al., 2012, p. e187). The culmination of this process was a realization that, regardless of the scenario chosen, continuing the status quo – recruitment and training of nurses alone – was not a viable option.

Although couched in the language of quality improvement, no data about hospitalized patients' care needs was publicly available, and there is no evidence that any assessment of patient needs (other than historical staffing precedent) was taken into account. The College and Association of Registered Nurses of Alberta countered by citing over 30 years of research demonstrating that reductions in RN staffing leads to increased death and complication rates.

An underlying issue is a continuing disconnect between postsecondary educators, practitioners, and policy-makers. While educators are well aware of best practices and scopes of practice, seeing these implemented in the workplace has been challenging. In short, health providers may receive the necessary training on interdisciplinary teams and scopes of practice, but they do not see it mirrored in the workplace. The net result is that graduated health providers are often unable to practise what they have learned once they are in the workplace. Ultimately, they revert to the existing status quo.

5.5.2 Collective bargaining

Collective bargaining in Alberta's health care system is conducted between the government of Alberta and Alberta Health Services as employers

---

4 It marked a departure from the traditional supply-side approach to workforce management.

5 As discussed further in chapter 8, in general, the connection between population health and health care resource allocation appears tenuous at best.

and one professional association and three major unions representing contractors or employees. A major issue in Alberta is the balance between management rights and union rights in collective agreements. AHS has limited flexibility in the redeployment of staff, and significant overtime costs are incurred due to the nature of current agreements.

The Alberta Medical Association negotiates an 8-year master agreement with the government of Alberta on behalf of all registered physicians (10,294 in 2017) in the province. While the agreement originally focused only on the schedule of fees, since the 1990s negotiations have broadened to include a wider range of issues. One analysis suggests that the current agreement holds the potential to improve the role of physicians as "stewards" in the health care system[6] (McIntosh, 2018).

The United Nurses of Alberta negotiate every 4 years with the government of Alberta and AHS on behalf of all regulated nurses (over 34,000 in 2015) on a range of issues, including rate of pay. The Health Sciences Association of Alberta negotiates multiple collective agreements with AHS and other health provider organizations on behalf of 27,000 paramedical and general support employees from over 240 disciplines (Health Sciences Association of Alberta, n.d.). The Alberta Union of Public Employees is the bargaining unit for LPNs and many other ancillary health care workers (United Nurses of Alberta, 2018; Alberta Medical Association, 2020).

5.6 Summary

Since the 1990s, Alberta has been attempting to develop a more effective means of health workforce planning. Over time, the province appears to have moved from a supply-side approach to planning to more of a needs-based approach. However, there is little evidence that this newer approach has yet had a positive effect on health workforce outcomes. Claims that planning is based on evidence and improvements in population health appear to be unsubstantiated, except possibly in the continuing care sector (see chapter 8 for more on this topic). There is currently no system of case-mix or activity-based costing beyond the long-term care system. Nor is there an explicit connection between health human resource planning and collective bargaining.

Administrative decision-making by AHS and effective lobbying have led to strategically adjusted scopes of practice for various health

---

6   The most recent agreement ties physician remuneration (for the first time ever) to a geographic needs-based physician resource plan (Alberta Medical Association, 2016).

professions and introduced new providers on the basis of arguments that these changes will increase cost efficiencies and improve access. The expanded scope of practice for LPNs has allowed health care decision-makers to increasingly substitute them for RNs in both the hospital and community settings. The expansion of the scope of practice has allowed pharmacists and RNs to assume a role in directly prescribing some pharmaceuticals and providing services previously only available through physicians. The expansion of scope for paramedics offers the opportunity to better stabilize patients before they reach the emergency room. The introduction of NPs, midwives, and PAs offers new opportunities to improve access to care in the community and institutional settings at lower costs. Many of these changes are designed to decrease the dependence on the physician as a single gatekeeper to the health care system while maximizing the ability of other health providers to practise to their full scope of practice.

However, continuing employment and funding arrangements do not support this theoretical commitment. The system continues to be physician-centric and funded mainly through fee-for-service. Although nurse practitioners as a cost-effective solution is well supported by evidence, it continues to be underutilized, and while evidence calls for significant investments in service delivery in community settings, the majority of health care workers continue to be employed in acute and hospital settings. Also, best practices about interdisciplinary teams learned through the education process do not seem to translate well into the practice setting.

As Alberta continues to spend more on health care than the majority of Canadian jurisdictions, its health workforce planning has yet to demonstrate that it can yield cost-effective solutions.

Chapter Six

Services and Programs Provided in Alberta's Health System

The previous two chapters described the physical and human resources that constitute Alberta's health care system. This chapter considers the actual services that Albertans receive through this system. In many cases, the effective delivery of services requires federal-provincial cooperation, as well as links to other government departments and sectors. The chapter looks at the volume, mix, and – to the degree it is known – quality of those services. Volume refers to the number of procedures, while mix refers to the different ways in which services can be combined or substituted for one another. Quality is defined, in the Alberta health context, as six dimensions: acceptability, accessibility, appropriateness, effectiveness, efficiency, and safety (Health Quality Council of Alberta [HQCA], 2005). This broad framework can capture many key aspects of health services delivery. For instance, acceptability may include cultural competency of health providers when working with Indigenous or ethnic minority populations. Wait times, as indicators of access to care, have been agreed among provinces and the federal government as important to measure in a comparative and ongoing fashion.

Implicit throughout this chapter are questions related to the ethical dimensions of how health services are prioritized, designed, and delivered. The handling of "exceptional" cases – for instance, when someone seeks access to a potentially life-saving experimental treatment not covered in Alberta or Canada – demands consideration of the ethics of health care resource allocation (Wasylenko, 2013). Unique religious communities, such as Hutterites, Christian Scientists, and Jehovah Witnesses, have beliefs about the acceptability of certain procedures (e.g., blood transfusions), which are not shared by most of the public or providers. Other procedures like vaccination are resisted among some ardent homeopathic and naturopathic adherents. Controversial cases where parents attempt to treat serious childhood illnesses by alternative means only keep an ethical spotlight on this issue. The implications of mandatory reporting of sexually transmitted illnesses such as HIV, which allows tracing the spread of disease but is also feared to have potentially negative impacts upon people's care-seeking behaviour, is another example of an ethical issue arising from health system design. In short, such considerations are always present when understanding and assessing the quality, acceptability, and appropriateness of the existing health care system.

6.1 Public health services

Public health services include both the prevention of disease and the promotion of optimal health and well-being within the population as a whole. Importantly, public health objectives are achieved not only through individual education and treatment, but also through population-level policies. The Ministry of Health has a lead role in planning for public health, while Alberta Health Services (AHS) performs the main delivery role. But successful public health goes beyond the health sector alone: across all sectors – including education, housing, transportation, and so on – policy decisions should be informed by consideration of their population health and health equity impacts.

6.1.1 Public health nursing and communicable disease control

It remains an important public health role to prevent, monitor, and respond to communicable disease. In Alberta, public health nurses deliver much of the province's immunization (or vaccination) schedule. A small number of physicians also immunize. In their expanded role, pharmacists provide some immunization as well, for those 9 years of age or older only. They play a particular role in providing community-based immunization for influenza during the fall season each year.

Vaccines have been key to the elimination of many once common communicable diseases, such as smallpox or polio, and are important in establishing individual- and population-level protection against others. Much of the vaccine schedule is intended to be delivered to children, such as measles, mumps, rubella, and varicella (MMRV). However, some vaccines are aimed at adolescent (e.g., HPV) or adult and older adult (e.g., international travel immunization, influenza)

Figure 6.1 Childhood vaccine coverage rates (receipt of all recommended doses), Alberta, 2019

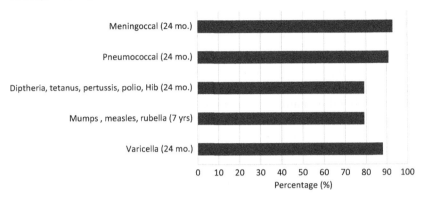

Source: Alberta Health, 2018d.

population groups. The province appears to achieve varying coverage rates on the vaccines contained in the recommended schedule for children (see Figure 6.1).

Any decline in vaccine uptake has implications in terms of the possible resurgence of potentially deadly childhood illnesses. While high-profile "anti-vax" movements may contribute to this decline, the relative absence of such diseases and their impacts may also contribute to parental lack of concern or commitment (Busby, Jacobs, & Muthukumaran, 2017).

Public health nurses provide sexual health education and counselling around sexually transmitted infections (STIs), including HIV/AIDS; family planning; genetic counselling; and contraception. Renewed attention is being devoted to sexually transmitted and blood-borne infections (STBBIs), which for the most part are easily treatable, as their rates have been increasing in Alberta and elsewhere (Neufeld, 2019; Singh & Romanowski, 2019). Public health nurses also work with expectant mothers to deliver prenatal support and provide postnatal education, home visits, and breastfeeding advice. This work takes place both in one-to-one and group settings. They also play a role in promoting population screening initiatives, such as pap smears (cervical cancer), mammography (breast cancer), and prostate cancer screening (for men).

6.1.2 Environmental health services

Delivery of environmental health services is largely, though not exclusively, the domain of public health inspectors. These consist of a variety of activities, as detailed below.

Restaurant and food safety: Public health inspectors assess whether or not restaurants sell food in a safe manner; all new establishments are inspected before opening, and thereafter all restaurants are inspected every 4 to 6 months (though inspections may be more frequent if an establishment has been previously found to fall foul of food safety practices). Health inspectors are also responsible for food safety in other venues where food is served or sold, such as daycares, group homes, work camps, farmers' markets, and festivals or special events. The volume of work involved can be judged using the estimate that there are approximately 10,000 restaurants, bars, and caterers operating in Alberta as of 2016. The safety of food manufacturing or production at source (processing plants, abattoirs, etc.) is the responsibility of the federal Canadian Food Inspection Agency (CFIA). Governments also support systematic education and training programs about food safety; for instance, Alberta Health Services staff developed the Serving Safer Food – Alberta program, while the CFIA requires or encourages its regulated industries to use the Hazard Analysis Critical Control Point (HACCP) system.

Water, air, and soil quality and housing: Inspectors monitor recreational water sources (swimming pools, beaches, and lakes) and drinking water wells to assess that they meet applicable public safety standards; medium- and large-scale water facilities are monitored through the Department of the Environment. Air quality monitoring and management, a related function in terms of public health and well-being, is carried out under the auspices of the province's Ministry of the Environment. Industrial activities, such as heavy manufacturing, gas stations, dry cleaning, and so on, can result in soil contamination with heavy metals and chemicals potentially injurious to human health. Local government by-laws will typically require such sites – referred to as "brownfields" – to be remediated and decontaminated before they can be redeveloped for other uses. Resistance to the fact that hazardous activities (known as "local unwanted land uses" or LULUs) are disproportionately sited within relatively disadvantaged communities has given rise in some jurisdictions to an environmental justice movement (Cole & Foster, 2001). As for housing, inspectors respond to complaints about rental units and can order defects to be remedied.

Animal and insect vectors: Animals can cause human injury (e.g., dog bites), and animals and insects can spread disease (e.g., Lyme disease and West Nile virus). Alberta's Rat Patrol, supported by the Agriculture Department, has attempted to prevent the Norway rat from establishing itself in the province (Bourne & Merrill, 2011); this program protects both the agriculture industry and human health. A rat control perimeter exists along the Saskatchewan border, and Alberta proclaims itself to be North America's – in fact, the world's – only rat-free jurisdiction. Most provinces have legislation that limits or bans the keeping of designated exotic animal species, and some, though not Alberta, have attempted to prohibit certain breeds of dogs as inherently dangerous.

Personal services: Inspectors are required to approve and monitor the safety of businesses that provide personal services to the public, including barbering, hair styling or hair replacement, body and ear piercing, body and facial waxing, electrolysis, make-up application (temporary or permanent), manicures and pedicures, and tattooing.

The problematic intersection of the economy and environmental health also raises a number of policy issues related to Alberta's major industries. The energy sector is implicated in matters such as fracking, remediation of abandoned well sites, downstream water and fish contamination, and climate change. Government agencies, too, must find ways to reduce their own carbon footprint. Such steps can include energy conservation and retrofitting measures, as well as reducing waste, encouraging recycling, and other pro-environment efforts.

Agricultural activity can impact on neighbouring residential areas through confined feeding operations (CFOs), antibiotic and pesticide overuse, and resistance. Forestry activities cause impacts upon watersheds, biodiversity, and habitat destruction. Tourism-related issues include potential spread of diseases through international travel, as well as degradation of natural and cultural values through overuse. Addressing such challenges frequently requires work across ministries or between levels of government, which contribute unique knowledge, skills, and regulatory powers.

6.1.3 Health promotion

The health promotion approach focuses on social determinants of health and healthy environments – in other words, the social, political, economic, and cultural circumstances that condition individual behavioural choices. Kotani and Goldblatt (1994) argue that health promotion principles have long historic roots in Alberta in the community services sector, exemplified by Family and Community Support Services (FCSS) programs. At the same time, the formal health sector has been slower to respond to such ideas. The Healthy Cities and Communities movement is an important vehicle for health promotion (Hancock, 1993, p. 7). While prominent in Europe and elsewhere as an intersectoral expression of health promotion, it has struggled to make headway in Alberta, which lacks the province-wide networks (with the possible exception of tobacco) that have been created in other provinces, although there have been a number of locally initiated projects (Sherwood, 2002).

Health promotion practice occurs in a variety of settings such as schools, workplaces, community spaces, and anywhere else where members of the public gather to work, live, or play (Poland, Green, & Rootman, 2000). Chronic disease and injury prevention programs use a variety of instruments and approaches: education, incentives, as well as regulation. For instance, both tobacco cessation and control through social marketing and smoke-free space legislation are employed. Reduction in smoking rates during recent decades is a major public health achievement and success story. Road safety requires a combination of engineering and enforcement. Healthy weight and obesity (e.g., healthy eating and active living) are addressed in Alberta via individual nutritional counselling offered by dietetic professionals, as well as by local food policies to support food security, urban design strategies that encourage walkable communities, and daily physical activity policies in schools.

6.2 Primary care

Primary care is normally the first line of contact for individuals seeking physician services; it deals with prevention, maintenance, and resolution of relatively minor complaints. As of 2018–19 in Alberta, family medicine practitioners provided a total of 20,467,750 consultations and visits, and performed 3,317,520 total procedures (Canadian Institute for Health Information [CIHI], 2020b).

The 2016 Commonwealth Fund International Survey found 80 per cent of Albertans reporting that they had a regular family doctor, and 78 per cent of respondents rated the quality of that care as excellent or very good (these results are comparable to the Canadian average). However, only one-third of respondents were able to get an appointment with their doctor on the same day, and 13 per cent reported having to wait more than a week to be seen (CIHI, 2016a; Commonwealth Fund, 2016).

Primary care does not only involve physicians; nurse practitioners and other allied health professionals can also play vital roles. The province has encouraged models of team-based care, such as the Primary Health Networks (described further in chapter 7).

6.3 Acute (secondary, tertiary) care including emergency services

Health care services can be provided on an inpatient or an outpatient basis. Inpatient services are those in which recipients remain in hospital for one or more days for recovery and/or observation; outpatient services are where procedures are performed either in hospital or in a separate clinic, but no overnight stay is required, and patients return to their own homes for recovery. Inpatient care is ideally reserved for the most serious and invasive procedures. Medical advances over recent decades have made it possible to deliver many procedures more simply and easily, reducing or eliminating the need for many hospital stays.

Rates of all-cause hospitalization in the province have been relatively stable at around 8,643 per 100,000 population on a 10-year average between 2006–07 and 2015–16 (calculated from the data in CIHI, 2021b). Rates in Alberta have been consistently higher than those for the country as a whole, as has the typical length of a hospital stay (Figure 6.2). This finding could reflect a population with greater health needs, a larger number of available beds, or differences in the management of patient illnesses. Due to the high costs of hospitalization, provincial governments are interested in ways to prevent hospital stays, use more outpatient care, and reduce lengths of stay.

Compared to 1996–97, the hospitalization rate in Alberta (as of 2018–19) has declined 25 per cent, down from 11,175 per 100,000; and length of stay has increased approximately 20 per cent, up from an average of 6.4 days (CIHI, 2021b). Around 406,000 people in total were discharged (separated) from an Alberta acute care facility in the 2019 calendar year (Alberta Health, 2018d).

Some quality of care measures that are tracked regularly relate to the dimension of safety, including hand hygiene: as of the end of the 2019–20 fiscal year, the percentage of opportunities for which health care workers clean their hands during the course of patient care was 88 per cent (Alberta Health Services, 2021d). Quality is also reflected by

Figure 6.2 Hospitalization rates per 100,000 population and average length of stay (days), Alberta and Canada, 2006–2016

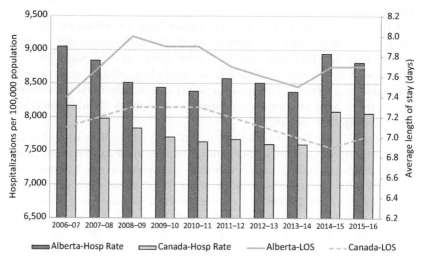

LOS = length of stay (days)
Source: CIHI, 2021b.

hospital productivity measures. In this case, Alberta hospitals "are less efficient than the average Canadian hospital ... [O]n average, over the three-year period 2007–09 it cost 15% more to treat a patient in Alberta compared to the cost of similar treatment in the average Canadian hospital" (Duckett, 2015, p. 305).[1]

6.3.1 Emergency services

Ground and air ambulance services are required to transport those who are ill or injured to the nearest (or to the most appropriate) facility where they can receive necessary care. Ambulance services historically were managed through local governments, but they have been incorporated into Alberta Health Services since 2009. The ground ambulance fleet in 2016 consisted of AHS-owned vehicles and those operated by over forty

---

1 Discussed further in chapter 8.

contracted operators; air ambulance included eleven contracted fixed-wing planes and helicopter services provided by not-for-profit charitable organizations.

Ground ambulances can provide either basic or advanced life support. Basic life support ambulances are staffed with emergency medical technicians or emergency medical responders and provide immediate patient assessment and treatment, including obtaining vital signs, administering oxygen, and splinting extremities. Advanced life support ambulances have at least one paramedic onboard, with additional life-saving equipment as well.

Alberta Health Services defines ambulance call-outs as one of three types: emergency response, nonemergency response, and patient transfer. In 2018–19, ambulances responded to approximately 130,000 individual events per quarter. About one-half of these were considered emergencies, and 20,000 per quarter were nonemergency responses; patient transfers made up the balance (Alberta Health Services, n.d.-q). STARS reports flying 1,325 air ambulance missions from its Alberta bases in the 2019–20 fiscal year; their website breaks this response down by community (STARS, 2021).

Ambulance response times are important in ensuring that patients receive care before they experience irreparable harm, but obviously responses will be more rapid in densely settled urban areas. AHS tracks response times. In 2018–19, the median response in urban centres and communities with a population over 3,000 was around 7.5 to 9 minutes; rural and remote regions had median response times of approximately 20 minutes. In all cases, these medians were better than AHS target times (Alberta Health Services, n.d.-q).

In 2017–18, a total of 1,155,229 patients made 2,286,421 visits to emergency departments in the province. About 11 per cent of patients were defined as frequent users with four or more visits each during the fiscal year; collectively these 11 per cent accounted for about 35 per cent of total emergency department use. The median length of stay in the emergency department for patients who were ultimately admitted to hospital was 9.1 hours, somewhat less than the wait time in four of the other six provinces for which data is available (CIHI, 2017b).

Canadian Blood Services (CBS) is a not-for-profit corporation established and funded by the provincial and territorial ministers of health. CBS collects blood from donors at clinics across the province, as well as purchases blood products from the United States and elsewhere. These products are distributed to hospitals for use in surgical procedures requiring transfusion. The blood supply system operates across the country, and Alberta is a net exporter of blood products (Alberta Health Services, 2015a). CBS was established following the tainted blood scandals of the 1990s in which many people received blood products that transmitted diseases such as HIV and hepatitis as a result of inadequate screening (Parsons, 2002).

Major natural or other disasters require the collaboration of multiple levels of government (Hale, 2013) – local, provincial, and federal – as well as coordination with efforts undertaken by not-for-profit agencies such as the Red Cross. Notable examples of natural disasters include the wildfires in Slave Lake (2011) and Fort McMurray (2016); southern Alberta floods (2013); and the Pine Lake tornado (2000). Disasters related to human industrial activity include such events as the Lodgepole sour gas well blowout (1982). Other industry-related incidents, such as train derailments or the potential of terrorist actions, might also be cause to trigger emergency response systems. Climate change will likely exacerbate environmental instability and make scenarios such as wildfires and flooding an ever-increasing threat across Alberta.

6.4 Diagnostic imaging and laboratory services

Alberta laboratories are funded by Alberta Health Services and perform approximately 75 million tests each year on about 2.3 million individual patients, reporting 2.9 million encounters (HQCA, 2017). Encounters occur in the following settings: community (65 per cent), emergency room or outpatient (23 per cent), inpatient (10 per cent), and long-term care (1 per cent; HQCA, 2017). Most of these tests occur in public facilities (Table 6.1).

The quality of Alberta's laboratories is maintained through external accreditation via the College of Physicians and Surgeons of Alberta, as well as through internal monitoring and assessment. While failures in

Table 6.1 Laboratory tests in Alberta, 2015–2016, by provider

Lab	Alberta Health Services	Calgary Lab Services	Covenant Health	Total public	DynaLife	Medicine Hat Diagnostic Labs	Total private
Tests (millions)	24.7	28.8	3.0	**56.5**	17.8	1.2	**19.0**

Source: HQCA, 2017.

Table 6.2 Publicly funded diagnostic imaging tests in Alberta, 2017

	CT	MRI	SPECT	PET-CT	SPECT-CT
Recorded number	405,332	192,375	17,996	11,005	8,134
Exams per machine	7,238	4,692	4,28	2,751	254

CT = computerized tomography; MRI = magnetic resonance imaging; PET = positron emission tomography; SPECT = single-photon emission tomography
Source: CADTH, 2017.

test reading have resulted in scandals in other provinces, there have been no such prominent reports from Alberta in recent years. However, the provision of unnecessary testing is another matter. The Health Quality Council of Alberta (HQCA, 2017, p. 38) cites Canadian Agency for Drugs and Technology in Health (CADTH) studies suggesting that from 20 to 50 per cent of laboratory tests may be inappropriately ordered. As one example of such practices, when Alberta Laboratory Services made changes to its order forms, a 92 per cent decrease in vitamin D testing occurred (CIHI & Choosing Wisely Canada, 2017).

Alberta reports about 3 million diagnostic imaging scans of all types annually. Table 6.2 provides data for the most common types. As of 2018, the median wait time to receive an MRI scan was around 10 weeks, and CT scans took a median wait time of around 15 weeks (Alberta, n.d.-a).[2]

As with laboratory services, a large proportion of the diagnostic imaging tests delivered for Canadians may also be unnecessary (CIHI & Choosing Wisely Canada, 2017). Again, to use an Alberta example, the Physician Learning Program found that about 28 per cent of bone mineral density scans were being inappropriately ordered (CIHI & Choosing Wisely Canada, 2017). There is great variability among provinces in the rate of diagnostic imaging testing per 100,000 population. In this regard, Alberta has a lower rate than other provinces where data are available (Naugler & Wyonch, 2019). However, the province's cost per test is one of the highest.

6.5 Long-term and continuing care services

This subsection considers institutional care and community-based home health services.

---

2 Discussed further in chapter 8.

6.5.1 Long-term care

Chapter 4 presented data about the number of continuing care facilities and beds in Alberta. It has been estimated that long-term care (LTC) has a turnover rate of about 18 per cent, or that almost one-fifth of residents will die over the course of a year. In addition to the normal course of aging and illness, congregate living facilities such as LTC are also highly susceptible to the spread of contagious viral illnesses such as Norovirus or, most recently, COVID-19. Changes to the health care system over recent years have meant that LTC residents are increasingly frail before they are admitted and so require higher levels of care and support.

A demographic profile of LTC residents indicates that, in 2016–17, the median age was 85 years. Unsurprisingly, most LTC clients were elderly, but not all – approximately 9 per cent were younger than 65. Sixty-two per cent were female. Nearly 60 per cent of residents had a dementia or Alzheimer's disease diagnosis; 66 per cent were assessed as being moderately or severely impaired in their decision-making ability (Alberta, 2018p). For the 2018–19 year, 58 per cent of those who are determined to be eligible for placement in a LTC facility receive a bed within 30 days (Alberta Health Services, 2019a). While Albertans can choose the facility in which they would like to be placed, AHS and its health zones have made attempts to centralize wait lists and to assign people, on an intended temporary basis, to the first-available appropriate living option (HQCA, 2014a).

The Alberta government inspects facilities for the cleanliness and safety of physical spaces in accommodations on an annual basis. Continuing Care Health Service Standards are assessed by AHS, sometimes jointly with Alberta Health, and include aspects related to the quality of care provided. The province is one of only three in Canada (besides Ontario and Nova Scotia) that can fine LTC operators for failing to meet minimum standards of care, though it has never done so (Graff-McRae, 2021). Alberta families generally report that their family members in care are treated with kindness and respect, according to surveys by the HQCA, which found 85 per cent agreement with this claim on average across facilities in 2017 (range of 68 to 99 per cent; HQCA, 2018). Facilities that choose to seek accreditation also benefit from site visits and feedback provided by teams of trained and experienced surveyors.

A shortage of LTC beds may mean that patients who are healthy enough to leave hospital, but unable to return to independent living, may remain in acute care beds that might be used more appropriately if other appropriate community or institutional options were available for patient care. Duckett and Peetoom (2013) suggest that an average of 5,200 beds per day are so occupied, which is why governments use alternative level of care (ALC) as one of their performance measures. In Alberta, approximately 16 per cent of inpatient-occupied acute care bed days were considered to be ALC (Alberta Health Services, 2021d); Alberta's rate is higher than other large provinces such as Ontario or British Columbia (McIntosh, 2020). An alternative approach to building additional LTC capacity is to increase home and community supports.[3]

6.5.2 Home and community care

Home care includes both professional health care services, such as nursing or rehabilitation, and personal supports, such as cleaning, cooking, and personal grooming. In Alberta, home care services are defined as either short-term (up to 90 days) or long-term (more than 90 days). Short-term clients comprise about 20 per cent of those receiving home care, but 50 per cent of services delivered (Harrison, Pablo, & Verhoef, 1999). In one estimate, up to 2017, "the number of home-care recipients in Alberta has increased about 20 percent in the last six years from 97,000 to 116,000" (Gerein, 2017a). McIntosh (2020) does note, however, that there are other widely different estimates of the home care population, with little to no explanation for the discrepancies.

Like LTC, home care is predominantly a service used by the elderly. According to a Canadian Medical Association report, "seniors [are] the most likely to receive care at home: 10% of those 65 to 74, 21% of those 75 to 84 and 45% of those 85 and older received this service" (Canadian Medical Association, 2016, p. 12).

Services are primarily delivered by private or nonprofit organizations contracted by AHS. A search for efficiencies and greater standardization for quality control purposes led the province to consolidate many contracts in 2013, reducing the number of providers in the province from seventy-two to thirteen (Wright, 2013). As a consequence, there was some concern that long-standing local and not-for-profit providers were losing contracts to large companies, often based outside the province (Mahaffey, 2013). Some of the largest private providers include Extendicare, We Care (CBI Home Health), and Bayshore.

---

3 Discussed further in chapter 8.

The Canadian Institute for Health Information (CIHI) has found that about one in five seniors admitted to long-term residential care nationwide (and 30 per cent in Alberta) could likely have remained at home with additional home care supports (CIHI, 2017d). Supportive living facilities with specialized expertise in dementia care are identified as one positive approach being undertaken in Alberta to relieve the pressure to institutionalize the elderly. Sutherland and Crump (2013) note that evaluations have supported the effectiveness of intensive home support programs in the United States that address complex care needs and incentivize providers to keep clients out of hospital; evidence from Quebec suggests such models could work in the Canadian context as well. Other successful Canadian programs from British Columbia and Ontario are profiled by Accreditation Canada and Canadian Home Care Association (n.d.).

6.6 Prescription drugs

As noted earlier, only prescription drugs dispensed during hospital care fall within the Canada Health Act parameters. Thus, the Alberta government provides at no charge to the patient any medically necessary drugs prescribed for inpatients in acute care hospitals and residents of auxiliary hospitals and nursing homes. For other contexts, the provincial government provides a range of plans to cover certain groups of Albertans, such as those over 65 years, those in palliative care, and those receiving social assistance benefits (Table 6.3).

In addition to the population-based programs noted in Table 6.3, the province also operates programs that provide coverage for specific types of pharmaceuticals: cancer drugs, very high-cost drugs, acid reflux treatments, and drugs for tuberculosis and sexually transmitted infections.

The plans described in Table 6.3 are provided to Albertans as non-group supplemental plans administered through the Alberta Blue Cross. In the 2017–18 fiscal year, the Blue Cross paid for the dispensation of 17.1 million prescriptions for seniors and almost 32,000 prescriptions for persons on palliative care; a total of 560,881 persons in these categories were enrolled with the program that year (Alberta Health, 2018a).

Albertans aged 18 to 64 may also voluntarily buy prescription drugs and other supplemental health benefit coverage through the Alberta Blue Cross, with a sliding scale of premium payments based on individual or family income. In 2017–18, this drug program covered 71,425 people at full premium rates and a further 4,381 paying reduced rates.

Table 6.3 Public programs providing prescription drug coverage for Albertans

Public drug program	Eligibility	Pharmaceutical benefits provided	Other benefits
Coverage for seniors	Alberta residents over 65 years of age	Drugs on the Alberta Benefit List – 30% co-payment required, to a maximum of $25 per prescription	· Diabetic supplies · Ambulance · Clinical psychology · Chiropractic services · Home nursing · Dental and optical
Palliative coverage	Alberta residents diagnosed as palliative and residing at home or in a hospice	Drugs on the Alberta Benefit List and Palliative Care Drug Benefit Supplement –30% co-payment required, to a maximum of $25 per prescription, to a lifetime maximum of $1,000	· Diabetic supplies · Ambulance
AISH (assured income for the severely handicapped)	Low-income adults on long-term or permanent disability	Prescription drugs on the Alberta Benefits List	· Diabetic supplies · Ambulance · Dental and optical · Assistive devices
Income Support	Low-income adults receiving social assistance payments who are able to work or attend training programs	Prescription drugs on the Alberta Benefit and Supplement Lists Some OTC products	· Diabetic supplies · Ambulance services · Dental and optical
Alberta Adult Health Benefit	Low-income adults leaving AISH or Income Support Refugees or refugee claimants	Prescription drugs on the Alberta Benefit and Supplement Lists Some OTC products	· Diabetic supplies · Ambulance services · Dental and optical
Alberta Child Health Benefit	Children in low-income households up to 18 years of age, and children 18–19 years old who live at home and attend school	Prescription drugs on the Alberta Benefit and Supplement Lists Some OTC products	· Diabetic supplies · Ambulance services · Dental and optical

OTC = over-the-counter
Source: Constructed from subpages of Alberta, 2021b.

A total of 69,831 persons from this group (92 per cent of all enrollees) obtained at least one prescription drug through the program during that year, with 1.6 million eligible prescriptions filled overall. Across all these groups, an additional 672,000 otherwise over-the-counter products were paid for as well (Alberta Health, 2018a).

The Alberta Blue Cross is also the largest provider of employer-sponsored drug benefit plans in the province; its group offerings cover 1.6 million employees working in slightly more than 5,000 firms and organizations. Other major insurers, such as Manulife, Sun Life, and Great-West Life, are also active in providing employee benefits to Alberta employers. Overall, about two-thirds of employed Canadians receive health benefits from their employer; younger workers, part-time workers, and those at the lowest end of the earning spectrum are least likely to have such coverage (Wellesley Institute, 2015). About one in ten Canadians have reported being unable to fill a prescription due to cost (Morgan et al., 2015).

Policy-makers and insurance providers use a variety of means to control drug costs. Among public plans, including in Alberta, requirements for generic substitution of brand-name drugs are common. Academic detailing, where trained professionals educate physicians about prescribing practices, is another strategy, meant in part to counter drug industry advertising. Alberta was one of several provinces to pilot such an approach but did not continue with it (Jin et al., 2012). Provinces have begun to bulk-buy drugs through the pan-Canadian Pharmaceutical Alliance, using their collective purchasing power to obtain cost relief. As described in chapter 2, Alberta also participates in pan-Canadian review processes for the approval of expensive new pharmaceutical products.

6.7 Occupational health services and rehabilitation care

6.7.1 Occupational health and safety

Occupational health and safety policies secure the well-being of workers in their places of work. They derive both from a demand for government regulation, due to fear that the profit motive will lead employers to neglect safety considerations that might involve additional expenditures, and from arguments suggesting that it is in fact positive for profit and business success to cultivate a safe and healthy workforce and that workplace wellness expenditures contribute to the bottom line as well as being of moral value in themselves.

Part of ensuring workplace safety is the Canada-wide Workplace Hazardous Materials Information System (WHMIS), which includes product labelling, safety information, and worker education and training. This system was adopted into law through a set of complementary federal and provincial parliamentary acts. In Alberta, the provincial Ministry of Labour enforces WHMIS and other occupational health and safety laws.

Alberta's Workers' Compensation Board (WCB) was created in 1918 as part of the wave of government policy choices that formed the twentieth-century welfare state. Workers who are injured on the job receive no-fault compensation funded by employer premiums. Industries with poor safety records are penalized through higher premiums. Until the Notley NDP government passed Bill 6 in December 2015, most farm workers were exempt from both WCB and employment standards legislation; the change brought Alberta into conformity with other provinces. However, the Notley NDP's successor, Jason Kenney's United Conservative Party government, repealed this legislation and replaced it with something they believed to be more employer friendly, the Farm Freedom and Safety Act.

In 2018, Alberta recorded 51,033 WCB claims for disabling injury, 40,361 claims for modified work duty requirements, and 27,463 lost time claims for workplace injury. Rates of injury both year over year and relative to the number of person-years of employment have been declining. The province reported 126 work-related fatalities; approximately half (45 per cent) were due to occupational exposure; 33 per cent resulted from worksite incidents; and 21 per cent were motor vehicle accidents during working hours (Alberta Labour and Immigration, 2018). Labour organizations in the province mark 28 April as a day of mourning for the victims of workplace injury and a catalyst for lobbying and advocacy.

The workplace is also, as noted earlier, a common setting for health promotion programming. Canadian data suggest that about half of workplaces offer such benefits, more commonly seen among larger employers and those in the public sector (Sanofi Canada, 2020). Within organizations, an Alberta environmental scan of select employers suggested that 40 per cent or fewer employees tend to take up such program opportunities (Bengoechea, Pasco, Thiem, & Langhout, 2004). It should be noted, however, that most workplace prevention programs are individualistic in nature, for instance encouraging physical activity, healthy eating, or tobacco cessation, and relatively few are designed to address structural or institutional features of the workplace that might affect workers' health and well-being, such as control over the pace of work, task scheduling, work-life balance, opportunities for self-development, and meaningful acknowledgment and recognition for workplace contributions (Jackson, 2004; Polanyi, 2004).

6.7.2 Rehabilitation care

Rehabilitation services in Alberta are provided by AHS on both an inpatient and outpatient basis; there are also a considerable number of private or not-for-profit organizations involved in care delivery in this field. These services are available to those with inherent and acquired, permanent or temporary disabilities. Inherent disabilities include, for instance, congenital conditions such as cerebral palsy, spina bifida, autism, fetal alcohol spectrum disorder, or hearing impairments. Acquired disabilities include those sustained from trauma (e.g., brain injury, spinal cord injury, burns) and from recent or past physical illness (e.g., strokes, postpolio syndrome). Core disciplines involved in rehabilitation include audiology, speech-language pathology, physiotherapy, occupational therapy, recreation therapy, and physiatry (doctors with expertise in rehabilitation medicine or doctors of osteopathy). Various ancillary disciplines, such as respiratory therapy, also play a role in assisting patients achieve the best possible health (Alberta Health Services, 2012).

Edmonton's Glenrose Rehabilitation Hospital is the largest free-standing tertiary rehabilitation facility in Canada. It serves children and adults, and its services include specialized geriatric care. On an annual basis, Glenrose reports 1,890 inpatient admissions and 79,648 outpatient visits (Alberta Health Services, 2021b). Community rehabilitation services and access to them vary substantially across the province.

6.8 Mental health care and addictions services

Up to one in five Albertans will experience some form of mental ill health, and up to one in ten will develop problematic behaviours related to alcohol or other drugs during their lifetime (Canadian Mental Health Association, n.d.); these often go together as concurrent disorders. For some, severe and persistent mental health disorders will last throughout their lives and will require ongoing specialized care and supports. Thus, mental health and addiction services are an important component of the health care landscape. Over time, drug use and addiction have been seen less as moral or criminal matters and more as health issues; policy approaches have shifted from enforcement alone to a combination of pillars including treatment and harm reduction.

Community-based mental health services are provided in each of Alberta Health Services' zones. They can include early intervention, individual and group counselling, as well as anti-stigma campaigns and mental health promotion. Some of these services are delivered directly, while others are contracted out to community not-for-profit agencies. There is no centralized reporting for such services, and even AHS itself can only produce ad hoc reports by extracting from a variety of different clinical information systems (CIHI, 2017a).

In the early twentieth century, concerns about the detrimental effects of alcohol led to a powerful temperance movement and the introduction of prohibition following a popular vote. While prohibition was short-lived (1916–24), liquor sales were reintroduced under the strict control of the Alberta Liquor Control Board, which had a monopoly over both sales and distribution. This monopoly lasted until 1993, when the Klein government legalized private liquor stores. Alberta is the only province in which there is now no government-owned system of liquor sales. Liquor outlets proliferated in the wake of this decision, increasing from 208 in 1993 to 1,010 in 2003 (almost 400 per cent growth). Critics have argued that the increased availability (more places from which to purchase alcohol, longer operating hours) has had negative public health consequences, as it can be correlated with increased suicides, domestic violence, and alcohol-related mortality (Campanella & Flanagan, 2012); correlational studies do not prove causation, however. Governments in Canada tend to use pricing policy as a means of discouraging consumption; taxes explain why alcohol prices in the various provinces are substantially higher than in the United States.

After alcohol and tobacco, the most widely used non-pharmaceutical drug in Canada and Alberta is cannabis (or marijuana). Survey data from 2015 suggests that 12 per cent of the Canadian population had used cannabis in the previous year; about 25 per cent of respondents stated that it was for medicinal purposes. (Canada, 2017). Medical use of cannabis was authorized by regulation in 2001. Usage in Alberta has grown rapidly in recent years. At the end of 2016, 329 doctors were registered to authorize medical marijuana for 5,254 people; within 4 months, the number of authorized physicians had grown by 50 per cent (to 495) and the number of patients by 90 per cent (to 9,995; Lee, 2017). The recreational use of cannabis was legalized across Canada as

Figure 6.3 Unintentional fentanyl-related deaths in Alberta, 2011–2018

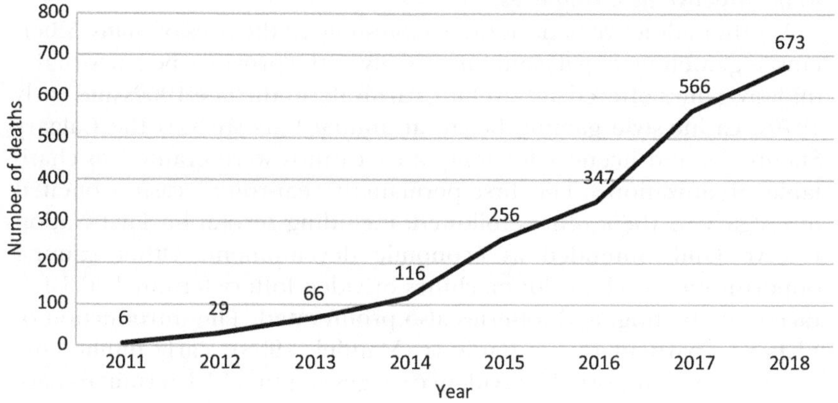

Source: Alberta, 2021f.

of October 2018, and cannabis is now distributed (by government) and sold legally (by the private sector) in Alberta.

Albertans use and misuse a variety of other drugs, even though these have long been illegal (e.g., cocaine, heroin, and methamphetamine). Some residents have also become dependent upon and abuse legal prescription medications. There is some suggestion that policy changes related to the drug OxyContin have pushed many people towards using street drugs, particularly heroin. In the years since 2010, the street supply has been found to be increasingly laced with the powerful opioid fentanyl, which can cause overdose death when consumed in even very small quantities. Unintentional fentanyl-related deaths in Alberta increased from 6 in 2011 to 116 in 2014, and then to 673 in 2018 (Figure 6.3).

Alberta's government, following that of other provinces, has made the overdose rescue drug naloxone more widely available. From the start of 2016 to the end of 2017, Alberta Health Services' naloxone program dispensed 37,737 naloxone kits (Alberta Health, 2018f). Needle exchange and other harm reduction policies have been pursued. In June 2017, Alberta requested federal permission to open supervised injection sites in Edmonton and Calgary (Kury de Castillo, 2017); these sites are modelled after existing facilities, such as British Columbia's

Insite, which have been found through rigorous peer-reviewed research to be effective in saving lives.

Another addictive behaviour, troublesome in the lives of many Albertans, is gambling. Legal gambling activity in the province began with the midway games offered at travelling carnivals; in the late 1960s and early 1970s, casino-style gaming began at annual fairs such as the Calgary Stampede, and licences for temporary casinos were granted to charitable organizations. The first permanent year-round casino opened in Calgary in 1980; others followed, including several on First Nation reserve lands intended as economic development. Other gaming opportunities, such as slot machines or video lottery terminals (VLTs), race track betting, and lotteries also proliferated. The introduction of VLTs was particularly contentious (Mandel, 1998); early public concerns may be supported by evidence suggesting that VLT terminals have the most addictive impacts (Maclaren, 2016). The Alberta Gambling Research Institute was established to study the economic and sociocultural impacts of legalized gambling in the province (Alberta Gambling Research Institute, 2021).

As of 2017–18, the province's addictions services enrolled 18,039 people, and 90 per cent of those waiting to be admitted for adult outpatient treatment services were enrolled within 13 days from referral or first contact (Alberta Health Services, 2019a). Waits can be longer in rural areas (2–3 weeks), while in Edmonton and Calgary it is often possible to access same day services. Overall, the wait time has declined from 18 days in 2013–14.

6.9 Dental health care services

Canada overall has among the best dental health of the OECD countries (Canadian Dental Association, 2017). Two-thirds of Albertans have private dental insurance, while another 9 per cent belong to publicly funded coverage programs; this overall proportion has increased by 24 per cent since 1996–97 (Quinonez, 2020). As noted in section 6.6 above, seniors, those in palliative care, those receiving disability payments, those on income assistance, and other low-income adults and families also receive some access to dental services through supplemental health benefit programs offered by the provincial government. While Alberta provides benefits for seniors and those on disability, which few other provinces do, it does not have coverage for children's oral health, which at least half the other provinces do provide (Canadian Academy of

Health Sciences, 2014). Alberta Health Services directly provides some basic dentistry to low-income individuals and families through its public health dentistry program, with clinics in Calgary and a mobile outreach program in Northern Alberta (Alberta Health Services, 2016a).

The addition of fluoride to drinking water has been long advocated as a population health-focused dental policy. Fluoridation of drinking water began in Edmonton in 1967 and was implemented in Calgary between 1991 and 2011. The removal of fluoride in Calgary allowed for a "natural experiment," and some research suggests that, while dental caries in children appear to be increasing overall, they increased more in Calgary, a statistically significant finding (McLaren et al., 2016).

6.10 Complementary and alternative medicines and care

Complementary and alternative medicine (CAM) refers to medical and health care models, services, practices, and commodities that are not considered to be established and proven approaches to medical care and treatment. Blending practices from both conventional and complementary or alternative therapies is referred to as "integrative health care."

The US National Center for Complementary and Integrative Health (formerly the National Centre for Complementary and Alternative Medicine, NCCAM) has developed a fivefold classification of CAM therapies: (1) alternative medical systems that use theories other than Western medicine, such as homeopathy, naturopathy, or Chinese or Aboriginal approaches (see Ries & Fisher, 2013); (2) mind-body medicine, such as meditation or hypnosis; (3) biologically based therapy, using foods, vitamins, and herbs to promote health; (4) body-based methods, such as chiropractic or massage; and (5) energy therapies, such as reiki (NCCAM, 2000; Institute of Medicine, 2005).

A series of studies conducted by the Fraser Institute found that lifetime use of CAM among Albertans increased from 75 per cent in 1997 to 84 per cent in 2006 and 2016 (Esmail, 2017). This finding appears consistent with other studies in concluding that the "use of APs [alternative practitioners] increases from east to west, with the highest rate of use in Alberta" (Simpson, 2003, p. 12). The seven therapies used by at least 20 per cent of respondents in 2016 included chiropractic, massage, yoga, acupuncture, relaxation techniques, prayer/spiritual practice, and herbal therapies (Esmail, 2017).

How does the establishment view integration of CAM and Western medicine? A survey of Alberta physicians published in 2008 suggested some techniques such as acupuncture, massage therapy, and chiropractic were viewed as legitimate, while others such as homeopathy, naturopathy, or reflexology were considered more dubious (Fries, 2008). Up to one-fifth of Alberta physicians have some training in CAM, with most of them integrating it to some degree into their practices (Ries & Fisher, 2013). As noted in the introduction to this chapter, ethical and legal issues can arise when parents use alternative therapies as a substitute for rather than complement to traditional medical care.

6.11　Targeted services for Indigenous and/or minority groups

Provincial and local health promotion programs in the province offer a number of services based on health equity and social justice principles, and aimed at ameliorating and improving the lives of "vulnerable populations," for example, Indigenous peoples; other racialized groups such as new immigrants, refugees (some of whom may be victims of state-sponsored torture), and non-English speakers; those with low literacy; homeless and "street-entrenched"; and LGBTQ+ and other gender-specific groups.

Alberta Health Services has an Indigenous health program that "partners with Indigenous peoples, communities and key stakeholders to provide accessible, culturally appropriate health services for First Nations, Métis and Inuit people" (Alberta Health Services, n.d.-g). Population, public, and Indigenous health is also a specific focus of one of the province's strategic clinical networks (SCNs; described further in chapter 7). Over time, a range of programs to address poor health status and determinants of ill health among Indigenous peoples have been initiated. In Alberta, as in all provinces, primary care services for Indigenous people are delivered through a combination of federal services, provincial services off reserves, and band-run programs; there is often poor integration among these various entities and squabbles over which government ought to be responsible for which services.

Alberta is one of only two provinces in which responsibility for health care in the provincial corrections system is handled by the Health Department rather than Justice Department (College of Family Physicians of Canada, 2016). Prison populations tend to be high needs when it comes to care, with many having mental health and addictions issues, as well as histories of sexual abuse. Chronic conditions such as hepatitis or HIV are also common. Health care for inmates of federal prisons is provided through Correctional Services Canada.

6.12 Palliative (end-of-life) care

6.12.1 Palliative care

Palliative care services focus on providing pain and symptom relief and maximizing quality of life among people living with serious illnesses. While current thinking does not restrict the value of such services to those who are in the final stages of life, Alberta does continue to base eligibility (such as for drug benefits) on the basis of a terminal diagnosis (Alberta, n.d.-b). These services can be offered at home, in hospital, or in designated palliative care beds or facilities such as hospices. About 85 per cent of palliative care patients are in terminal stages of cancer, and the palliative population includes about 900–1,400 children with "life-limiting illnesses" (Alberta Health Services, 2014).

6.12.2 Medical assistance in dying

In February 2015, the Supreme Court of Canada ruled that criminal prohibitions on the provision of medical assistance to persons seeking to end their own lives (assisted dying) were unconstitutional violations of the Charter of Rights and Freedoms. The federal government and provinces responded with new laws and regulations to allow those with severe and incurable illnesses to seek aid to bring about death. The Alberta government conducted public consultations to determine its response; health disciplines such as medicine, nursing, pharmacy, physiotherapy, occupational therapy, dietetics, and social work have also all worked to provide guidance for their members and clients. The approach initially adopted in Alberta has been argued to be one of the better models in the country (Downar & Francescutti, 2017), though, as noted earlier, faith-based institutions in the health care system do not make these services available. From 17 June 2016, when data collection began, through to December 2020, a total of 1,507 Albertans took advantage of the provisions of the law; the number has increased each year at a rate between 23 and 50 percent (Alberta Health Services, n.d.-e).

6.13 Summary

This chapter reveals two prominent themes. First, despite the province's formal authority over health care delivery, it must work closely with other levels of government on policy and programming that promotes the best overall health of the population as a whole. Second, there are challenges in using information about the quality of health care services to make good allocation decisions.

Federal and provincial/territorial governments interact in providing many health care and prevention services. Examples mentioned above include the blood supply, environmental health, and workplace health and safety regulations and policy. Other examples include the pan-Canadian immunization strategy and development of common drug formularies as part of pharmaceutical benefit program design. Local governments and Indigenous communities are also important partners for achieving population health promotion.

While data exist about the quantity of many services that are delivered, less information appears to be available about the quality of care. This lack is a concern, as poor quality care wastes resources and can even cause harm. Up to 30 per cent of many common tests and procedures are potentially unnecessary (Born, Huynh, & Levinson, 2019). Use of quality measures is valuable, yet overemphasis can drive provider behaviour into unintended negative patterns; for instance, over-focusing upon wait times for selected procedures can lead to "gaming" the system and to diversion of resources.

Chapter Seven

Recent Health Reforms

In this chapter we describe the major health reforms that have occurred in Alberta since 2003, specifically the creation of primary care networks (PCNs) in 2003 and the replacement of geographically based health regions with a single provincial health authority, Alberta Health Services, in 2008. The chapter discusses reforms to the governance and delivery of services, including advances in quality assurance (scientific clinical networks, patient safety, and patient advocacy), primary care governance, and wait times management.

7.1 Alberta Health Services

As discussed in chapter 2, Alberta, like most other Canadian jurisdictions, introduced health regions during the 1990s. In 2008, the remaining nine health regions and several other provincial agencies were merged into a single provincial authority, Alberta Health Services (AHS). The move to consolidate existing governance and administrative structures came after a decade of experimentation in which the health regions failed to live up to the expectations of the provincial government. Stephen Duckett, former CEO of AHS, stated:

> An inevitable consequence of regional autonomy is regional variability; indeed, regional variability, labelled as "regional responsiveness," is among the arguments for regionalization. The positive side of this is regional innovation and harnessing the benefits of competition ... [and] the downside is inequity. And this is what happened in Alberta, in both clinical and non-clinical service choices. (Duckett, 2010, p. 156)

Duckett also notes that, while innovation happened, unhealthy competition also occurred, particularly between the two major cities, leading to what he characterized as a "medical arms race" where the interests of the individual region superseded the interests of the population of Alberta as a whole (Duckett, 2010, p. 156).

This logic would seem to fit with the government's rationale for restructuring. Former health minister Ron Liepert put it this way:

> Many reasons for this particular decision have been cited, but in my view the purpose was to reverse the siloed and fragmented approach to the delivery of health care that had developed in Alberta – not by any devious means, but by evolution. This created barriers to good care that various entities had originally been created to provide. These silos did not just develop between cancer, mental health and other areas, but also between regions. Initially, the desire was to promote healthy competition between regions in their coordination of the delivery of acute care, public health and continuing care. And individual regions did become leaders in certain fields of delivery. But what struck me in taking over this portfolio ... was the reluctance to adopt winning strategies developed in other regions. (Liepert, 2009, p. 1)

Perhaps of greater importance are the external forces that have bedeviled efforts to reform Alberta's health system regardless of the choice of administrative and governance structures. The collapse of the price of oil in 2008 ended the 10 per cent annual growth rate in health expenditures, leading to a return to deficit spending. In addition, the centralization of governance administration has been a double-edged sword. While it has created improved opportunities for synergy between the Ministry of Health and AHS, and greater stability in funding, it has also created a crisis of legitimacy with local stakeholders (Rusnell & Russell, 2013).[1]

The crisis of legitimacy is well illustrated by the perception of political interference in the day-to-day operations of AHS that has occurred since 2008. This general trend has been punctuated by very public battles between the government and the CEO and board of AHS, including the removal of the CEO and the board in separate incidents due to fundamental disagreements between government policy and AHS

---

1 This topic is discussed further in chapter 8.

operational decision-making.[2] This battle indicates a lack of clarity between who is responsible for the steering and rowing (or perhaps what distinguishes steering from rowing) functions in Alberta's health care system. The net result is that AHS has lacked stable organizational leadership since its inception. In essence, the autonomous nature of health regions, which had ultimately resulted in their demise, appears to have continued under AHS.[3] Having said this, the appointment of a new board of governors in November 2015 and the appointment of a new CEO in 2016 has created greater stability in leadership. A chronology of changes in the AHS leadership is as follows:

- Stephen Duckett (CEO and President): 2009–2010
- Dr. Chris Eagle (Acting CEO and President): 2011–2013
- Janet Davidson, 12 June 2013, as Official Administrator replacing Board
- John Cowell, 12 September 2013, as Official Administrator replacing Davidson
- Dr. Duncan Campbell: Interim CEO, October 2013 to November 2013
- Brenda Huband and Rick Trimp (co-CEOs): November 2013 to March 2014
- Carl Amrhein, as Official Administrator: 17 November 2014 to 30 June 2015
- Vickie Kaminski (CEO and President): May 2014 to November 2015
- Linda Hughes, Dr. Brenda Hemmelgarn, David Carpenter, Hugh D. Sommerville, Marliss Taylor, and Glenda Yeates appointed as new Board of Governance, 23 October 2015
- Dr. Verna Yiu (interim CEO and President): January to May 2016.
- Dr. Verna Yiu (CEO and President): June 2016 to present (Office of the Auditor General of Alberta, 2017, 24)

---

2 Ironically, on the day that the board was fired in 2013, the government posted a governance review report designed to clarify responsibility between Alberta Health and AHS.

3 As noted in chapter 2, part of the original rationale for creating health regions was to provide them with fixed budgets and allow them to make decisions within these budgets. In essence, the government saw this approach as a way to allow for local (regional) variation in the delivery of services, but within fixed budgets. Unfortunately, regional health authorities (RHAs) and AHS (when it was first established) demonstrated that they had their own ideas about how to run the health care system, and these ideas are at odds with those of the government.

7.2 Strategic clinical networks

In 2012, Alberta launched the first of what would become sixteen strategic clinical networks (SNCs) within AHS (Figure 7.1). SCNs bring together "clinicians, patients, operational leaders, and other stakeholders" with the purpose of using evidence to improve patient care in areas that each network identifies as a priority. SCNs have created the opportunity to take a multidisciplinary approach to patient/population care focused on five main goals: (1) improving patient outcomes and access; (2) improving clinical practice; (3) ensuring quality and patient safety; (4) applying clinical expertise to strategic and service planning; and (5) supporting the teaching and research responsibilities of Alberta Health Services. The sixteen SCNs address the following areas: Addiction and Mental Health; Bone and Joint Health; Cancer; Cardiovascular Health and Stroke; Critical Care; Diabetes, Obesity and Nutrition; Kidney Health; Population, Public and Indigenous Health; Respiratory Health; Seniors Health; Maternal, Newborn, Child and Youth; Neurosciences, Rehabilitation and Vision; Emergency; Digestive Health; Primary Care Integration Network; and, Surgery (Alberta Health Services, n.d.-x, n.d.-o).

The clinical networks are structured to include a core team of approximately twenty-five strategic, operational, and clinical content experts and patients, and an Alberta Health and Wellness representative with appropriate experience. Outside of this core team, a range of AHS administrative and operational personnel, relevant community partners, and Alberta Innovates and Alberta Health Network researchers are included. Through the application of best evidence and grassroots input, SCNs will develop strategies to realize value for money and improvement in the quality of patient care (Alberta Health Services, 2019b). In this sense, SCNs are conceived as mechanisms for spreading innovation and addressing variation in care, as well as for accelerating quality improvement, sustainability, and innovation. Alberta's SCNs are modelled on precedents from the United Kingdom and Australia. While some early successes in the province are reported, overall the evidence base remains scant as to whether or not clinical networks are an effective means of achieving these goals (Beeson, Robert, & White, 2019).

7.3 Primary care

Stemming from intergovernmental policy agreements between federal, provincial, and territorial governments (Canada, 2016, 2007), Alberta launched an 8-year Primary Care Initiative in 2003 to improve access to

Figure 7.1 Alberta Health Services strategic clinical networks

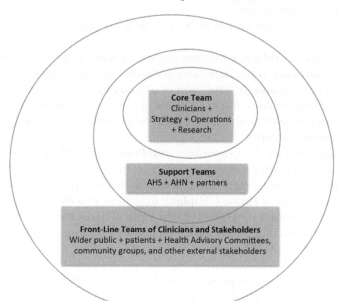

AHN = Alberta Health Network; AHS = Alberta Health Services

primary care.[4] It represented the first effort to bring together the department, the health regions, and the Alberta Medical Association to collaborate on primary care reform. The central aspect of the initiative was the creation of forty-one primary care networks (PCNs) involving 3,800 physicians (approximately 80 per cent of family physicians) and 1,000 full-time–equivalent additional health care providers. These networks provide services to approximately 70 per cent (3.5 million) of all residents (Alberta Health, 2016b; Office of the Auditor General of Alberta, 2012; Spenceley et al., 2013, p. 6).

A PCN is a joint venture between Alberta Health Services and a group of family physicians, which is funded by Alberta Health. A board of governance comprising physicians, AHS, and Alberta Health

---

4 For a discussion of recent primary care reforms in Alberta, see Church, Skrypnek, & Smith, 2018.

representatives makes policy decisions, while physicians control the daily clinical operations.

The four key objectives of PCNs are the following:

1. Accountable and Effective Governance – Establish clear and effective governance roles, structures and processes that support shared accountability and the evolution of primary healthcare delivery.
2. Strong Partnerships and Transitions of Care – Coordinate, integrate and partner with health services and other social services across the continuum of care.
3. Health Needs of the Community and Population – Plan service delivery on high quality assessments of the community's needs through community engagement and assessment of appropriate evidence.
4. Patient's Medical Home – Implement patient's medical home to ensure Albertan's have access to the right services through the establishment of interdisciplinary teams that provide comprehensive primary care (ACTT, n.d.).

Although physician compensation is distinct from PCN funding, PCNs receive $62 per panelled patient, the majority of which is used to hire allied health providers.

PCNs submit 3-year business plans to the Ministry of Health for review and approval. They also provide regular financial reporting to ensure compliance with ministry policies and business plan goals and objectives (Alberta Health, 2016b).

During the 2012 provincial election campaign, Premier Alison Redford announced an ambitious plan to create 140 independent family care clinics (FCCs) with interdisciplinary teams paid through grant funding and salaried staff. Subsequently, significant logistical issues and resistance from physicians resulted in abandoning the idea, although three FCCs were created. In the wake of this initiative, there was a renewed focus on PCNs, with a specific emphasis on greater integration and leadership between Alberta Health, AHS, and the Alberta Medical Association (CBC News, 2012).

In 2014, Alberta introduced a primary health care strategy that established three strategic directions: (1) enhancing the delivery of care; (2) bringing about cultural change; and (3) establishing building blocks for changes. Embedded within this strategy is the notion that all Albertans should be attached to a primary care home that has a focus on wellness, prevention, and chronic disease management.

Clinics are expected to provide improved access through longer hours of service and care provided by multidisciplinary teams. Shared governance with local community members,[5] improved information systems, and physician payment mechanisms are also part of the strategy (Alberta Health, 2014a).[6] In 2017–18, Alberta Health established a reformed primary care governance structure based on five geographic zones defined by AHS to support greater collaboration in planning and service delivery across PCNs in each zone (Alberta Medical Association, n.d.).

7.4 Wait times

Wait times have been an issue in Alberta since the mid-1990s when expenditure reductions reduced the capacity of the health care system significantly. While initially the government response was to periodically inject additional targeted money to address specific surgical pressure points, it gradually came to better understand the complexity of wait times. Along with other provinces and territories, in 2004 Alberta committed to reducing wait times in priority areas including heart, diagnostic imaging, hip and knee replacement, and eye surgery. To this end, Alberta has developed a voluntary centralized wait times registry, launched online in 2011, which provides a real time estimate for everything from major surgery to emergency room visits. Currently AHS provides information on province-wide targets, quarterly and annual performance data, and improvement strategies. (Church & Smith, 2009; Alberta, n.d.-a; Health Council of Canada, 2013). Consistent with other provinces, Alberta has used a mix of publicly and privately delivered surgical services through nonhospital and surgical facilities. The role of private facilities and non-urgent elective surgery within a constrained budget is a continuing issue. Recent litigation on the right to timely care in the public system may pose a challenge to the public system, depending on the outcome of the litigation.

---

5 Guidelines have been developed for community involvement in governance at the zone and individual PCN level. However, how community members are to be engaged has been left to individual PCNs to determine.
6 Reforms to information systems and physician payment mechanisms are discussed further in chapter 8.

7.5 Patient safety

Since the release of a report in the United States in 2000 on the high rate of medical error, governments in Western democracies have increased their focus on improving patient safety in health care (Baker et al., 2004; Levinson, 2010). In Alberta specifically, the Health Quality Council of Alberta (HQCA) is responsible for overall quality assurance for the health care system and was created, in part, in response to the issue of medical error. To this end, HQCA was asked by Alberta Health to assume responsibility for developing a patient safety framework. Building on previous work initiated in 2006, HQCA began work on a comprehensive patient safety framework in 2009. Introduced in 2010, the patient safety framework for Albertans is based on five principles: (1) patients are the primary focus; (2) organizations create a patient safety culture; (3) information about adverse events is shared in a transparent manner; (4) a systems approach is required to understand and address the complexity of factors that contribute to error; and (5) a continuous improvement approach strengthens an organization's ability to make informed patient safety improvements (Health Quality Council of Alberta [HQCA], 2010, pp. 4–5).

The framework identifies several "building blocks for patient safety": governance and leadership; building a patient safety culture; safety management; transparency and information sharing; effective teams; and patient engagement (HQCA, 2010, p. 5).

In tandem with the HQCA's framework, AHS has been developing its own patient safety initiative, introducing a quality and patient safety strategic outline in 2009 and a quality and safety dashboard in 2010. The dashboard is designed to allow AHS to monitor performance and facilitate quality improvement (Alberta Health Services, 2009, 2010).

Currently, AHS employs an electronic (and telephone) system for self-reporting and tracking adverse events. Data from this system is used to conduct human factor and system analysis. Alberta has also developed a cutting edge supply chain management program with bar code technology for tracking supplies and care processes that employ technology.

7.6 Patient advocacy

As mentioned in chapter 2, in 2010 the Alberta government introduced a Health Charter, although there are no formal accountability or performance measures. While a laundry list of rights was outlined, the document was poorly worded and was never revised based on feedback to provide greater clarity.

Following up on the Health Charter, in 2014 Alberta created the Health Advocate to assist the minister of health in addressing patient concerns about the health care system. Under the umbrella of this newly created office are the Health Advocate, a Seniors Advocate to address concerns related to seniors care, and the Office of the Mental Health Patient Advocate, which was created in 1990 to investigate patient complaints within the mental health system (Alberta Health Advocate, 2021b; Lesage, 2006, pp. 300–1).

While a positive step, the Office of the Health Advocate has been plagued by staffing shortages and is viewed by many as "largely toothless." Its main function to date has been to assist patients to "navigate" the system, including where to direct complaints. However,

> in most cases, the office can't handle such complaints directly and instead must direct callers to other complaint resolution systems. Even this can get tricky, because someone who had a bad experience as a patient may go through several complaints processes run by separate organizations, including AHS patient relations, the College of Physicians and Surgeons and the College of Registered Nurses ... [E]ach of these areas is siloed. (Gerein, 2016b, 2018)

AHS has also created new structures to enhance opportunities for patient input in health care decision-making. Twelve geographic health advisory councils allow input for local communities. In addition, four population advisory councils (Addictions and Mental Health; Cancer; Seniors and Continuing Care; and Sexual Orientation, Gender Identity, and Expression) allow for a voice for these perspectives. A Wisdom Council allows for participation from Indigenous peoples (Alberta Health Services, n.d.-b).

Complementing these councils, patient and family advisors (volunteers) use their experiences with health care to advise all sorts of community and governmental entities grappling with the challenges of health care. They speak at conferences, advise government committees, become involved with groups wishing to influence government, or more generally are available whenever a group feels left out of the health care system (Alberta Health Services, 2021c). Finally, the AHS board itself includes a committee dedicated to community engagement (Alberta Health Services, 2021a).

7.7 Health research

As discussed in chapter 2, Alberta created the Alberta Heritage Foundation for Medical Research (AHFMR) in 1980 to support biomedical and population health research. This organization was later renamed Alberta Innovates – Health Solutions (AIHS). In 2016, AHIS was consolidated with other (nonhealth) sector research initiatives to create Alberta Innovates. The mandate of the new organization is to support innovative research to enhance and diversify Alberta's economy. What is most noteworthy about this new organization is its closer alignment with the needs of government and industry, as opposed to the individual preferences of researchers (Graham et al., 2012).

7.8 Summary

Since 2008, Alberta's health sector has undergone significant integration in governance, service delivery, and research funding infrastructure. In addition, the province has invested significant resources to improve access and wait times, quality of care, and governance and accountability. Chapter 8 will look more critically at the challenges associated with these changes.

Chapter Eight

Assessing Alberta's Health Care System

So far, this book has focused largely on describing in detail the various key aspects of Alberta's health care system. As discussed in chapters 2 and 7, the organization of this system has undergone significant change over the past three decades. Reorganization began in 1994 with the creation of seventeen health regions with broad responsibilities for health services, and in 2003 the health care system was reorganized into nine health regions. In 2008, the nine regions and several existing provincial health agencies were merged into a single administrative entity, Alberta Health Services. Included in this evolution has been the development of an increasingly robust system of performance management supported by the collection of system-level service delivery and costing information and data on population health outcomes. The purpose of this chapter is to assess Alberta's health care system by examining some key indicators of system performance and population health.

Although Alberta spends more per capita than almost all other jurisdictions in Canada, it continues to underperform. While this underperformance is, in part, attributable to the instability of the province's economy (boom and bust) and a lack of consistent leadership in the health sector, it is equally attributable to the effects of provincial political culture on health resource allocation and the relative political strength of major health care providers, especially physicians.

8.1 Stated objectives of the health system

The Ministry of Health vision calls for "healthy Albertans in a healthy Alberta." Its mission statement calls for the provision of "the right health care services, at the right time, in the right place, provided by the right health care providers and teams" (Alberta, 2021e).

In its most recent business plan, Alberta Health articulated the following outcomes:

- A modernized, seamless health care system built around Albertan and patient needs, that provides effective and timely health care services and leads to improved health outcomes.
- A safe, high quality health system that is sustainable into the future and provides the best care for each tax dollar spent.
- Albertans have increased access to health care professionals and the mix of professionals that best meets their needs.
- Albertans are supported by accessible and coordinated mental health and addiction services and supports.
- The health and well-being of Albertans is supported through population health initiatives. (Alberta, 2020b, p.85)

To support accountability and quality assurance, the department collects information annually on a variety of performance measures. A health system classification approach supports the collection of information in four major domains: population health, health services delivery, governance and community engagement, and health system sustainability (Table 8.1).

In Domain #1 (population health), information is collected on both health status and the nonmedical determinants of health based on the same framework used by the Canadian Institute for Health Information (CIHI) and Statistics Canada. Alberta also includes various subdimensions of health status and nonmedical determinants of health.

Domain #2 (health services delivery) focuses on six dimensions of quality found in the Alberta Quality Matrix for Health: acceptability, accessibility, appropriateness, effectiveness, efficiency, and safety (Health Quality Council of Alberta [HQCA], 2005).

Domain #3 (governance and community engagement) is focused on assurance, specifically the relationship between Alberta Health and Alberta Health Services (AHS), and community involvement in system-level planning and assurance (Alberta Health, 2013, p. 2).

Domain #4 (health system sustainability) measures the impact of resource allocation decisions and sustainability of the health system, including health technologies, health workforce, information management/technology, and fiscal efficiencies.

Table 8.1 Alberta Health performance measurement classification approach

	Population health						
Well-being	Health conditions	Human function	Death	Health	Living and working conditions	Personal resources	Environmental factors
	Health services delivery						
Acceptability	Accessibility	Appropriateness		Effectiveness		Efficiency	Safety
	Governance and community engagement						
Governance			Community engagement				Accreditation
	Health system sustainability						
Health technologies		Health workforce		Information management information technology			Fiscal efficiencies

Source: Alberta Health, 2013.

As for AHS, the vision is summarized as "Healthy Albertans. Healthy Communities. Together." Its mission is "to provide a patient-focused, quality health system that is accessible and sustainable for all Albertans" (Alberta Health Services, n.d.-y). AHS's articulated goals include the following:

Goal 1: Improve patients' and families' experiences.

Goal 2: Improve patient and population health outcomes.

Goal 3: Improve the experience and safety of our people.

Goal 4: Improve financial health and value for money. (Alberta Health Services, 2017, p. 15)

8.2 Financial protection and equity

In compliance with the Canada Health Act, Alberta provides universal access to publicly financed health care services. However, like other provinces and territories, the distribution of major service providers is uneven across the province. As noted in chapter 5, over 90 per cent of physicians are based in urban centres, and it has been so for many years. Geographically, physicians are concentrated in Calgary and Edmonton, the two major census metropolitan areas in the province. However, as noted below (section 8.5), geographic distribution since 2010 has overwhelming favoured Calgary and the southern part of the province. In particular, the North zone has the fewest physicians per 100,000 population relative to the rest of the province, although remote northern areas within Canada are generally hard to serve.

In response to this challenge, the government established the Physician Resource Planning Advisory Committee. With membership from all major medical stakeholders,[1] the committee advises the minister on the appropriate supply, distribution, and mix of physicians. In particular, the ministry will focus on improving physician distribution to rural, remote, Indigenous, and underserved urban communities (Alberta Health, 2018b).

---

1 The committee consists of representatives of Alberta Health, Alberta Health Services, the two medical school faculties (deans), the College of Physicians and Surgeons of Alberta (CPSA), the Provincial Association of Resident Physicians of Alberta (PARA), and both medical schools' medical student associations (MSAs).

8.3 Health system and service outcomes

In addition to a growing number of external comparative measures since introducing business planning during the 1990s, Alberta has developed an increasing array of performance measures and health outcomes measures for tracking both the efficiency of the health system and population health outcomes. In this section, a number of these performance measures (access to care, wait times, patient safety, and continuity of care) are discussed. Comparisons are drawn with other Canadian provinces; in particular, Saskatchewan and Ontario are used because Saskatchewan has a similar geography, population, and economy to Alberta and Ontario has maintained relatively decentralized health care governance as compared to Alberta.

8.3.1 Access to care

Table 8.2 provides the results of a number of indicators of access to care.[2] While Alberta is better than the Canadian average in several categories, overall the results suggest that there remains significant work to improve access for the province's older residents and the average wait times to see a specialist for all residents.

Alberta physicians have been slow to comply with their contractual obligation to provide after-hours coverage. A 2016 survey by the College of Physicians and Surgeons of Alberta found that fewer than 30 per cent of physicians were providing after-hours coverage. For primary care networks, about 30 per cent provide extended hours coverage (24/7), and 50 per cent provide after-hours coverage (evenings and weekends).[3] The college has issued guidelines requiring physicians to either collaborate with colleagues or contract a service provider to ensure that after-hours coverage is available (Gerein, 2016a; Yourex-West, 2015).

8.3.2 Wait times

As noted in chapter 7, since the late-1990s Canadian governments have become increasingly concerned with wait times for major medical

---

2 This issue is also discussed under section 8.4 User experience and satisfaction.
3 Coverage may be underestimated because many rural physicians also staff emergency departments.

Table 8.2 Access to medical services

Indicator	Alberta	Canadian average
Percentage of people who needed medical attention and were able to get a same day or next day appointment to see a doctor or a nurse (%)	46.3	39.2
Percentage of people who went to the ED for a condition that could have been treated by their regular doctor (%)	30.1	41.1
Percentage of older Canadian (55+) who went to ED for a condition that could have been treated by their regular doctor (%)	39.0	37.0
Percentage of population who report having a regular primary health care provider (medical doctor) (%)	80.1	85.1
Percentage of people who report having a difficult time accessing medical care in the evenings or weekends (%)	49.0	55.3
Percentage of older Canadians (55+) who have a difficult time accessing medical care after hours (%)	45.0	51.0
Wait time to see a specialist – from a GP to specialist	12.0 weeks	10.2 weeks

ED = emergency department; GP = general practitioner
Sources: Peckham et al., 2018; Commonwealth Fund, 2016; Canadian Institute for Health Information (CIHI), 2015; Barua, 2017.

procedures. Within Alberta, the former Capital Health Authority (Edmonton) began publishing data publicly in 1995 that showed increasing wait times for cardiac and major joint replacement surgeries. Subsequently, the provincial government began publishing data on cardiac surgery wait times using data collected from the two cardiac care centres in Edmonton and Calgary.

In 1994, federal, provincial, and territorial governments created the Canadian Institute for Health Information (CIHI) to facilitate the collection of comparative information on wait times and a range of other health system indicators. The federal government at about this same time also provided a one-time infusion of cash to allow provincial and territorial governments to expand the capacity of their health care systems to offer advanced diagnostic testing, particularly MRIs. During the early 2000s, the federal and provincial/territorial levels of government came to a consensus on the measurement and reporting of wait times on an annual basis through CIHI (Church & Smith, 2009).

Figure 8.1 Wait times for common medical procedures (90 per cent of patients treated)

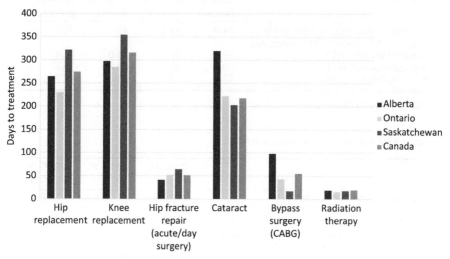

Source: CIHI, 2017e.

Along with other provinces and territories, in 2004 Alberta committed to reducing wait times in priority areas including heart surgery, diagnostic imaging, hip and knee replacement, and eye surgery. As previously noted in chapter 7, Alberta has developed a voluntary centralized wait times registry to address this issue (Church & Smith, 2009; Alberta, n.d.-a).

Despite significant developments in tracking wait times and providing this information online to decision-makers and patients, wait times in Alberta have continued to grow. While not alone among Canadian jurisdictions, wait times in Alberta have basically doubled since 1993 (Barua & Ren, 2016). The increase is attributable to a continuing shortage of resources and integration and/or coordination strategies for services provided outside of hospitals. In short, as long as there are insufficient resources for primary health care, seniors care, and community mental health, many individuals will end up in institutional settings when they might have received care in the community or have avoided needing care at all (Office of the Auditor General of Alberta, 2014a).

Table 8.3 Alberta surgery wait times, 2014–2018, in weeks

Surgery	2014–15 (weeks)	2015–16 (weeks)	2016–17 (weeks)	2017–18 (weeks)
Coronary artery bypass graft, ready to treat (RTT), Urgency III – scheduled	14.9	12.1	10.7	22.2
Cataract surgery, RTT	29.9	33.0	34.0	38.4
Hip replacement, RTT	28.7	31.4	32.9	36.7
Knee replacement, RTT	33.0	34.7	36.9	40.7

Source: Alberta Health Services, 2018b.

Table 8.4 Emergency department wait times

	2014–15 FY	2015–16 FY	2017–18 FQYTD
ED LOS for admitted patients (median in hours at busiest sites)	10.5	10.0	10.7
ED patients treated and admitted to hospital within 8 hours (LOS < = 8 hours) (All sites)	46.0%	46.9%	43.9%
ED patients treated and admitted to hospital within 8 hours (LOS < = 8 Hours) (busiest sites)	36.1%	37.9%	35.3%
ED LOS for discharged patients (median in hours at busiest sites)	3.2	3.2	3.4
ED patients treated and discharged within 4 hours (LOS < = 4 hours) (all sites)	78.5%	78.3%	76.0%
ED patients treated and discharged within 4 hours (LOS < = 4 hours) (busiest sites)	63.3%	69.2%	60.1%
ED time to physician initial assessment (median in hours at busiest sites)	1.4	1.3	1.4
ED patients left without being seen and left against medical advice	4.3%	3.9%	4.3%

ED = emergency department; FY = fiscal year; LOS = length of stay
Source: Alberta Health Services, 2018b.

Recent information on wait times for common medical procedures (Figure 8.1) suggests that Alberta is better than the Canadian benchmark in some but not all categories.[4]

Nonetheless, wait times for several of these procedures have increased significantly since 2014 (Table 8.3). The current government is tackling this issue by seeking to contract out the delivery of a variety of surgical procedures (Babych, 2019).

---

4 While Alberta fares well at the 90th percentile, it does much worse at the 50th percentile. Relative performance thus depends on which measurement one chooses to report.

Figure 8.2 Wait times for cancer treatment (90 per cent of patients treated)

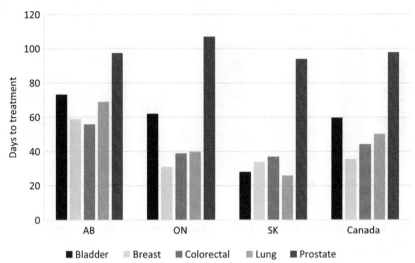

AB = Alberta; ON = Ontario; SK = Saskatchewan
Source: CIHI, 2017e.

Wait times in Alberta's emergency departments have not improved significantly since 2014–15 (Table 8.4). One of the major reasons for this relates to hospital throughput (particularly for seniors), which is discussed further in section 8.5.

When it comes to access to cancer treatment, Alberta performs comparatively poorly on access to three of the five cancer treatments and below the Canadian average for all cancer treatments (Figure 8.2).

Finally, access to diagnostic imaging has long been an issue in Canada's health system (Church & Smith, 2009). Alberta does not compare well for access to MRI compared to certain other provinces (Figure 8.3). Nor does it compare well for CT scans (Figure 8.4).

8.3.3 Patient safety

When looking at comparative provincial and territorial data, Alberta (13.2 per 100,000 population) is above the Canadian average (9.3 per 100,000) for patient safety indicators and is the highest in Canada for

Figure 8.3 Access to MRI (90 per cent of patients treated)

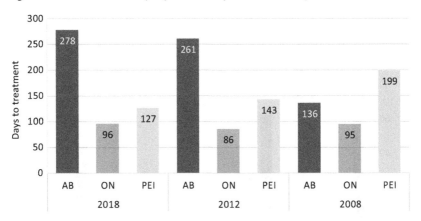

AB = Alberta; ON = Ontario; PEI = Prince Edward Island; MRI = magnetic resonance imaging
Source: CIHI, 2017e.

Figure 8.4 Access to CT scans (90 per cent of patients treated)

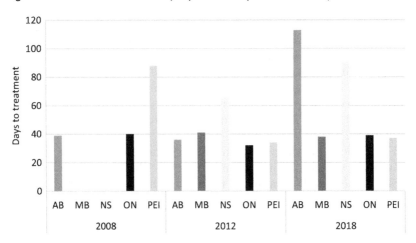

AB = Alberta; MB = Manitoba; NS = Nova Scotia; ON = Ontario; PEI = Prince Edward Island; CT = computerized tomography
Source: CIHI, 2017e.

Figure 8.5 Trend over time: Hospital deaths (hospital standardized mortality ratio)

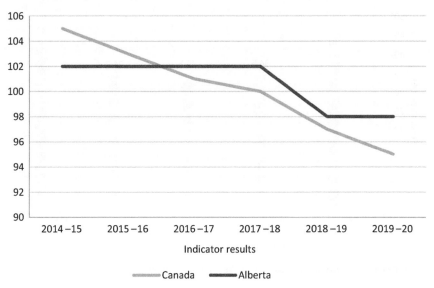

Indicator results

Source: CIHI, 2021e.

at least one measure of adverse events, the rate of foreign bodies such as surgical sponges or medical tools left inside a patient's body during a procedure (Canadian Institute for Health Information [CIHI], 2018e).

As Figure 8.5 illustrates, Alberta has shown modest improvements in the number of patients dying in hospitals since 2013, although the average for Canada has improved steadily.

At the current time, the only publicly available data within Alberta relates to the patient. Figure 8.6 depicts the percentage of Albertans experiencing and being informed of unexpected harm over the past decade after an initial decline. Overall, there has been little improvement in either reducing harm or informing patients and their families who have experienced harm over the past decade. As mentioned above, both increased awareness and improved reporting might partly explain this finding.

Figure 8.6 Percentage of Albertans who experience and are informed of un-expected harm during interaction with the health care system (self-reported)

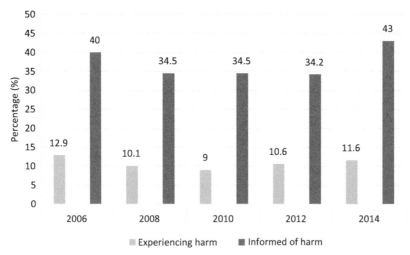

Sources: HQCA, 2014c, pp. 126–7; Alberta Health, 2018b, p. 58.

8.4 User experience and satisfaction

Since the mid-1990s, Alberta has been tracking the user experience through a growing number of indicators. Some major indicators are highlighted in the discussion below: access, patient satisfaction, handling of complaints, and continuity of care.

8.4.1 Access

As discussed previously, since at least the mid-1990s access to health care services has been a major concern for Albertans. An examination of data collected since 2004 shows that the majority of Albertans have not found access to be easy (Figure 8.7). The terms "actual" and "perceived" used in this data distinguish perceptions based on actual recent experiences from more general perceptions about health care accessibility overall, which might not reflect any recent contact with the system. In this sense, those who have had cause to use the system seem to express less concern than the public at large.

When health status is factored in, those who see themselves as being less healthy are less likely to view access as easy (Figure 8.8).

Figure 8.7 Percentage of Albertans rating access as very easy/easy

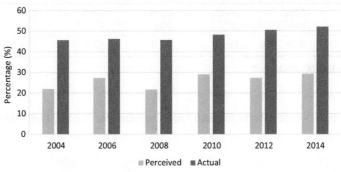

Source: HQCA, 2014c, pp. 19–20.

Figure 8.8 Ease of access by health status (very easy/easy)

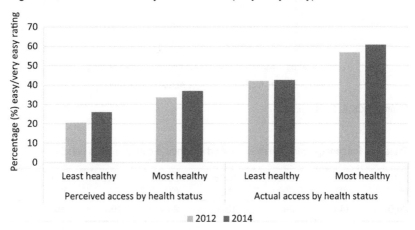

Source: HQCA, 2014c, pp. 142–3.

8.4.2 Satisfaction

When looking at overall satisfaction (Table 8.5), approximately two-thirds of Albertans are satisfied with the health care services they receive, a marked improvement over the past decade.

Table 8.5 Overall satisfaction with health services received (very satisfied or satisfied)

2004 (%)	2006 (%)	2008 (%)	2010 (%)	2012 (%)	2014 (%)
51.7	57.9	59.8	61.9	63.5	66.4

Source: HQCA, 2014c, p. 7.

Figure 8.9 Overall satisfaction with health services received by health status

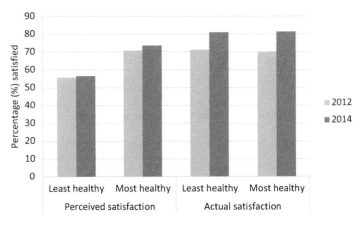

Source: HQCA, 2014c, p. 139.

Table 8.6 Percentage very satisfied/satisfied with how a complaint was handled

2003 (%)	2004 (%)	2006 (%)	2008 (%)	2010 (%)	2012 (%)	2014 (%)
20.9	14.8	24	18.9	20.4	19.7	20.8

Source: HQCA, 2014c, p. 34.

When this data are disaggregated by health status (Figure 8.9), again those who are less healthy are less likely to be satisfied about health services.

As Table 8.6 depicts, when asked about their satisfaction with how complaints were handled, fewer than 25 per cent of Albertans surveyed were very satisfied/satisfied.

8.4.3 Continuity of care

Although there are significant innovations occurring within the province, managing patient transitions between acute care, specialists, and community care continues to be a challenge (especially for complex patients).[5] The reliance on several electronic systems and a legacy paper-based approach is "problematic and ultimately does not support or protect Albertans' continuity of care" (HQCA, 2016a, p. 9). Most physicians do not actively monitor the health status of their patients between visits or effectively share and use clinical information (Alberta Netcare, 2018; Office of the Auditor General of Alberta, 2017); this issue is discussed further below.

When Albertans are asked about their overall coordination of care (Table 8.7), only about 50 per cent rate it as excellent or very good. Improvement in this area has been marginal over the past decade.

In an effort to address this gap, Alberta is implementing several solutions. The Central Patient Attachment Registry (CPAR) is a province-wide database designed to capture the attachment of primary care physicians and their patients. About 70 per cent of PCN physicians have established or are working to establish patient panels.[6] To support this effort, the Health Quality Council of Alberta uses administrative health data to provide standardized reports on patient panels, including patient demographics, health conditions, select aspects of patient management, and health system utilization.

Table 8.7 Coordination of care rating (excellent/very good)

2004 (%)	2006 (%)	2008 (%)	2010 (%)	2012 (%)	2014 (%)
47.7	46.4	49.2	48.3	48.6	51.8

Source: HQCA, 2014c, p. 28.

---

5 The information infrastructure aspects of continuity of care are discussed below in section 8.7, Information, performance measurement and quality assurance.

6 Patients formally registered with a physician practice. Attachment and panelling indicates that the patient who is registered with a particular physician is actually receiving services from that physician. In some cases, as a result of being formally registered with a physician, patients have been found to be receiving services from more than one physician.

Figure 8.10 Personal doctor informed about specific health care services

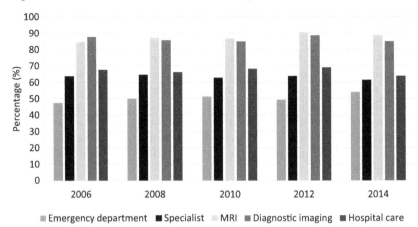

MRI = magnetic resonance imaging
Source: HQCA, 2014c, p. 27.

The sharing of information among health providers is also a good indicator of continuity of care. When it comes to the transfer of medical records, only 54.4 per cent of Albertans were confident that their medical records had been transferred when they switched providers (HQCA, 2014c, p. 66). As Figure 8.10 demonstrates, when it comes to sharing information with family physicians, only about half of the time do emergency rooms and about two-thirds of the time do specialists share information about services provided to those patients.

Although there are currently no jurisdiction-wide practices in place to support two-way communication between primary and specialist care, some locally based efforts are underway. In Calgary, for instance, Specialist Link allows family physicians to connect with specialists by telephone (Bahler, 2018; HQCA, 2016b; Patients Collaborating with Teams, 2017; Alberta Health Services, n.d.-l, n.d.-v).

8.5 Efficiency (technical and allocative)

The following section provides an overview of a number of areas in which there remain important questions about whether the province's allocation of health system resources is achieving the best outcomes for the dollars being spent.

Figure 8.11 Provincial government health spending per capita (current $)

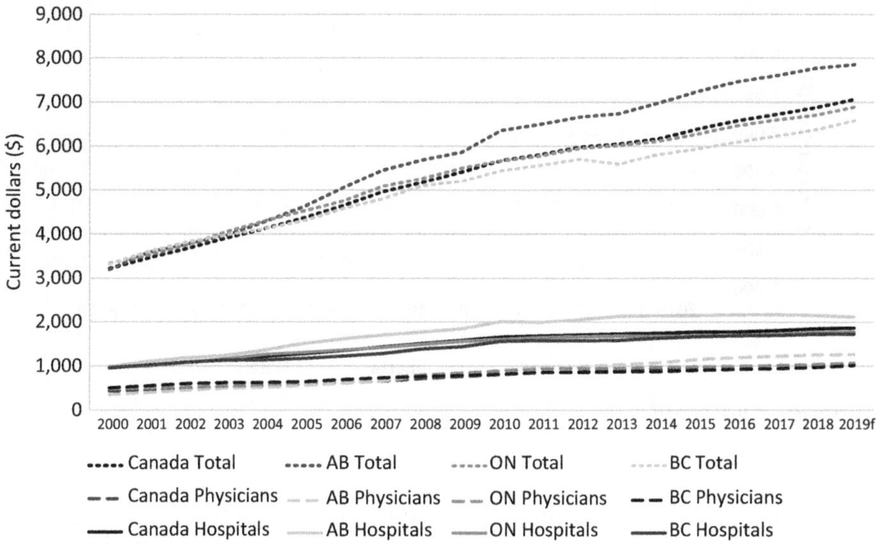

AB = Alberta; BC = British Columbia; ON = Ontario; f = forecast
Source: CIHI, 2020a.

8.5.1 Financial costs

As discussed in chapter 3, Alberta has had the highest per capita expenditures on health among provincial governments since the early 2000s. Duckett noted: "In 1996 Alberta's provincial government health expenditure was about 12% below that of other provinces. By 2008, however, Alberta was spending about 15% more per person" (Duckett, 2015, p. 299). Fast forwarding to 2019–20, the health care expenditure forecast of $7,855 per capita is 10 per cent higher than the national average and 21 per cent higher than Ontario. This situation has remained largely unchanged since 2010 (2 years after AHS was created). Hospital (operating) expenditures are 12 per cent higher than the national average and 17 per cent higher than Ontario. Expenditures on physicians are 17 per cent higher than the national average and 15 per cent higher than Ontario (Figure 8.11).

Further unpacking this comparison, Figure 8.12 reveals that the cost per standardized hospital inpatient case in 2018-19 was 30.1 per cent higher in Alberta than the national average and 45.7 per cent higher than in Ontario (lowest in Canada). Central to this cost are provider compensation, staff mix, and hours per patient.

Figure 8.12 Trend over time: Cost of a standard hospital stay (current $)

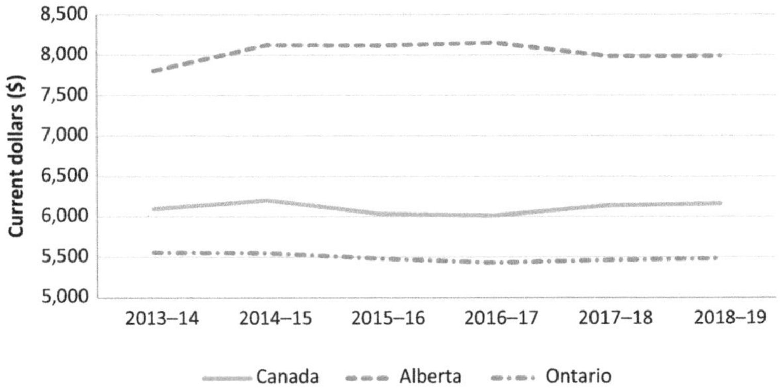

Source: CIHI, 2021d.

And this problem is not limited to acute care. Expenditures per capita in 2019 on continuing care were close to the national average but 23 per cent higher than Ontario. Finally, Alberta's utilization rate for major indicators is 10 per cent higher than the Canadian average (CIHI, 2020a).

To address this expenditure discrepancy in 2015, AHS began a process of operational efficiency benchmarking at fifteen acute care sites. Operational benchmarking compares the costs, expenses, and productivity of a specific hospital unit to the costs and expenses of other similar units at similar hospitals. The intent is to improve efficiency without adversely affecting quality of care (Alberta Health Services, 2015b). One other cost consideration is the estimated $8 billion needed to replace existing hospitals that are over 40 years old. Over $1 billion alone is needed to address existing deferred maintenance (Gerein, 2015b).

However, while Alberta is struggling with the cost of service delivery, in 2019–20 it spent less on administration per capita (3.5 per cent) than the Canadian average (4.5 per cent; CIHI, 2020b). This figure might be attributed to the economies of scale realized through administrative consolidation.

8.5.2 Utilization

Hospitalization rates for Albertans under the age of 75 have been declining over the past several years (Alberta Health, 2018b, p. 38). However, a

Table 8.8 Wait times for placement from acute/subacute hospital bed into continuing care

Continuing Care	2014–15	2015–16	2016–17	2017–18
Total number of people placed into continuing care	7,310	7,379	7,963	7,927
Number of patients placed from acute/ subacute hospital beds into continuing care	5,548	5,405	5,395	5,218
Number of clients placed from community (at home) into continuing care	2,262	2,474	2,568	2,709
Average wait time in acute/subacute care hospital bed for continuing care placement (in days)	42 days	44 days	46 days	51 days
Total number waiting for continuing care placement	1,544	1,411	1,873	1,937
Number of persons waiting in acute/subacute hospital bed for continuing care placement	690	628	846	676
Number of persons waiting in community (at home) for continuing care placement	854	783	1,027	1,261
Number of unique home care clients	113,778	11,6415	118,744	121,021

Source: Alberta Health Services, 2018b.

number of hospital admissions could have been prevented if appropriate care were available in an ambulatory care setting (Table 8.8). Figure 8.13 indicates that Alberta's ambulatory care sensitive conditions rate was above the Canadian average and 15 per cent higher than Ontario by 2016. In fact, the rate stalled for 5 years after AHS was created. However, by 2019–2020, Alberta was approaching the Canadian average and is now 4.7 per cent higher than Ontario.

One important population affecting hospitalization rates is seniors. While the rate of placement in continuing care facilities has improved over the past several years, 40 per cent (the same as reported in 2015–16) of seniors requiring placements still do not receive their placement within 30 days, leading to unnecessary or extended hospital stays (Alberta Health Services, 2020, p. 24). As Figure 8.14 demonstrates, this delay contributes to a shortage of acute care beds through the well-recognized challenge of patients who are stranded in hospitals because of the lack of timely availability of alternative care. Thus, they are failing to receive the most appropriate care in the most appropriate setting.

Table 8.8 illustrates the continuing deterioration of hospital through-put associated with the seniors population; specifically, there have been significant increases in the number of patients waiting for placements

Figure 8.13 Ambulatory care sensitive conditions rate – avoidable admissions per 100,000 population (age-standardized)

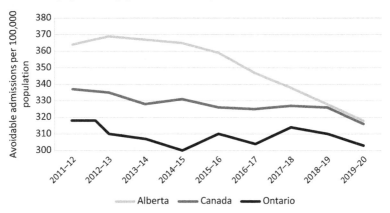

Note: 2010–16 based on 2011 standardized population; 2007–09 data is based on 1991 population, values shown are estimated. (The comparison shown here is unpublished because of the break in the data in 2010; graph is illustrative only.)
Source: CIHI, 2021c.

Figure 8.14 Alternate level of care: Annual percentage of acute beds occupied by patients awaiting placement in continuing care or other services/care settings

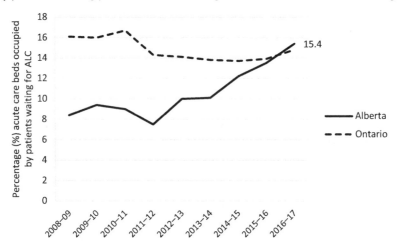

ALC = alternative level of care
Note: The long Alberta series and the comparison shown here are unpublished; AB-ON data is not fully comparable; graph is illustrative only.
Sources: Alberta Health Services, 2018c; Health Quality Ontario, 2018.

in continuing care in the community and in the number of home care clients. The number of patients placed from acute to subacute hospital beds and the average wait time in acute/subacute care hospital beds has also been increasing.

Wait times for patients in hospitals rose between 2014 and 2018, with 17.4 per cent of hospital beds in 2017 occupied by patients waiting for other care. Meanwhile, expenditures on home care have grown at barely 2 per cent during this time. Of Alberta seniors placed in continuing care, 30 per cent have low to moderate needs that could be met if there were sufficient home care available. This figure compares to 23 per cent for Ontario and 15 per cent for British Columbia (CIHI, 2017d).

One final population that might be better served if appropriate resources were available outside of the hospital is those experiencing mental health issues. In 2019–20, Alberta had 11.6 per cent repeat stay average for mental illness compared to 12.8 per cent average for Canada (CIHI, 2021f). However, one in five Alberta adults[7] has experienced addiction or mental health issues, so there is room for improvement. Despite this, 48.7 per cent of Albertans experiencing an addictions or mental health issue reported that they could not access sufficient care. Possible reasons include the reactive, acute care model configuration of existing services (including limited hours of operation, limited assessment and treatment, and lack of peer support and follow-up), institutional barriers to access (refusal criteria), limited efforts to connect rejected clients with appropriate services, and very limited prevention and promotion services (Wild, Wolfe, Wang, & Ohinmaa, 2014).

In particular, mental health services for children and youth are under resourced (Wild et al., 2014, pp. 18–20). Access to services for children (receiving an appointment within 30 days) has fallen from 82 per cent in 2014–15 to 67 per cent by the end of 2017–18 (Alberta Health Services, 2018b).

8.5.3 Public health

Immunization is considered to be one of the major means of preventing the spread of disease. The percentage of Albertans who get an annual flu shot is relatively low (40 per cent). The reason for this low compliance

---

7 The Canadian Mental Health Association website also lists one in five as the average for Canada (see Fast facts about mental illness, https://cmha.ca/fast-facts-about -mental-illness).

Figure 8.15 Childhood immunization rates (by age two)

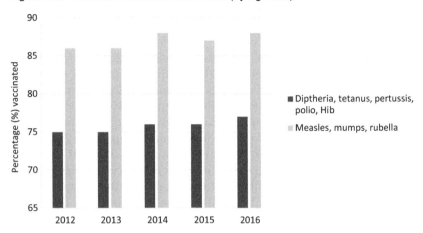

Source: Alberta Health, 2018b, p. 93.

rate appears to be primarily linked to a lack of concern for the possible adverse effects of influenza (HQCA, 2014c, pp. 122–4). With an immunization rate for seniors of 60 per cent in 2017–18, Alberta is slightly below the 65.4 per cent national average for this indicator (Alberta Health, 2018b p. 46; HQCA, 2014c, pp. 122–4).

When it comes to childhood vaccinations (Figure 8.15), the rates are significantly higher. However, given the nature of the diseases associated with these vaccines, achieving an even higher compliance rate would be beneficial. To this end, public health officials will start asking the parents of students in grades 1–9 who do not appear to have up-to-date vaccinations to verify that their children have received all the necessary vaccinations and to justify why they have not (Alberta Health, 2018b, p. 49).

8.5.4 Integration

A major theme across the health policy literature has been the importance of creating a more integrated health care system. Integration allows for a more efficient and effective use of health care resources leading to improved health outcomes. Since the creation of AHS in 2008, Alberta has made significant strides in creating a more integrated health care system. Regionalization initially brought acute care, continuing care, and public health services under a single management structure; other services such as cancer care, mental health, and ambulances were subsequently rolled into AHS. Thus, the opportunity to overview a spectrum of services, plan linkages among them, and reallocate resources has grown considerably. As noted previously (chapter 7), the integration of administrative support services has allowed Alberta to achieve the lowest per capita health care spending on administration in Canada. It might be argued as well that consolidation in the not-for-profit sector, such as among home care providers, or in the private lab sector also holds potential to decrease integration challenges, since logically, if there are fewer players, it is easier for them to coordinate their activities.

AHS has also created a quality management framework (discussed below) that has allowed for the development of various quality initiatives, such as strategic clinical networks (see chapter 7), that have already realized measurable quality gains through better integration. Other initiatives have been designed specifically to support the work of physicians:

• Primary care networks provide formal linkages between family physicians and programs and services provided through AHS.
• Access Improvement Measurement Program provides support for physicians in chronic disease management.
• Patient First Strategy supports a patient-centred approach to care.
• CoAct[8] designs tools and processes for collaborative care.
• Netcare connects health providers (mainly physicians) with diagnostic testing services and pharmacies for the transfer of diagnostic test results and drug prescriptions. Alberta is considered a leader in Canada in this area.
• Dyad (co-lead) management (managers and physicians) structure in hospitals and zones facilitates better coordination of decision-making between managers and physicians.

Despite these achievements, the provincial auditor general has noted that, while Alberta has made significant investments over the past two decades in efforts to integrate various aspects of the health care system, problems remain.

---

8   CoAct is a program designed to better coordinate and integrate patient care by linking patients, family members, and care providers and ensuring smoother transitions between care providers and services.

We identified the following underlying challenges to healthcare integration in Alberta:

- the fragmented structure of the public healthcare system
- the lack of integration of physician services and of services of other care providers
- the lack of sharing and use of clinical information. (Office of Auditor General of Alberta, 2017, p. 18)

The system that has developed in Alberta has done so in a piecemeal fashion over the past century. As discussed in a number of chapters in this book, historically the allocation of resources for health care services has been skewed towards acute care. While significant integration and coordination of care has been achieved within the walls of the hospital, far less has occurred to ensure continuity of care either between the hospital and other organizational and individual care providers in the health care system or across the broad spectrum of health providers in the community. As noted by the provincial auditor, "simply bringing organizations and providers under one management umbrella has not automatically integrated patient care" (Auditor General of Alberta, 2017, p. 28).

For example, a major reason for this lack of integration is the structure of health care financing. In essence, there are currently three disconnected streams of funding. As discussed in chapter 3, historically health care funding was structured through federal-provincial fiscal arrangements related to health care. These arrangements gave funding for services provided in hospitals and by physicians outside of hospitals. Services not covered through these two main funding streams were either covered through other funding streams introduced by provincial governments over time or through private insurance.

With the advent of health regions and more recently AHS, the hospital services funding stream was merged administratively with other services provided through AHS. However, the current configuration of funding streams in Alberta includes a budget for physician services (not controlled by AHS), a budget for services provided through AHS, and funding for a range of other health care services through private insurance. None of these funding streams are linked in a meaningful way for planning, continuity of care, or quality assurance. For instance, patients can experience gaps when they leave inpatient settings, where necessary pharmaceuticals are provided, for outpatient settings, where they must rely upon the insurance market as to what costs are covered. When you add to this mix that physicians and other providers (e.g., chiropractors) bill for each discreet service they provide or each diagnostic test that they order, the results are often extremely disjointed.

The province's costs for family medicine consults are almost one-third greater than the Canadian average (Duckett, 2015). As a result of research and experiential learning (policy learning), the government has attempted to address this issue through a range of possible payment options beyond fee-for-service, currently referred to as alternative relationship plans or ARPs (Alberta Health, 2018c; Alberta Medical Association, 2018a; Church & Smith, 2013b). However, despite these efforts to shift physician method of payment away from fee-for-service, relatively little progress has been made to date. In 2015–16, Alberta had the lowest percentage among all provinces of total physician payments delivered through ARPs (13.2 per cent) and has been consistently well below the Canadian average over the past 15 years (CIHI, 2020a).

One explanation for this lack of progress is the disconnect between the expectations of the government that ARPs will lead to immediate cost savings and the reality that such models are designed to improve quality of care in the short run with a cumulative long-term effect of saving money. This disconnect has led to frustration on the part of participating physicians and increasing bureaucratic rigidity on the part of government. As a result, there is untapped potential to expand ARPs in the province.

Overall, the combination of separate funding streams and the continuing role of physicians as independent contractors responsible for most clinical decisions in health care, but not accountable for the associated costs, has hampered efforts to integrate the delivery of services. While there have been significant efforts to better integrate the work of physicians into the rest of the system for greater continuity of care, such as primary care networks (PCNs), these initiatives have been only partially successful.

A good example of this challenge is the lack of a direct relationship between physicians practising in hospitals and the hospitals. Another example is the lack of a formal referral system between specialists and family physicians to manage patient transitions from acute care to community care (especially for patients with complex needs), even though family physicians are commonly seen as the coordinators of care for their patients. As previously noted, most physicians do not proactively monitor the health status of their patients between visits. In general, there is no formal agreement between physicians and AHS on mutual goals for health care (Office of the Auditor General of Alberta, 2017, pp. 33–7; HQCA, 2013, p. 4). Disconnects between institutional and community-based mental health services have also been a perennial problem for patient care in the province.

While PCNs were envisioned to facilitate integration and continuity of care through interdisciplinary teams, there has been little incentive to develop these teams (Office of the Auditor General of Alberta, 2017, pp. 37–8). Admittedly, the funding provided to PCNs may be insufficient to support the development of multidisciplinary teams (Theman, 2016). Additionally, while PCNs were seen as a way to increase access to primary care, most PCNs have failed to provide consistent after-hours care (Gerein, 2016a).

Finally, at the broad level, the need for different government departments and other provincial partners to collaborate in intersectoral action to create healthy public policy is another integration challenge for the province (Carey, Crammond, & Keast, 2014).

8.5.5 Resource allocation

As was mentioned earlier, when we examine the geographic distribution of physicians, those practising in urban settings are clearly predominant and becoming increasingly so (Figure 8.16). This trend has continued despite the presence of the Rural Physician Action Plan (since 1991–92) intended to provide incentives and policy tools to attract physicians into rural and underserved locations (Wilson, Woodhead-Lyons, & Moores, 1998).

Figure 8.17 suggests a more interesting story. Since the creation of AHS in 2008, the ratio of physicians per 100,000 population has continued to increase in the southern part of the province, including Calgary, at a significantly higher rate than the rest of the province. The current government is attempting to address the issue of the geographic distribution of physicians through legislation that would give it the power to influence where new physicians might practice (Bellefontaine, 2019).[9]

When it comes to the allocation of resources by AHS, the reliance on per capita funding has not resulted in technical efficiency. A comparison of medical conditions and spending patterns suggests that, while

---

9 The government of British Columbia attempted to address the issue of geographic distribution of physicians during the 1990s, but the provincial medical association launched a successful constitutional challenge, claiming that the legislation constituted a violation of Charter mobility rights.

Figure 8.16 Alberta physician urban/rural distribution

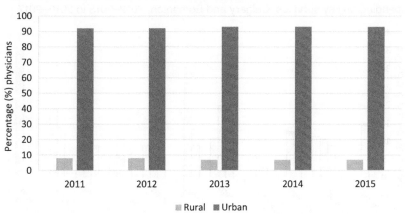

Source: CIHI, 2016c, Alberta profile.

Figure 8.17 Alberta physicians percentage change in geographic distribution by zone, 2010–2014

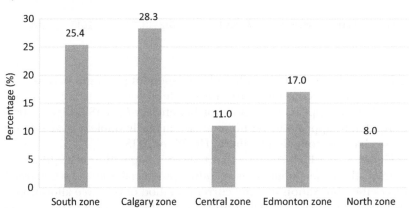

Source: CIHI, 2016c, Alberta profile.

Calgary has a lower disease rate than other AHS zones, it is nonetheless allocated far more health care resources.[10]

---

10 As an example, for Figure 8.19 the total AMI for Alberta is 165 and for Calgary it is 116. 165 – 116 = 49; 49 divided by 165 = .3. Thus, Calgary is 30 per cent below the

Figure 8.18 Alberta Health Services percentage changes over 4 years in spending on key services, Calgary and Edmonton, 2012–2013 to 2016–2017

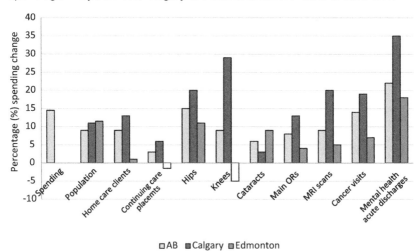

Sources: Alberta Health Services, Annual reports 2012–13, 2014–15, 2015–16, and 2016–17.

Figure 8.18 presents a crude index of spending changes because the different health conditions are not weighted for the average cost per case. Calgary appears to be a major beneficiary of AHS budget allocations. There appears to be no analysis currently publicly available on these changes from either Alberta Health or AHS.

Figure 8.19, which suggests that Calgary's population is healthier on average than the populations in other provincial zones, further reinforces the observation that the current method of resource allocation is technically inefficient in that it provides greater resources to those areas in which the need is least. Figure 8.20 further demonstrates this trend.

While administrative outcomes are important, of equal importance is the way in which services affect the health of the population.

provincial average. The overall average for each zone is just the simple average of the +/- provincial average for all the indicators. To calculate disease rates per 100,000 for each zone, take the number of occurrences and divide by the zone population. So again for Calgary, 1,812 occurrences divided by 1,556,569 (15.57) = 116.

Figure 8.19 Relative rates of major chronic conditions, plus birth rates and injuries, in the Alberta Health Services zones, percentage difference from provincial average

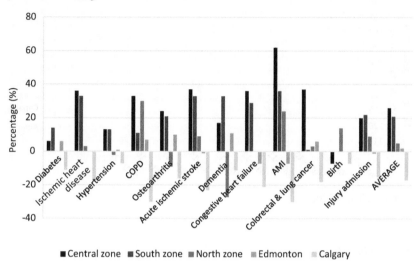

■ Central zone ■ South zone ■ North zone ■ Edmonton ▨ Calgary

AMI = acute myocardial infarction; COPD = chronic obstructive pulmonary disease
Source: Alberta Health IHDA website: Chronic disease; Demographics; Injury; 2016 or latest data.

Figure 8.20 Alberta potential years of life lost, by zone (age standardized by cause of death, 2000–2015)

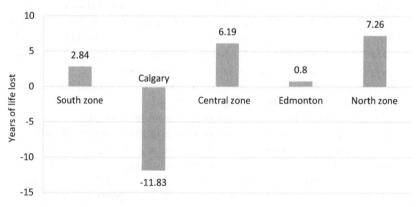

Source: Alberta Health IHDA website: Potential years of life lost by zone, age standardized by cause of death, 2000–15.

Figure 8.21 Potentially avoidable deaths (age-standardized rate per 100,000 population) from *preventable* causes (e.g., lung cancer due to smoking)

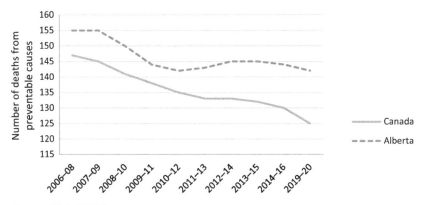

Source: CIHI, 2020d.

8.5.6 Mortality

As mentioned in chapter 1, while the life expectancy of Albertans is on a par with the rest of Canada, there are several areas (infant mortality, obesity, respiratory diseases, heart disease, suicide, and illicit drug use) where Alberta faces significant challenges. As Figure 8.21 illustrates, Alberta's progress in reducing avoidable deaths stopped after 2010, while overall Canada's continued to improve. Alberta is 10 per cent higher in preventable death overall and 20 per cent higher in potential years of life lost (PYLL; more Albertans appear to be dying younger). The AHS *2017–18 Annual Report* shows that PYLL for men has increased significantly since 2013, suggesting a link with the economic downturn.

As with avoidable deaths, Alberta is above the national average for deaths from treatable causes (Figure 8.22).

Substance abuse is another preventable condition. As discussed in chapter 1, the nature of Alberta's economy and the resultant lifestyle patterns have created a perfect storm for substance abuse. Although it has shown a gradual improvement, Alberta's smoking prevalence rate was 18.9 per cent in 2019 compared to 15.8 per cent in 2015. It is still above the national average of 15.1 per cent (Reid et al., 2019, pp. 15, 26). As previously noted in chapter 6 and depicted in Figure 8.23, opioid-related deaths have been increasing steadily over the past several years and appear

Figure 8.22 Potentially avoidable deaths from *treatable* causes (age-standardized rate per 100,000 population)

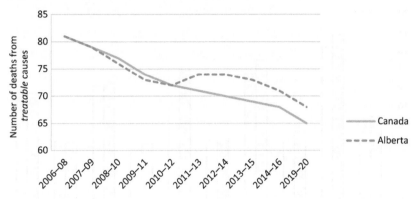

Source: CIHI, 2020e.

Figure 8.23 Rate per 100,000 person-years of apparent accidental drug poisoning deaths related to fentanyl, by zone (based on place of death), 1 January 2016 to 31 May 2018

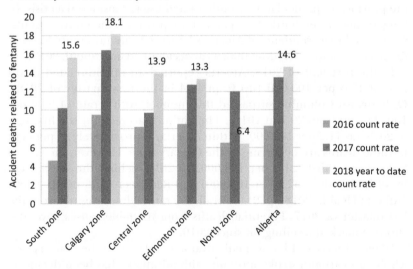

Sources: Alberta Health, 2018e, p. 9, Table 3; Alberta Health, 2018f p. 2, Table 1.

Figure 8.24 Acute myocardial infarction (heart attack) and stroke in-hospital mortality within 30 days of admission, Alberta and Canada

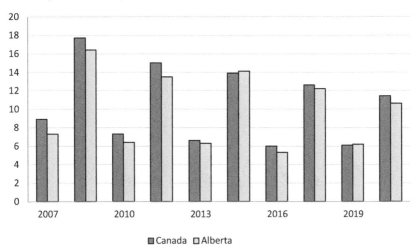

■ Canada □ Alberta

Source: CIHI, 2021a (risk-adjusted % rate, 3-year average).

to be concentrated in major urban centres and in the southern half of the province in particular. Currently, opioid use is considered a crisis. In Calgary, one of the hardest hit parts of the province, the mayor recently announced that "residents of Alberta's largest city are now more likely to die from an opioid overdose than a car accident" (Giovannetti, 2019).

In the first half of 2018, Alberta reported an opioid-related death rate of 17.6 per 100,000 (up from 14.4 in the first quarter of 2018). Only British Columbia surpassed this number, with a rate of 30.2 per 100,000 (up from 20.7 in 2016). The national average for the first half of 2018 was 11.2 per 100,000. Within Alberta, approximately 47 per cent of these deaths are occurring in the Calgary zone. However, the City of Calgary was third (21.6 per 100,000) in 2018, behind the smaller cities of Lethbridge (32.1 per 100,000) and Red Deer (37.3 per 100,000) (Alberta Health, 2018f, p. 9). Overall, the rate is down slightly from the last quarter of 2017. Potential deaths from treatable causes have also shown a marked levelling off since 2010.

While Alberta still has a small advantage relative to the country as a whole in heart and stroke mortality, this advantage has been declining over the past decade (Figure 8.24).

Figure 8.25 Indigenous life expectancy at birth (years)

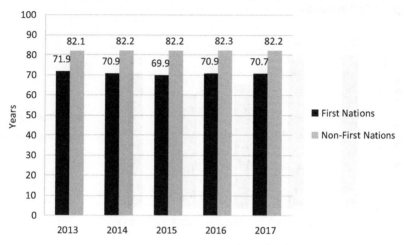

Source: Alberta Health, 2018b, p. 50.

The Ministry of Health acknowledges that Indigenous peoples, especially Indigenous youth, continue to experience significantly poorer health outcomes (Alberta Health, 2018b). A report by the Office of the Child Youth Advocate for Alberta indicated that, between 2012 and 2017, over half (52.8 per cent) of the death notifications for children in the care of the state were for Indigenous children. Nearly three-quarters of the notices for serious injury were for Indigenous youth (Office of the Child and Youth Advocate Alberta, 2018).

As Figure 8.25 indicates, the life expectancy for an Indigenous Albertan as of 2017 is significantly lower (by 11.5 years) than for non-Indigenous Albertans (Alberta Health, 2018b, p. 50).

As Figure 8.26 indicates, infant mortality rates for Indigenous Albertans are approximately double those of non-Indigenous Albertans.

One final observation about Indigenous Albertan youth: the age-standardized mortality rate due to suicide of 12.2 per 100,000 for all Alberta Indigenous youth (18.3, male) is above the Canadian average of 10.4 per 100,00 (17.9, male; Tait, Butt, Henry, & Bland, 2017, p. 59, Table 1; Statistics Canada, 2017a).

Recognizing these enormous disparities, the government is partnering with First Nations of Alberta to examine existing health services and

Figure 8.26 Indigenous and non-Indigenous infant mortality rates in Alberta (per 1,000 live births)

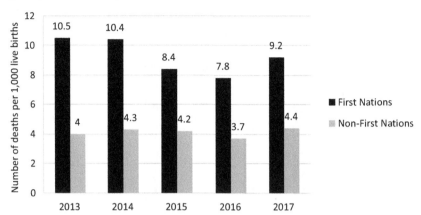

Source: Alberta Health, 2018b, p. 52.

programs, the collection of health systems information, and health outcomes data, including the effects of racism. Specific immediate emphasis is also being placed on addressing the opioid crisis in Indigenous communities (Alberta Health, 2018b).

8.6 Accountability

Since the 1990s, the Department of Health and other major health care organizations that receive public funding are required to submit annually a 3-year business plan and annual report. This requirement was part of the shift in government thinking during the Klein government era to incorporate the neoliberal ideas of New Public Management and the adoption of more business-like practices (Goodkey, 2001; Peach, 2004; Speers, 2005). As discussed at the beginning of this chapter, embedded within these documents are clearly articulated vision and mission statements and performance targets. Public reporting and access to various forms of performance information is also a potential means by which the health system's decision-makers can be scrutinized, which contributes to a more accountable system.

Implicit in the major restructuring that has taken place in Alberta since the 1990s was an effort to increase accountability (see chapter 2). Within the context of health care, accountability means "the obligation to answer to an authority that conferred a responsibility, by an agent

Table 8.9 Alberta provincial health strategies

Strategy	Year	Detailed action plan?	Progress reported?	Status
Advancing the Mental Health Agenda: A Provincial Mental Health Plan for Alberta	2004	×	×	Replaced before implemented
Alberta Infection Prevention and Control 10-Year Strategy	2008	×	×	Replaced before implemented
Becoming the Best: Alberta's 5-Year Health Action Plan 2010–15	2010	×	√	Not followed through
Alberta's 5-year Health System IT Plan 2011–16	2011	×	×	Not followed through
Creating Connections: Alberta's Addiction and Mental Health Strategy	2011	√	×	Active
140 Family Care Clinics	2012	×	×	Discontinued
Alberta's Primary Health Care Strategy	2014	×	×	Active

Source: Office of the Auditor General of Alberta, 2017, p. 23. Table reproduced with permission of the Office of the Auditor General of Alberta.

who accepted it, with the resources and delegated answer necessary to achieve it, and with the understanding that inadequate performance will result in intervention" (Shortt & Macdonald, 2002, p. 27).

The creation of AHS was tainted by a lack of clarity in roles and responsibilities leading to the firing of the first CEO and the dismissal of the first board of directors. Prior to this action, the government had removed the boards of health regions on several occasions for the same reason. However, as the provincial auditor noted in 2017, accountability relationships continue to be weak:

There is a lack of clear roles and responsibilities for major entities in the health system. There is a poor link between funding and results. It is not clear who is responsible for the overall cost and quality of care that individuals receive over time. (Office of the Auditor General of Alberta, 2017, p. 7)

This lack of clarity is the result of several trends that have emerged since the 1990s. The first is a series of "piecemeal aspirational strategies" (Office of the Auditor General of Alberta, 2017). Table 8.9 summarizes

Figure 8.27 Average tenure of Alberta health leaders, 2008–2016

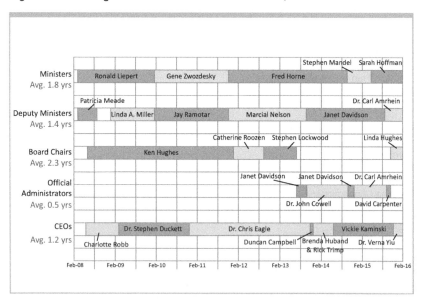

Note: The table includes those who held office in February 2016, but their tenure is not included in the averages presented. The election of the NDP government in 2015 resulted in the appointment of a new minister of health and a board chair for AHS. The subsequent election of the UCP government in 2019 once again resulted in the appointment of a new minister of health and AHS board chair.
Source: Alberta Office of the Auditor General, 2017, p. 24. Table reproduced with permission of the Office of the Provincial Auditor of Alberta.

strategies announced by the government between 2004 and 2014, and shows the status of those strategies. The fact that the government has initiated successive strategies and subsequently dropped them has been a major contributing factor to fragmentation of policy and a growing "saturation psychosis"[11] among managers and care providers (Laframboise, 1971).

A second challenge for accountability has been the constant turnover in the senior management of the health care system. As Figure 8.27

[11] According to Laframboise (1971, p. 304), saturation psychosis has two major components: (1) the psychological immobilization of managers in the face of insistent and conflicting demands; and (2) a revolt by managers against innovators leading to an outright hostility to change, whatever its real or apparent merit (aggression).

indicates, the average tenure of the CEO of AHS is well below the industry standard for hospital CEOs in the United States (Khaliq, Walston, & Thompson, 2005; Office of the Auditor General of Alberta, 2017, p. 24).

A third challenge has been a parallel management structure in which the continuing policy legacy of department involvement in operational decision-making has created significant confusion and undermined the authority of AHS. Under Section 5 of the Regional Health Authorities Act, AHS is supposed to have "final authority" over "operational decisions," which begs the question of whether or not AHS, its board, and senior management can reasonably be held accountable (even if the government can fire the CEO and board) if it does not in fact have final authority over operational decisions. This point is important in terms of both achieving budget control and health outcomes (discussed at greater length later in the chapter).

Two good examples of this parallel management are Department of Health administrative structures that mirror those of AHS (e.g., mental health, continuing care, infection surveillance, etc.) and the continuing operational control by the department over key clinical information systems (e.g., Netcare and the Pharmaceutical Information Network). A good illustration of the operational effect of this duplication took place in 2012 when the department announced that it intended to establish 140 family care clinics, the first 3 of which were to be part of AHS. Not only did AHS learn about this initiative just shortly before the public notification, but the clinical information systems stipulated by the department were incompatible with AHS clinical information systems (Office of the Auditor General of Alberta, 2017, p. 26). The overruling of AHS proposals around such matters as closure of institutional psychiatric beds – on largely political grounds – is another example of ministerial actions that undermine the AHS authority (Duckett, 2015) and perhaps its legitimacy in the eyes of stakeholders.

The net result of this constant policy and administrative "churning" is a demoralized workforce and a growing sense of system paralysis (Rose & Davies, 1994, pp. 114–15; Office of the Auditor General of Alberta, 2017, p. 26). At the heart of this issue has been a loss of trust between major actors that has occurred since the creation of AHS. As was discussed in chapter 7, the lack of leadership and policy stability has allowed major players in the health care system to resist proposed policy changes at the implementation stage. The appointment of a new CEO and board in 2016 has led to greater stability in leadership, although a new board chair was appointed when the UCP government was elected in 2019.

A fourth challenge relates to the government as funder in the system. Even though the government pays for most physician services and services provided by AHS, funding is not based on ongoing evaluation of the cost effectiveness or quality of the services provided. In particular, physicians as "stewards" of the public health care system direct the use of many diagnostic and treatment resources. However, the department has indicated "it has limited ability to manage how physicians consume resources" (Office of the Auditor General of Alberta, 2017, p. 26). In essence, physicians who make numerous decisions related to referral, diagnostics, and treatment that account for a significant portion of AHS expenditures are not held accountable to either the department or to AHS (pp. 26–8). Some aspects of this practice, such as potential referral of patients to diagnostic providers in which the physicians have an ownership stake, raise troubling ethical concerns as well (Green, 1990).

A good example of the lack of accountability is primary care networks (a cornerstone of health reform), discussed in chapter 7. As noted, both the auditor general and the Health Department have evaluated PCNs and have found them to be lacking in sufficient internal financial accountability or external accountability to the department or to AHS for expenditures or program and service outcomes. In addition, there is no formal accountability to patients (Office of the Auditor General of Alberta, 2017, pp. 32–41).

In response to these concerns, Alberta implemented a new PCN governance framework in 2017, which is intended to (1) improve integration between PCN services, AHS programs, and services provided by community-based organizations; (2) align services across communities through zone-wide service planning; and (3) share administrative services across the zone, leading to more PCN resources applied to direct patient care (Alberta, n.d.-c).

A key feature of the governance model is the creation of zone PCN committees that bring AHS operational leaders together with PCN physician leaders to jointly develop and implement service plans. There is also a provincial PCN committee that advises the minister of health on key matters related to PCNs and primary health care in Alberta. These changes strengthen the structural alignment between PCNs and AHS, and should lead to greater accountability for making improvements in priority areas.

The provincial PCN committee is examining the funding model to ensure PCNs promote team-based care and are accountable for services provided. Alberta also has a demonstration project underway to implement a blended capitation compensation model for family physicians (Alberta, n.d.-c; Alberta Health, 2018c).

For both general practitioners and specialists, the College of Physicians and Surgeons evaluates physician performance through the Physician Achievement Review Program (PAR). The review involves a general assessment by survey and feedback, and more recently, a more intensive on-site competency assessment of a sample of practices (College of Physicians and Surgeons of Alberta, n.d.-b). This evaluation process suggests that, in the future, individual physicians will be more accountable for the decisions they make and the quality of the care they provide.

Another important service area where accountability is weak is continuing care. A 2014 review of quality assurance in continuing care by the Health Quality Council of Alberta indicated:

> Quality and safety management in continuing care lacks clarity in roles, responsibilities, and accountabilities among the Ministry of Health, AHS, and contracted service providers. Within AHS alone there is a lack of clarity regarding roles and responsibilities for quality and safety management. This results in confusion and duplication of effort. (HQCA, 2014b, 7)

An audit by the auditor general in the same year found that, while the Health Department had made significant improvements since a 2005 review, problems remained:

> Our audit found fragmented responsibility. It found unnecessary duplication of monitoring. It found that the Department of Health and AHS now have the information, but are not using it to assess performance and report on results. Making this performance information available to the public would go a long way towards enhancing trust in the system. (Office of the Auditor General of Alberta, 2014b, p. 73)

The theme of the collection and use of information is underpinned by the lack of an integrated information system, something that is explored below.

8.7 Information, performance measurement, and quality assurance

A well-integrated health information system has several inherent functions. First, efficient and effective management of diagnostic test results is crucial to ensuring continuity and quality of care. While AHS has conducted a proactive safety analysis of its management of critical test results, it determined that there were over 180 failure points in the existing system. The lack of a comprehensive and accurate provider registry and concerns with privacy are major barriers to implementing a critical test monitoring system (HQCA, 2016a, p. 10).

A second important function of an integrated information system is supporting performance management and quality assurance. AHS has developed a provincial quality management framework. However, the framework is in the early stages of implementation. Currently, significant gaps remain in performance and quality management. For example, even though the department, AHS, and the regulatory college have the required information to assess physician performance, they do not use the information individually, share it with each other, or share it with individual physicians for quality improvement purposes (Office of the Auditor General of Alberta, 2017, p. 39).

Conversely, physicians complain that their capacity to function as stewards of health care resources is impeded because they are unable to get meaningful information on the cost of services (Office of the Auditor General of Alberta, 2017, p. 35). As for the patients, the department leaves it up to them to assess the quality of their care and to change providers if they are not satisfied, without providing appropriate tools for the evaluation of the services provided (p. 27).

An integrated clinical information system (CIS) based on a single electronic health record would lead to better management of chronic conditions, improved continuity of care, reduced hospital-acquired conditions, reduced adverse drug events, and improved personal health (Office of the Auditor General of Alberta, 2017, p. 52). While Alberta has invested significantly in the development of information technology infrastructure to support quality oversight and to inform decision-making in health care (see chapter 4), there are still significant barriers to achieving a comprehensive and integrated clinical information system, including a single electronic health record.

Currently, physicians use at least sixteen different electronic medical record systems that are not compatible with each other or with the systems used by AHS. In AHS, there are 1,300 stand-alone clinical information systems. Most are either outdated or not compatible. Significant parts of the system still rely on paper-based information management (HQCA, 2016a, pp. 5–6).

In addition, management for the existing CIS (Netcare), which was previously a provincial responsibility, has been delegated to AHS moving forward. This change means that family physician offices and the majority of primary care data will not be included. It also means that family physicians will no longer be able to realize the benefits of Netcare, despite the recognition that "successful electronic health record systems are centred around primary care and primary care data" (Office of the Auditor General of Alberta, 2017, p. 51).

When it comes to providing patients with information about their own health, in 2011 the Ministry of Health launched a limited (internal) pilot for a personal health portal (PHP) to give patients access to their personal health profile and upload personal fitness tracking data. Ideally, such a portal should include medication, laboratory, and diagnostic imaging information. Due to technical and privacy concerns, no full rollout has been announced (HQCA, 2016a, p. 7).

Having an integrated system for referral to specialized care is essential to ensuring continuity of care. To this end, AHS launched a limited pilot of an electronic referral system through Netcare in 2014. However, there are several other electronic referral systems being tested by other organizations in the health care system. The Health Quality Council of Alberta noted:

> Having more than one electronic referral system, along with paper-based processes (mail or fax), is problematic and ultimately does not support or protect Albertan's continuity of care. It is undoubtedly more burdensome to physicians and physician office staff when more than one e-referral system exists in the province. (HQCA, 2016a, p. 9)

In response to these challenges, Alberta has successfully linked over fifty provincially held databases. This information system, presently known as Netcare, is mainly used by physicians, laboratories, and pharmacies and includes the following types of information: personal demographic information, hospital visits, surgeries, immunizations, laboratory test results, diagnostic images, medication information, and allergies (Alberta, 2018a).

The province has also successfully developed several means of gathering and sharing management and clinical information:[12]

• Netcare, which allows for the electronic storage and sharing of diagnostic images, test results, medical reports, drug prescriptions, immunization

---

12 Discussed earlier but summarized again here.

records, and general patient information so that health care providers can access information about patients in a timely fashion;

- A comprehensive website for providing information to the public on wait times for diagnostic and specialist services (Alberta, n.d.-a);
- Real time tracking by AHS of wait times for access to emergency departments in hospitals in Calgary, Edmonton, Lethbridge, Red Deer, and Medicine Hat (Alberta Health Services, 2010);
- A comprehensive AHS patient safety program, including an electronic adverse event reporting system (Alberta Health Services, 2010); and an array of quality oversight mechanisms, including external accreditation of health facilities and laboratories, and professional regulation including requirements for ongoing continuing education, driving system improvements, and protecting patient safety (as described in chapter 6 earlier).

Additionally, the Physician Office System Program (POSP), a tripartite initiative of the province, the Alberta Medical Association, and the health regions (now AHS), spearheaded the adoption of electronic medical records (EMRs) in physician offices. POSP ran in several phases, beginning in 2001, and was credited with bringing Alberta physicians to the forefront in Canada for the use of EMRs, achieving 70 per cent uptake by 2012–13 (OECD, 2010, p. 106; Alberta Health, 2014b).

In 2017, the province committed an additional $400 million to health information infrastructure over the next 5 years. This funding will facilitate implementation of Connect Care, a single clinical information system that will replace the 1,300 currently used across AHS. Implementation began in 2019 and is expected to roll out across the province over the next several years. Family physicians who do not currently use an AHS system will then have access to patient and physician portals, which will enable e-referrals, viewing of patient information, and exchange of secure messages with patients and other providers. A Community Information Integration Initiative is underway to link community EMRs with Netcare and Connect Care. The ultimate goal is to create a common electronic health information platform across the province, including a single patient record that can be accessed by health care providers and patients from anywhere in the province (Alberta Netcare Learning Centre, 2018; Gerein, 2017b).

In the case of continuing care, the lack of a standardized contract for providers and the diffusion of responsibility for compliance oversight have created confusion about who is ultimately responsible for quality assurance. There are also issues with continuous performance measurement because there is not currently a consistent review mechanism in place for measuring quality or client and family experience; nor is there a single repository for continuing care safety information (HQCA, 2014b, pp. 57–64).

To begin to increase accountability in continuing care, the government passed the Resident and Family Council Act in 2018, facilitating the establishment of resident and family councils. The councils will provide a forum for residents and their families to discuss ways to improve the quality of life in supportive and long-term care facilities. AHS has also created a Provincial Advisory Council for Seniors and Continuing Care.

In 2014, AHS created a Continuing Care Quality Indicator Working Group to support continuous quality improvement. The Alberta Long-Term Care Quality Indicators report provides comparative (zone-level) data to CIHI and is publicly available (Alberta Health Services, 2018a, 2017b, pp. 9, 22; Alberta Health, 2018b, p. 66).

8.8 Summary

While Alberta has made significant progress in developing a more integrated health care system, there still remain significant challenges related to service delivery and health outcomes, performance management and quality assurance, and accountability. The effectiveness of a single organization mandated with responsibility for the delivery of most health care services in the province has been hampered by frequent changes in senior leadership, constant policy change, and a lack of clarity about roles and responsibilities.

Alberta has developed a robust framework to support performance management, but the lack of an integrated health care information system has limited effective evaluation of many services for efficiency or quality. In short, there are many islands of health care information but little meaningful connectivity between these islands. In part, this situation is due to ongoing technical and privacy concerns. However, continuing delays in creating a single data repository or even a linked decentralized repository for information to support health care decision-making continues to be problematic.

Overall, the centralized structure of AHS has realized some scale and scope efficiencies by consolidating some administrative services. However, the existing funding infrastructure has failed to sufficiently incentivize major health providers to integrate and coordinate the delivery of services to achieve continuity of care. In a health care system that lacks meaningful continuity of care, patients are often left to navigate a complex system and are by default their own care coordinators. There remain significant gaps in continuity between acute, primary, and continuing care, as well as significant issues related to timely access to care.

Current evidence suggests that Alberta Health is not meeting three of the four objectives (patient and population health, patient safety, financial health, and value for money) outlined in its most recent business plan (discussed at the beginning of this chapter). The bottom line is that Alberta spends more than any other Canadian provincial government on health care, yet does not realize significantly better results on many comparative indicators. In fact, the performance of the system seems to have deteriorated in some key areas since the introduction of AHS in 2008.

Chapter Nine

Conclusion

Like other jurisdictions, Alberta has been struggling for several decades to reform its health care system so that it performs in a more cost-effective way. To do this requires substantive change to one or all of the dimensions of health policy (governance, funding, delivery, and programming). To be truly effective, these changes must directly affect the "governing coalition" – the policy network of health professionals, experts, and policy-makers – who determine how the system functions (Denis & Forest, 2012). This concluding chapter will revisit several major themes emerging throughout this book (the economy and people, health care costs, health system governance, health workforce, professionalism, infrastructure and services, performance measurement, and performance outcomes) and reflect on the extent to which substantive change has been achieved.

9.1 The economy and people

Although one of Canada's newer provinces, Alberta has risen to become the economic powerhouse of Canada's economy. The discovery of oil and gas in 1947 shifted Alberta's economy from predominantly agricultural to one in which the prosperity of the oil and gas sector preoccupies the minds of both politicians and the public. In short, many Albertans are employed either directly in the oil and gas sector or indirectly through other sectors (e.g., construction) that provide support services. More generally, all Albertans benefit because of the government revenues generated through oil and gas production in the province. These revenues have allowed Alberta to make significant investments in the development of its health care sector, including significant investments in medical and population health research.

The nature of Alberta's economy and its growing importance in the Canadian economy has made Alberta a destination of choice for a growing number of young skilled and unskilled workers (many of whom are transient), both Canadian and foreign. In fact, Alberta is increasingly dependent on workers from other provinces and countries to support its economic growth. Alberta also has a higher than average number of Indigenous peoples.

The combination of this population mix and a resource-based economy punctuated by sharp, cyclical market adjustments has created a number of unique health challenges. Albertans have higher than average consumption rates for alcohol, tobacco, and illicit drugs and a higher rate of addiction to gambling. They also carry the highest personal debt load among Canadians. Many of these trends are contributing factors to higher than average rates of infant mortality, obesity, heart and respiratory ailments, and suicide.

9.2 Health care costs

As was noted in chapters 3 and 8, Alberta spends more per capita on health care than other provincial jurisdictions in Canada. However, this expenditure pattern over the past two decades does not appear to have yielded significant major advantages compared to other Canadian jurisdictions that spend less. In 2019–20, Alberta spent 10 per cent above the national average. Hospital expenditures are expected to be 12 per cent higher, and physician expenses will top out at 15 per cent higher. Higher unit costs combined with high utilization have made Alberta consistently the highest of the provinces in age-adjusted per capita expenditures on health care. However, further unpacking this analysis reveals that Alberta's labour costs during the economic boom years (1998–2008) were significantly higher than those of other provinces, especially costs for health professionals and other front-line workers. While utilization rates on select administrative and management costs were closer to the national average, utilization rates on major service indicators were 10 per cent higher than the national average.

9.3 Health system governance

To a large degree, Alberta's health care system remained geographically localized and professionally and administratively fragmented until the reforms of the 1990s. It had the effect of creating a hypercompetitive environment for resource allocation, punctuated by parochial considerations (similar to other Canadian jurisdictions). Like most other provinces, Alberta implemented regional governance structures in health care at the beginning of the 1990s. Informed by a growing concern about provincial deficits and debt and the prevailing neoliberal logic of New Public Management (NPM), these structures were expected to save money through greater integration and coordination of service delivery, improve responsiveness to local communities, realize economies of scale, rationalize service delivery, and shift the focus of the system away from hospitals towards less costly services provided in the community. Politically at the time, the government wanted, first and foremost, to cut costs in health care and, secondly, to reduce the predominance of parochialism in decision-making (Barker & Church, 2017, pp. 335–6).

In the case of Alberta, it was also clear that the provincial government was looking to shift the role of the Ministry of Health away from the direct provision of services (mental health) and programs (home care), and to shift local governance away from the approximately 200 local hospital and public health boards to a much smaller number of regional governance boards. Thus, Alberta collapsed existing local boards (with the exception of Catholic organizations) into seventeen regional health authorities (RHAs) in 1994 and nine by 2003. Separate provincial governance structures were maintained for mental health, addiction and alcohol services, and cancer care.

Initially, the regional health authorities appeared to be containing costs, but by the late 1990s, any cost-saving advantages of health regions appeared to have evaporated. Significant growth in the provincial economy, a related growth in the population (and shifting demographics), and steadily increasing labour and service costs led to a return to the pattern of local expenditures beyond provincial health care budget allocations that were characteristic of the 1980s. RHAs had simply replaced hospital boards as the advocates for these overexpenditures. Additionally, the hypercompetitiveness and parochialism that characterized the health sector prior to regionalization prevailed (Duckett, 2011, p. 24). A good example is the primary care reforms through Health Transition and Primary Health Transition funding during the late 1990s and early 2000s. There were many geographically dispersed pilot projects that died a silent death once the pilot funding was exhausted, because there was no commitment to scale up good ideas either within or beyond regional boundaries.

Like other provinces (Marchildon, 2015), the Alberta provincial government, having found that regionalization failed to realize cost savings, significant improvements in service delivery, or less parochialism, doubled down on the consolidation of governance by creating a single governance structure, Alberta Health Services (AHS), with responsibility for all health services, including mental health, addictions and alcohol, and cancer care.[1] While there was an expectation that this new configuration would lead to less conflict between the province and local stakeholders and less local competitiveness, the CEO and board of AHS found themselves increasingly at odds with the province about expenditure and operational decisions. After only 2 years (2010), the government fired the CEO, and after 5 years (2013) removed the board. Only in 2015 were a new permanent CEO and board appointed.[2]

What happened in Alberta reflects what Aucoin characterizes as a tension between the principles of NPM and those of New Public Governance (NPG) – the one calling for decentralization and/or devolution of authority and the empowerment of managers, the other calling for tighter political oversight of public bureaucracies. Senior political officials have grown concerned with maintaining authority within the increasingly "turbulent environment" in which governments now find themselves (Aucoin, 2012, p. 183). As Lewis and Kouri have noted about health care regionalization in Canada generally, governments have never really been clear about what they expected health regions to be (Lewis & Kouri, 2004, p. 30).

In the case of Alberta, this shift in decision-making arenas was reflected in two important ways. First, prior to the reforms of the 1990s, public servants in health care had often led provincial planning and consultation initiatives. During the 1990s, elected officials replaced public servants in the leadership of these initiatives, with the public servants acting in a supportive (secretariat) role. Second, the communications function, which had traditionally resided at the department level, was centralized to the Office of the Premier. Thus, government MLA-led committees formulated health reform plans, while messaging

---

1 Canada was not the first country to "recentralize" its health care system. As Saltman (2008) noted, European countries had already begun this process.

2 Although these developments have created greater stability in governance of the health system, they also reflect a larger trend in Alberta, as a single-party dominant petrostate, towards a consolidation of power at the provincial level (AHS is a province-wide authority).

was controlled through the Premier's Office. As the new system of governance unfolded, it was not uncommon for the minister of health to make a major policy announcement followed closely by the premier making a contradictory announcement. Health policy appeared to be emanating directly from the Office of the Premier with the Ministry of Health playing a secondary and servile role[3] (Church & Noseworthy, 1999, p. 194).

Another inherent problem with regionalization is that governments have never been willing to transfer authority for the allocation of either physician or community-based pharmaceutical budgets. Thus, from the beginning, RHAs were hamstrung by a lack of sufficient authority to fully integrate and coordinate the delivery of health care services or effectively control costs. Nowhere is this problem more apparent than with primary care services (Marchildon, 2015).

Although PCNs in Alberta have begun this process, several independent reviews have been highly critical of the lack of accountability, integration, and coordination of primary care services. The combination of recently announced reforms to the governance of primary care, the creation of an integrated information system, and accountability requirements built into the new master agreement with physicians hold promise to resolve some of these long-standing issues, although a fix does not appear likely in the short term.

One final observable trend in governance has been a distinct move away from formal roles for citizens in decision-making. Numerically, the 200 local elected boards that populated the health care governance landscape prior to regionalization provided numerous formal opportunities for local citizen involvement. Although there was a brief experiment with partially elected regional boards, it was quickly abandoned with remarkably little concern. The consolidation of governance to a single provincial authority has minimized these opportunities. However, the more recent introduction of patient advocates, a formal role for patients in the governance of PCNs, and various patient advisory committees supporting AHS governance may allow for greater citizen input into health care decision-making in the future.

---

3 If we fast-forward to the current context, the authors discovered while writing this book that requests for basic information were often referred from content experts to public relations specialists, at both the ministry and AHS levels. Usually, this referral didn't yield favourable results. Basically, if something isn't written down in a publicly available document, there is no available information.

9.4 Health workforce

While Alberta has realized a significant benefit from its economic prosperity in attracting health workers (often from other less wealthy Canadian jurisdictions), it has not escaped challenges in effectively planning for health workforce needs. Although Alberta has comparatively generous labour agreements, increasingly nurses have been challenged by a focus on substituting less skilled workers for registered nurses as a means of reducing costs, in spite of mounting evidence that such strategies may endanger the health of patients. The steady increase in hospital mortality rates would seem to support the concerns of nurses about their continuously declining numbers. In the case of both nurses and physicians, labour negotiations have focused largely on wages, which have increased steadily over the past several decades.

Having said this, scopes of practice for a number of professions (nurses, pharmacists, and paramedics) have recently been expanded to allow Albertans more efficient access to some services that previously were only accessible through physicians' offices. Thus, the role of the physician as the single gatekeeper to the system is beginning to shift, although the shift is glacial in nature. The slow implementation of an expanded role for nurse practitioners is a case in point.

9.5 Professionalism

At the heart of many issues related to governance and workforce planning is the relative distribution of power among the various occupational groups and between the occupations and other health system actors such as politicians and health managers. While governance arrangements have strengthened the power of politicians and managers, and the expansion of scopes of practice have increased the roles of some providers, for the most part these reforms constitute policy changes at the margin. The distribution of power still overwhelmingly privileges physicians. Physicians have been slow to respond to efforts to reduce costs and improve access to services, especially where their financial interests are threatened.

Alberta has the lowest uptake of alternate payment methods for physicians and has been slow to reform primary care, although PCNs hold significant promise if implemented effectively. Other jurisdictions, such as Ontario, appear to have had greater success in introducing a diversity of ways of paying physicians and delivering primary care services. Additionally, as previously mentioned, health regions were hamstrung as they were not given control of physician budgets because physicians opposed this idea. Conversely, nurses, who had assumed increasing roles in policy and clinical management positions, have seen this trend reversed through labour substitution and other cost-saving measures. Overall, a lack of trust between government and the health professions has limited the successful implementation of workforce innovation into the system.

9.6 Infrastructure and services

Over time, the health sector in Alberta has become increasingly diverse, with the government providing funding for a range of services including acute care, long-term care, primary care, rehabilitation, public health, mental health, and addiction treatment services. However, recent evaluations have identified a growing infrastructure deficit, particularly in the acute care sector, and significant gaps in the availability, continuity, and integration of services. Overcoming the infrastructure deficit before it becomes a crisis will require significant creative thinking, especially if the current continuing focus on hospitals does not shift.

Despite the major efforts to reform governance structures, the associated goal of shifting the emphasis from acute care to community-based services has remained elusive. Current resource allocation patterns continue to largely reinforce the status quo across service categories. Additionally, current resource allocation appears not to be based on population health needs and to represent a distinct geographic bias.

Although Alberta is considered to be a leader in health care IT in Canada, one of the underlying unresolved infrastructure issues has been a lack of an integrated information system to support the collection of relevant information to inform planning, operational, and clinical decision-making. The government has now initiated the process of creating a single, integrated information system for the province that holds great promise to address this issue. However, significant changes in how information is used to inform decision-making and data-sharing practices will be required to take full advantage of any new integrated information system.

9.7 Performance measurement

Related to information infrastructure is the growing range of resources devoted to supporting research and performance measurement. Alberta was the first province in Canada to substantially invest directly in supporting medical research. Investment was possible through the creation of the Alberta Heritage Foundation for Medical Research (now Alberta Innovates) to provide funding support for health sciences scholarly research. Initially, the nature of the research that was funded approximated and complemented academic research funded through national and international processes. More recently, the focus of research has shifted towards more directly supporting operational decision-making (an industry-driven focus). Greater integration of research into operational decision-making is currently being achieved through strategic clinical networks, which bring together researchers and decision-makers around current and emerging issues.

Alberta Health has also developed a publicly accessible database that includes a wide range of economic and population health indicators. AHS has a publicly accessible wait times website that allows the public to see real wait times for access to emergency rooms and wait times for access to common medical procedures. Both of these developments enhance the ability of political decision-makers, researchers, and the public to assess the performance of the system. However, much of this information is focused on identifying the quantity and outputs of services available. Relatively little information is available about the quality of the services provided. Much of the current information on quality is generated through public surveys conducted by the Health Quality Outcomes Commission and reviews of services conducted by the commission and the Office of the Auditor General.

9.8 Performance outcomes

Despite significant expenditures, Alberta performs below the Canadian average on a number of performance outcomes relating to wait times, avoidable admissions, mortality, and potentially avoidable deaths. Much of this poor performance is attributable to the lack of an effective strategy for coordinating and integrating the delivery of care outside of hospitals and between hospitals and other aspects of the health care system and the broader community. Alberta admits and re-admits more patients than the average in Canada and keeps them longer. Deaths while in the hospital also exceed national averages. On a number of population health outcomes associated with lifestyle factors tied to the nature of the economy, Alberta is also experiencing some significant challenges.

9.9 Final thoughts

While Alberta was the first province to move to a centralized governance structure, it does not appear to be realizing either significant financial or population health benefits in comparison to other Canadian jurisdictions.[4] In fact, it continues to struggle with many of the issues encountered by other Canadian jurisdictions and to perform poorly relative to the level of expenditures. However, a number of recent initiatives hold significant promise to improve the governance and accountability of Alberta's health care system and the efficiency and effectiveness of health care services. If these initiatives reach fruition, Alberta will be well positioned to better serve the health care needs of its population. However, achieving this goal will require a clearer linkage of population health to resource allocation, a better use of evidence to inform health workforce planning, and improved governance and accountability. Despite recent changes in political regime, historical expenditure patterns, both across services and geographically, and mediocre performance outcomes have persisted.

There are three possible explanations for this pattern. The first relates to the inability of government or AHS to control the geographic distribution of physicians. The fact that the greatest growth in physician numbers (see chapter 8) is concentrated around Calgary and the south may be skewing the allocation of health services to these areas. In short, resources tend to follow physicians. A second relates to the high number of young, transient workers who are not attached to a regular physician and may pursue high-risk lifestyles. A third possible explanation is that, because Calgary is politically strategic for political parties (see chapter 1), politics may be trumping population health. Regardless of the cause, this continuing pattern suggests that Alberta has not yet been successful in implementing reforms that significantly disrupt the governing coalition in health care to effectively meet the needs of its population.

---

4 In part, this outcome is attributable to trying to provide services across a large geographic area that is relatively sparsely populated.

Afterword

Shortly after we completed writing this book, Alberta (along with the rest of the world) found itself in the midst of a major pandemic, COVID-19, unlike any seen since the 1918 outbreak of Spanish flu. Currently (4 May 2021), Alberta leads North America with the most actives cases per capita (Yun, 2021). It has recorded 2,090 deaths, with 23,608 actives cases (194,914 total so far). While most deaths have occurred in individuals over 80 years of age, younger populations are now being more directly affected. Alberta is third behind Quebec and Ontario for the number of total cases and deaths in Canada at this point, although the gap is narrowing (CBC News, 2021; Alberta, 2021a).

As Alberta's premier said in his first televised address on 7 April 2020, Alberta was "facing not one crisis, but three" (Dryden, 2020). The three crises were the direct costs of responding to the pandemic, the effects on the economy of public health measures to address the pandemic, and the collapse of oil prices.

Alberta had been experiencing economic decline since the 2008 market collapse. It was further exacerbated in 2014 when the world oil market collapsed. Although the market bounced back modestly in 2016, the shock of 2014 lingered, and the oil and gas market remained soft. The net result is that, while in 2007 Alberta "had net assets equivalent to 15 percent of GDP" (Tombe, 2020), current predictions suggest a debt to GDP ratio of 20 per cent. The recent collapse of oil prices because of COVID-19, and a subsequent price war between Saudi Arabia and Russia, now threatens to throw Alberta into a third recession.

The effects of this gradual economic decline have been visible in Alberta for some time. Empty commercial buildings in downtown Calgary and increasing unemployment have become the new normal.

From a low of around 3.5 per cent in 2008, Alberta's unemployment rate has climbed to 13.4 per cent, jumping from 7 per cent in 2019 alone (Alberta, 2020c).

In the midst of this situation, Jason Kenney and the United Conservative Party were elected in 2019 on a platform of a return to fiscal austerity. The Kenney government moved quickly to begin implementing expenditure cuts similar to what the Progressive Conservative government of Ralph Klein had implemented during the mid-1990s. Arguably, the timing of the announced budget cuts and the resultant fallout has further contributed to increasing unemployment in the province and created increasing chaos for public sector workers. The almost total shutdown of the economy due to COVID-19 has further exacerbated what was already a precarious employment climate.

In some respects, Alberta has made its own economic bed and is now lying in it. The long-term government trend of pursuing low personal and corporate tax rates, low oil and gas royalty rates, and refusing to implement a provincial sales tax has left Alberta with serious limitations on revenue sources. And while the government has consistently framed the issue as an expenditure problem, the current economic crisis makes it hard to ignore the fact that these largely untapped revenue sources might go a long way to relieving the financial strain that Alberta is under. In fact, if the government had used its available fiscal tools more effectively in the past, it might have avoided much of the current financial hole in which it finds itself.

Instead, the government has based its economic planning on the continuing prosperity of the oil and gas market alone, which (as was discussed in chapter 1) is volatile and unstable. The current situation makes this crystal clear. While the Progressive Conservative government of the 1990s benefitted from a major bounce-back in the market that would last for 15 years and reach unprecedented heights (close to $150US per barrel of oil in 2008), those halcyon days are unlikely to return, with the current oil price hovering around the $30US mark. Consistent overproduction of oil since 2010 and increasing environmental concerns have raised the spectre of a decline in the importance of oil as an engine of sustainable economic growth. Yet, the current Alberta government has shown no sign of shifting its economic strategy to reflect this emerging reality (Macrotrends, 2020).

In fact, while cutting expenditures to education and postsecondary education, resulting in significant job losses, the government allocated $30 million to create an energy "war room" to combat the negative publicity that the energy sector has encountered over the past several years. It also launched a public inquiry into who is behind the anti-oil campaign (Anderson, 2019; Dawson, 2019).

Turning to health care, while the government did not openly cut expenditures, because it provided no new money, in effect the health care sector will experience budget cuts, including planned layoffs for nurses and reductions in physician funding. Specifically, the government legislated the elimination of incentives for physicians to see patients between 15 minutes per visit and up to 24 minutes, although they did not eliminate incentives to see patients beyond 24 minutes. This legislation was publicly rejected by the Alberta Medical Association (AMA) on the basis that it violated the rights of physicians to collective bargaining and, more specifically, that it penalized individual physicians (particularly in rural areas) who spent more than 15 minutes with patients. The government justified the change on the basis that Alberta physicians are paid more than in other provinces and that physicians were routinely abusing the 15 to 24 minute incentive. The government has now walked back this change after the AMA membership recently rejected the proposed new collective agreement (Hardcastle & Ogbogu, 2021).

In response to COVID-19, the government announced that it would inject an additional $500 million into the health care sector, including a boost for mental health services. In addition, AHS has agreed to delay the layoff of thousands of nurses until the COVID crisis subsides. However, the government has not relented on its plans to cut the budget for physician services, and the AMA has threatened a court challenge. In the midst of the biggest health crisis in Alberta's history, all is not well with the relationship between the government and physicians (Bennet, 2020).

At the operational level, a number of issues have emerged that reflect the ongoing tension between Alberta Health and AHS, and the challenge concerning coordination of services across public and private providers. Some of this strife is attributable to the emergency powers granted to government ministers to write ministerial orders without legislative oversight (French, 2020).

On the positive side, Alberta had a comparatively good inventory of personal protective equipment (PPE) and ventilators when the pandemic began, which was attributable to the effective procurement process and bulk-buying power that was possible because of the integrated governance structure of AHS (Staples, 2020). On the downside, when

AHS began to develop a method of tracking the inventory, based on current and projected usage patterns and current and projected supply and shipments, Alberta Health stepped in and assumed control of this information for a period of time. This move resulted in the premier publicly sharing information on PPE inventory, without adequate context, before AHS released the information internally to their employees and to relevant external stakeholders, such as the health care unions (Global News, 2020).

The Premier's Office also began making announcements about the AHS inventory that seemed to contradict AHS's understanding of its own inventory. At one point, the premier announced on Twitter that the Alberta government had directly purchased 2 million KN95 masks from China, which were approved for use by AHS. These masks were not procured by AHS and were not being stored by AHS; nor had AHS fit tested these masks for use in health care settings, so it was unclear how they were going to be used and why the government had procured them (Kenny, 2020). Further, Premier Kenney announced that Alberta was donating PPE and medical equipment to other provinces in need, including 4.5 million surgical/procedural masks and 750,000 N95 respirators.

There were two issues with this announcement. First, the announcement occurred the day after Alberta Health and AHS released continuous masking public health orders and guidelines, which required all health care workers to wear a surgical/procedure mask at all times while working in all health care settings, including continuing care sites. This decision resulted in an exponential increase in demand for surgical/procedure masks in Alberta, and AHS had to look at procuring and introducing new masks made by manufacturers other than Pri-Med, which was the preferred supplier of surgical/procedure masks in Alberta to date. One of the new masks (Vanch) that was introduced resulted in widespread concerns from health care workers in relation to the fit, smell, and quality of the mask. The situation created concern and speculation among health care workers that the preferred Pri-Med masks had been sent to other provinces, while Alberta workers were left to use the problematic Vanch masks, because Premier Kenney's announcement took place in front of a large supply of Pri-Med boxes.

The second issue with the announcement was that the N95 respirators were in fact only going to be sent to other provinces if AHS ended up receiving the large orders they were expecting, which had not yet occurred at the time of the premier's announcement.

This misunderstanding again created concern among health care workers, as there was confusion about whether N95s were being sent before AHS had received the shipments. A month after the premier's announcement, N95s had not been sent to other provinces because AHS had not yet received the large orders they were expecting of 3M N95s; and it is not known whether these promised N95 respirators will ever be deployed to other provinces (Bellefontaine, 2020). In essence, the way in which the premier framed the announcement about the deployment of masks to other provinces made it look like Alberta expected cooperation from the other jurisdictions on the oil and gas file, a political tit for tat (Climenhaga, 2020).

The disconnection between the government and AHS was also reflected in the issue concerning the movement of health workers between institutional settings. Some health care workers, in particular nurses and health care aides, worked at more than one site. In the early stages of the pandemic, it was determined that these workers could transmit the virus from one site to another. The government developed a ministerial order, without consulting unions or employers, requiring employees to work at only one site (auxiliary hospitals and nursing homes); the employee was allowed to indicate a preference, and the employer determined the site.

Three problems with the original wording of the order came to the fore. First, health care workers could be working for more than one employer (public and private), and the employers might make different decisions. Although the unions worked with the Ministry of Labour to reach a consensus with some employers through a mediator, neither Alberta Health nor AHS agreed to participate. The recommendations from the advisory committee formed the basis of a new ministerial order, and Alberta Health developed an algorithm and process reflecting this order (Alberta Health, 2020).

Second, the order did not clarify which sites were included, and the majority of hospitals in Alberta were designated as both auxiliary hospitals and nursing homes. So, for example, some sites included both acute and long-term care beds (particularly in rural areas), but the order did not specify whether these sites were entirely included or whether only the long-term care beds were included. This issue took a month to resolve. In some parts of the province, as of 1 June 2020, the order had still not been implemented.

Third, there was an issue related to the variation in pay between private sector and public sector workers and across sites, with public sector workers being paid a higher wage. At the outset of the pandemic, some private operators gamed the system by offering increased pay as a means to entice workers to choose their site. The government stepped in and forbade the practice. However, enforcement has been uneven. The Ministry of Health announced a $2 per hour wage increase for health care aides, but only for those working in the private sector (Hunt, 2020). Again, there was significant confusion about how the order was to be implemented; because the private operators were in competition with each other, there was no effective institutional structure for coordinating the implementation of the order to ensure that all eligible workers were treated fairly.

There was also a more general issue of increasing compensation for some workers, but not others, potentially leading to animosity among some workers. Again, this decision was made without consulting either the unions or the employers, and again AHS indicated that it didn't want to get involved. The same advisory committee and mediator again worked to develop recommendations on how any pay increase would happen. Unlike the single-site issue, these recommendations were ignored. Contrast this chaos with British Columbia, where the government effectively took control of the industry temporarily so that wages could be standardized and overall efforts could be coordinated across the system.

Specific to long-term care, COVID-19 has revealed the inherent weakness of the existing business model in the long-term care sector in terms of the quality of care. As discussed in chapter 6, a provincial auditor's report in 2005, and again in 2014, highlighted the existing deficiencies in Alberta's long-term care system. These deficiencies included sole-source contracting, inadequate staffing levels and mix, and overall lack of quality assurance.[1] The fact that a significant number of pandemic-related deaths[2] have occurred in these facilities has cast a stark light on these inadequacies. Initially, Alberta resisted aggressive COVID-19 testing at long-term care facilities. However, the COVID-19 crisis has sparked national calls for significant revisions to long-term care in Canada (Lee, 2020; Wherry, 2020).

---

1 These inadequacies are common to all long-term care systems in Canada.
2 Large outbreaks have also occurred at meat packing plants in Alberta, although so far the number of deaths has been far less than in long-term care facilities.

Finally, as noted in chapter 8, the allocation of health care resources in the province has favoured Calgary in particular and southern Alberta more generally. This finding is noteworthy, because Calgary also has the healthiest population. It is somewhat surprising, then, that the largest number of reported cases of COVID-19 at the outset was in Calgary, although travel importation patterns, early large-scale spreading events, and inclusion of a meat packing plant (with the largest concentrated outbreak in Canada) within the Calgary health zone may explain the phenomenon. Overall, however, Alberta's relatively younger and geo-graphically dispersed population may have worked in its favour in terms of limiting the spread of COVID-19. Whether or not the weaknesses in Alberta's health care system revealed by COVID-19 will be remedied after the storm has passed remains to be seen. However, given that Alberta's performance on the COVID-19 issue has actually lowered the premier's popularity rating (currently at 40 per cent) and the UCP are now trailing the NDP by a growing margin, the government must be somewhat worried about the longer-term political implications once the COVID-19 pandemic has passed and it is left to deal with a depressed economy. The response will likely require making difficult choices that may not play well to its political base.

References

Accreditation Canada & Canadian Home Care Association. (n.d.). *Home care in Canada: Advancing quality improvement and integrated care.* Ottawa, ON: Author.

ACTT (Accelerating Change Transformation Team). (n.d.). PCN operational resources. Retrieved from https://actt.albertadoctors.org/pcns/Pages /default.aspx

Adams, A., & Theodore, D. (2005). The architecture of children's hospitals in Montreal and Toronto, 1875–2010. In C.K. Warsh & V. Strong-Boag (Eds.), *Children's health issues in historical perspective* (pp. 439–78). Waterloo, ON: Wilfred Laurier University Press.

Alberta. (n.d.-a). Alberta wait times reporting website. Retrieved from http:// waittimes.alberta.ca/

Alberta. (n.d.-b) Palliative care health benefits. Retrieved from https://www .alberta.ca/palliative-care-health-benefits.aspx

Alberta. (n.d.-c). Primary health care. Retrieved from https://www.alberta.ca /primary-health-care.aspx

Alberta. (1990). *Hospitals Act: Operation of Approved Hospitals Regulation.* Alberta Regulation 247/1990. Retrieved from https://www.qp.alberta.ca /documents/Regs/1990_247.pdf

Alberta. (2000a). *Health Disciplines Act: Revised statutes of Alberta 2000, Chapter H-2.* Retrieved from https://www.qp.alberta.ca/documents/Acts /H02.pdf

Alberta. (2000b). *Health Information Act: Revised statutes of Alberta 2000, Chapter H-5.* Retrieved from https://www.qp.alberta.ca/documents/Acts /H05.pdf

Alberta. (2000c). *Health Professions Act, Chapter H-7.* Retrieved from https:// www.qp.alberta.ca/documents/Acts/H07.pdf

Alberta. (2000d). *Hospitals Act, Revised Statutes of Alberta 2000, Chapter H-12.*
    Retrieved from https://www.qp.alberta.ca/documents/Acts/H12.pdf

Alberta. (2000e). *Mental Health Act, Revised Statutes of Alberta 2000, Chapter M-13.*
    Retrieved from https://www.qp.alberta.ca/documents/Acts/M13.pdf

Alberta. (2000f). *Pharmacy and Drug Act: Revised statutes of Alberta 2000, Chapter
    P-13.* Retrieved from https://www.qp.alberta.ca/documents/Acts
    /P13.pdf

Alberta. (2000g). *Regional Health Authorities Act, Revised statutes of Alberta 2000,
    Chapter R-10.* Retrieved from https://www.qp.alberta.ca/documents
    /Acts/R10.pdf

Alberta. (2003a). *Health Professions Act: Licensed Practical Nurses Profession
    Regulation.* Alberta Regulation 81/2003. Retrieved from https://www
    .qp.alberta.ca/documents/Regs/2003_081.pdf

Alberta. (2003b). *Public Health Act: Co-ordinated Home Care Program Regulation.*
    Alberta Regulation 296/2003. Retrieved from https://www.qp.alberta.ca
    /documents/Regs/2003_296.pdf

Alberta. (2004a). *Health Professions Act: Registered Dieticians and Registered
    Nutritionists Regulation.* Alberta Regulation 79/2002. Retrieved from https://
    www.qp.alberta.ca/documents/Regs/2002_079.pdf

Alberta. (2004b). *Mental Health Act: Mental Health Regulation.* Alberta Regulation
    19/2004. Retrieved from https://www.qp.alberta.ca/documents
    /Regs/2004_019.pdf

Alberta. (2005). *Health Professions Act: Registered Nurses Profession Regulation.*
    Alberta Regulation 232/2005. Retrieved from https://www.qp.alberta.ca
    /documents/Regs/2005_232.pdf

Alberta. (2006a). *Alberta Health Care Insurance Act: Alberta Health Care Insurance
    Regulation.* Alberta Regulation 76/2006. Retrieved from https://www.qp
    .alberta.ca/documents/Regs/2006_076.pdf

Alberta. (2006b). *Health Professions Act: Chiropractors Profession Regulation.* Alberta
    Regulation 277/2006. Retrieved from https://www.qp.alberta.ca
    /documents/Regs/2006_277.pdf

Alberta. (2006c). *Health Professions Act: Dental Hygienists Profession Regulation.*
    Alberta Regulation 255/2006. Retrieved from https://www.qp.alberta.ca
    /documents/Regs/2006_255.pdf

Alberta. (2007a). *Health Disciplines Act: Emergency Medical Technicians Regulation.*
    Alberta Regulation 48/1993. Retrieved from http://www.emslaw.ca
    /downloads/ar-48-93-april-2015.pdf

Alberta. (2007b). *Health Professions Act: Medical Laboratory Technologists Profession
    Regulation.* Alberta Regulation 255/2001. Retrieved from https://www.qp
    .alberta.ca/documents/Regs/2001_255.pdf

Alberta. (2009). *Health Professions Act: Medical Diagnostic and Therapeutic Technologists Profession* Regulation. Alberta Regulation 61/2005. Retrieved from https://www.qp.alberta.ca/documents/Regs/2005_061.pdf

Alberta. (2011). *Health Professions Act: Pharmacists and Pharmacy Technicians Profession Regulation.* Alberta Regulation 129/2006. Retrieved from https://www.qp.alberta.ca/documents/Regs/2006_129.pdf

Alberta. (2012a). *Health Professions Act: Dentists Profession Regulation.* Alberta Regulation 254/2001. Retrieved from https://www.qp.alberta.ca/documents/Regs/2001_254.pdf

Alberta. (2012b). *Health Professions Act: Social Workers Profession Regulation.* Alberta Regulation 82/2003. Retrieved from https://www.qp.alberta.ca/documents/regs/2003_082.pdf

Alberta. (2014). *Insurance Act: Diagnostic and Treatment Protocols Regulation.* Alberta Regulation 116/2014. Retrieved from https://www.qp.alberta.ca/documents/Regs/2014_116.pdf

Alberta. (2015). *Health Professions Act: Optometrists Profession Regulation.* Alberta Regulation 83/2003. Retrieved from https://www.qp.alberta.ca/documents/Regs/2003_083.pdf

Alberta. (2016a, 10 May). Amendments to Health Professions Act would make physician assistants and medical diagnostic sonographers regulated professions in Alberta. News release. Retrieved from https://www.alberta.ca/release.cfm?xID=417331B4942DD-D40C-5C90-6FAF259F570DEEA0

Alberta. (2016b). General practitioner and family physician. Retrieved from https://open.alberta.ca/publications/general-practitioner-and-family-physician

Alberta. (2018a). Alberta Netcare EHR: Privacy and security for Alberta Netcare. Retrieved from https://www.albertanetcare.ca/PatientPrivacy.htm

Alberta. (2018b). Industry profiles 2018: Health care and social assistance industry. Retrieved from: https://work.alberta.ca/documents/industry-profile-health-care-and-social-assistance.pdf

Alberta. (2018c). MyHealth.Alberta.ca: Medical specialists. Retrieved from https://myhealth.alberta.ca/health/pages/conditions.aspx?Hwid=specl

Alberta. (2018d). Occupations in Alberta: Dental hygienist. Retrieved from https://alis.alberta.ca/occinfo/occupations-in-alberta/occupation-profiles/dental-hygienist/

Alberta. (2018e). Occupations in Alberta: Dentist. Retrieved from https://alis.alberta.ca/occinfo/occupations-in-alberta/occupation-profiles/dentist/

Alberta. (2018f). Occupations in Alberta: Emergency medical responder. Retrieved from https://alis.alberta.ca/occinfo/occupations-in-alberta/occupation-profiles/emergency-medical-personnel/

Alberta. (2018g). Occupations in Alberta: Medical radiation technologist. Retrieved from https://alis.alberta.ca/occinfo/occupations-in-alberta/occupation-profiles/radiological-technologist/

Alberta. (2018h). Occupations in Alberta: Nurse practitioner. Retrieved from https://alis.alberta.ca/occinfo/occupations-in-alberta/occupation-profiles/nurse-practitioner/

Alberta. (2018i). Occupations in Alberta: Optician. Retrieved from https://alis.alberta.ca/occinfo/occupations-in-alberta/occupation-profiles/optician/

Alberta. (2018j). Occupations in Alberta: Optometrist. Retrieved from https://alis.alberta.ca/occinfo/occupations-in-alberta/occupation-profiles/optometrist/

Alberta. (2018k). Occupations in Alberta: Pharmacy technician. Retrieved from https://alis.alberta.ca/occinfo/occupations-in-alberta/occupation-profiles/pharmacy-technician/

Alberta. (2018l). Occupations in Alberta: Physiotherapist. Retrieved from https://alis.alberta.ca/occinfo/occupations-in-alberta/occupation-profiles/physiotherapist/

Alberta. (2018m). Occupations in Alberta: Public health inspector. Retrieved from https://alis.alberta.ca/occinfo/occupations-in-alberta/occupation-profiles/public-health-inspector/

Alberta. (2018n). Occupations in Alberta: Registered psychiatric nurse. Retrieved from https://alis.alberta.ca/occinfo/occupations-in-alberta/occupation-profiles/psychiatric-nurse/

Alberta. (2018o). *Pharmacy and Drug Act: Pharmacy and Drug Regulation.* Retrieved from https://www.qp.alberta.ca/documents/Regs/2006_240.pdf

Alberta. (2018p). *2016/2017 Alberta long-term care resident profile.* Retrieved from https://open.alberta.ca/dataset/90c128a6-3a8e-4c6e-8591-58e88fe6b6f9/resource/894a3a9c-8999-4487-b7e5-2850b3bb1a2e/download/cc-ltc-resident-profile-2017.pdf

Alberta. (2020a). Budget 2020: Fiscal plan – A plan for jobs and the economy, 2020–23. Retrieved from https://open.alberta.ca/dataset/05bd4008-c8e3-4c84-949e-cc18170bc7f7/resource/79caa22e-e417-44bd-8cac-64d7bb045509/download/budget-2020-fiscal-plan-2020-23.pdf

Alberta. (2020b). *Ministry Business Plan: Health.* Retrieved from https://open.alberta.ca/dataset/bb547784-e775-4eed-aa9c-0aa4a1aece8a/resource/891eadb9-b91b-48ab-99b4-33dbbf1b35a0/download/health-business-plan-2020-23.pdf

Alberta. (2020c). Unemployment rate. Economic dashboard. Retrieved from https://economicdashboard.alberta.ca/Unemployment

Alberta. (2021a). COVID-19 Alberta statistics. Retrieved from https://www .alberta.ca/stats/covid-19-alberta-statistics.htm

Alberta. (2021b). Drug coverage and health benefits. Retrieved from https:// www.alberta.ca/drug-coverage-health-benefits.aspx

Alberta. (2021c). Health care services covered in Alberta. Retrieved from https://www.alberta.ca/ahcip-what-is-covered.aspx

Alberta. (2021d). Heritage Trust Savings Fund. Retrieved from https://www .alberta.ca/heritage-savings-trust-fund.aspx

Alberta. (2021e). Ministry of Health: Our responsibilities. Retrieved from https://www.alberta.ca/health.aspx

Alberta. (2021f). Substance use surveillance data. Retrieved from https://www .alberta.ca/substance-use-surveillance-data.aspx

Alberta Association of Midwives. (n.d). What is a midwife? Retrieved from https://abmidwives.ca/what

AlbertaCanada.com. (2018). Economic results. Retrieved from http://www .albertacanada.com/business/overview/economic-results.aspx

Alberta College and Association of Chiropractors. (2020). About chiropractors. Retrieved from https://albertachiro.com/chiropractors/

Alberta College of Optometrists. (n.d.). Welcome to the Alberta College of Optometrists [Home page]. Retrieved from https://collegeofoptometrists .ab.ca/

Alberta College of Paramedics. (n.d.). About practice. Retrieved from https:// abparamedics.com/practice-guidelines/

Alberta College of Paramedics. (2020). *2019–2020 annual report: Redefining resilience*. Retrieved from https://abparamedics.com/wp-content/uploads /2021/02/2019-2020-Annual-Report-Final.pdf

Alberta College of Pharmacy. (2016). *Going the distance to care for Albertans: 2015/16 annual report*. Retrieved from https://abpharmacy.ca/annual-reports

Alberta College of Pharmacy. (2020). [Home page]. Retrieved from https:// abpharmacy.ca/

Alberta College of Social Workers. (2021). [Home page]. Retrieved from https://www.acsw.ab.ca

Alberta College of Speech-Language Pathologists and Audiologists. (2018). Governing legislation & bylaws. Retrieved from https://www.acslpa.ca/the -college/governing-legislation-bylaws/

Alberta Dental Association and College. (2021). Dental team. Retrieved from https://www.dentalhealthalberta.ca/visiting-your-dentist/dental-team/

Alberta Finance and Enterprise, Demography Unit. (2011). *Demographic Spotlight: The visible minority population: Recent trends in Alberta and Canada*.

Retrieved from https://open.alberta.ca/publications/visible-minority
-population-recent-trends-in-alberta-and-canada

Alberta Gambling Research Institute. (2021). *Alberta Gambling Research Institute. Consortium of University of Alberta, University of Calgary, and University of Lethbridge.* Retrieved from https://research.ucalgary.ca/alberta-gambling-research-institute

Alberta Health. (1997). *Health care '97: A guide to health care in Alberta.* Edmonton, AB: Author.

Alberta Health. (2008). *Vision 2020: The future of health care in Alberta: Phase one.* Retrieved from https://open.alberta.ca/dataset/9f312863-76ed-4d6f-b336-327bd7ae8fb6/resource/5e9160ea-9fac-469f-bb1b-47743c400aa1/download/vision-2020-phase-1-2008.pdf

Alberta Health. (2013). *Alberta's health system measurement classification approach.* Retrieved from https://open.alberta.ca/dataset/569c438b-b479-4ce7-a5f5-953775f055da/resource/176d5e6f-e831-493c-8d3b-d19778b76c1a/download/PMIS-Classification-Approach-2013.pdf

Alberta Health. (2014a). *Alberta's primary health care strategy.* Retrieved from https://open.alberta.ca/dataset/1cac62b5-a383-4959-8187-1b2a6798d0ac/resource/2ff5246a-bdd9-428a-ab04-62e5475c90ed/download/6849603-2014-albertas-primary-health-care-strategy-2014-01.pdf

Alberta Health. (2014b). *Performance measure definition: Physicians' use of electronic medical records (EMR).* Retrieved from https://open.alberta.ca/dataset/c7e3fc16-7aea-455c-96a1-20811a640b1a/resource/63eb8989-6521-4006-af33-eed63568cef0/download/PMD-Physicians-Use-EMR.pdf

Alberta Health. (2016a). *Continuing care health service standards: Information guide.* Retrieved from https://open.alberta.ca/dataset/8fd7f61d-7c16-435e-8181-dc9a38d761d5/resource/d0055ab3-3ec8-4d55-952f-fedeff446cba/download/Continuing-Care-Standards-Guide-2016.pdf

Alberta Health. (2016b). *Primary care networks review.* Retrieved from https://open.alberta.ca/dataset/3ca7c848-0112-467f-8230-2ee364a294f8/resource/a41ff408-5d52-4763-83b5-1171612ee8c7/download/PCN-Review-2016.pdf

Alberta Health. (2017a). *Alberta Health Care Insurance Plan statistical supplement, 2016/2017.* Retrieved from https://open.alberta.ca/dataset/3c9a0637-29c1-4cb2-93ba-c2ac090ab2b5/resource/220fdcad-3173-46f5-adb8-c6b47db0e93c/download/ahcip-stats-supplement-17.pdf

Alberta Health. (2017b). *Annual report 2016-17.* Retrieved from https://open.alberta.ca/dataset/4bb6bc99-ab59-47fd-a633-dfc27d7a049e/resource/7acc0ad0-bf1b-45dd-9a41-c64f3d85db04/download/Annual-Report-2017-Health.pdf

Alberta Health. (2018a). *Alberta health care insurance plan statistical supplement, 2017/18*. Retrieved from https://open.alberta.ca/publications /0845-4775

Alberta Health. (2018b). *Annual report 2017–2018*. Retrieved from https:// open.alberta.ca/dataset/4bb6bc99-ab59-47fd-a633-dfc27d7a049e /resource/94b95989-e03a-4acc-8bf9-f080f911abf0/download/health-annual -report-2017-2018.pdf

Alberta Health. (2018c). Blended capitation clinical ARP model. Retrieved from https://www.alberta.ca/blended-capitation-clinical-alternative -relationship-plan-model.aspx

Alberta Health. (2018d). Interactive Health Data Application. Retrieved from http://www.ahw.gov.ab.ca/IHDA_Retrieval/

Alberta Health. (2018e). *Opioids and substances of misuse: Alberta report, 2017 Q4*. Retrieved from https://open.alberta.ca/publications/opioids-and -substances-of-misuse-alberta-report

Alberta Health. (2018f). *Opioids and substances of misuse: Alberta report, 2018 Q2*. Retrieved from https://www.alberta.ca/assets/documents/opioid -substances-misuse-report-2018-q2.pdf

Alberta Health. (2018g). Vision, mission, values, & strategies. Retrieved from https://www.albertahealthservices.ca/about/Page190.aspx

Alberta Health. (2019). *Annual report, 2018–2019*. Retrieved from https://open .alberta.ca/dataset/4bb6bc99-ab59-47fd-a633-dfc27d7a049e/resource /32a0c20e-728d-4004-bc38-52f24ebd30cd/download/health-annual-report -2018-2019-web.pdf

Alberta Health. (2020a). *Annual report, 2019–2020*. Retrieved from https:// open.alberta.ca/dataset/4bb6bc99-ab59-47fd-a633-dfc27d7a049e/resource /04c7e15d-c88e-4172-b3fd-169be52ffe73/download/health-annual-report -2019-2020.pdf

Alberta Health. (2020b, 10 April). Record of decision – CMOH Order 10-2020 which rescinds CMOH Order 6-2020 and CMOH Order 08-2020. Retrieved from https://open.alberta.ca/dataset/b0483d64-254e-4d55-895a -1c1d9127c906/resource/76b47c6e-4ac9-41e1-ad7b-244fe1e149ee/download /health-cmoh-record-of-decision-cmoh-10-2020.pdf

Alberta Health & Alberta Medical Association. (2016). *Agreement to amend the Alberta Medical Association agreement: Exhibit A to schedule 7: Draft terms of reference for PRPC*. Edmonton, AB: Author.

Alberta Health & Premier's Commission on Future Health Care for Albertans. (1989). *The Rainbow Report: Our vision for health* (Vol. 2). Edmonton, AB: Queen's Printer.

Alberta Health Advocate. (2021a). Alberta's Health Charter. Retrieved from https://www.alberta.ca/alberta-health-charter.aspx

Alberta Health Advocate. (2021b). [Home page]. Retrieved from https://www.alberta.ca/office-of-alberta-health-advocates.aspx

Alberta Health Services. (n.d.-a). About AHS. Retrieved from https://www.albertahealthservices.ca/about/about.aspx

Alberta Health Services. (n.d.-b). Advisory councils. Retrieved from https://www.albertahealthservices.ca/ac/ac.aspx

Alberta Health Services. (n.d.-c). Audiologist. Retrieved from https://www.albertahealthservices.ca/info/Page8482.aspx

Alberta Health Services. (n.d.-d). Connect Care: Health professionals. Retrieved from https://www.albertahealthservices.ca/info/Page15449.aspx

Alberta Health Services. (n.d.-e). Data & statistics: Medical assistance in dying. https://www.albertahealthservices.ca/info/Page14930.aspx

Alberta Health Services. (n.d.-f). Dietician. Retrieved from https://www.albertahealthservices.ca/careers/Page11759.aspx

Alberta Health Services. (n.d.-g). Indigenous health. Retrieved from https://www.albertahealthservices.ca/info/Page11949.aspx

Alberta Health Services. (n.d.-h). Laboratory technologist. Retrieved from https://www.albertahealthservices.ca/careers/Page11698.aspx

Alberta Health Services. (n.d.-i). Midwifery services. Retrieved from https://www.albertahealthservices.ca/info/Page9271.aspx

Alberta Health Services. (n.d.-j). Nurse practitioners (NP). Retrieved from https://www.albertahealthservices.ca/info/page7903.aspx

Alberta Health Services. (n.d.-k). Occupational therapist (OT). Retrieved from https://www.albertahealthservices.ca/info/Page8493.aspx

Alberta Health Services. (n.d.-l). Patients collaborating with teams (PaCT). Retrieved from https://www.albertahealthservices.ca/info/Page15283.aspx

Alberta Health Services. (n.d.-m). Physician assistant (PA). Retrieved from https://www.albertahealthservices.ca/info/Page9882.aspx

Alberta Health Services. (n.d.-n). Physiotherapist (PT). Retrieved from https://www.albertahealthservices.ca/info/Page8489.aspx

Alberta Health Services. (n.d.-o). Primary Care Integration Network. Retrieved from https://www.albertahealthservices.ca/info/page15353.aspx

Alberta Health Services. (n.d.-p). Public health inspector. Retrieved from https://www.albertahealthservices.ca/careers/Page12298.aspx

Alberta Health Services. (n.d.-q). Quarterly Emergency Medical Services Dashboard. Retrieved from https://www.albertahealthservices.ca/assets/info/ems/if-ems-dashboard.pdf

Alberta Health Services. (n.d.-r). Registered nurse. Retrieved from https://www.albertahealthservices.ca/careers/Page11733.aspx

Alberta Health Services. (n.d.-s). Registered psychiatric nurse (RPN). Retrieved from https://www.albertahealthservices.ca/info/Page8492.aspx

Alberta Health Services. (n.d.-t). Respiratory therapist (RT). Retrieved from https://www.albertahealthservices.ca/info/Page8496.aspx

Alberta Health Services. (n.d.-u). Social worker. Retrieved from https://www.albertahealthservices.ca/careers/Page11723.aspx

Alberta Health Services. (n.d.-v). Specialist link. Retrieved from https://www.specialistlink.ca/

Alberta Health Services. (n.d.-w). Speech language pathologist (SLP). Retrieved from https://www.albertahealthservices.ca/info/Page8483.aspx

Alberta Health Services. (n.d.-x). Strategic clinical health networks. Retrieved from https://albertahealthservices.ca/scns/scn.aspx

Alberta Health Services. (n.d.-y). Vision, mission, values & strategies. Retrieved from https://www.albertahealthservices.ca/about/Page190.aspx

Alberta Health Services. (2009). *AHS quality and patient safety strategic outline.* Retrieved from https://www.mindbank.info/item/1683

Alberta Health Services. (2010, 21 January). Quality and Patient Safety Dashboard indicators. New release. Retrieved from https://www.albertahealthservices.ca/news/releases/2010/Page1329.aspx

Alberta Health Services. (2012). *Rehabilitation conceptual framework.* Retrieved from http://rehabcarealliance.ca/uploads/File/knowledgeexchange/Alberta_Health_Services-Rehabilitation-Conceptual-Framework.pdf

Alberta Health Services. (2014). Palliative and end of life care: Alberta provincial framework. Retrieved from http://albertahealthservices.ca/about/Page10774.aspx

Alberta Health Services. (2015a). *Alberta blood contingency plan.* Retrieved from https://open.alberta.ca/dataset/5eea94dd-ecf4-40e4-91da-572c46a4f7a8/resource/969aa2ec-e869-4eee-886b-7ce0c62b5d2c/download/2015-Alberta-Blood-Contingency-Plan-2015.pdf

Alberta Health Services. (2015b). *Annual report 2014–2015.* Retrieved from https://www.albertahealthservices.ca/assets/about/publications/ahs-pub-2014-2015-annual-report.pdf

Alberta Health Services. (2015c, 11 February). Beyond the headlines: Operational benchmarking. Retrieved from https://www.albertahealthservices.ca/Blogs/BTH/Posting248.aspx

Alberta Health Services. (2016a). *Oral health action plan.* Retrieved from https://www.albertahealthservices.ca/assets/info/oh/if-oh-action-plan.pdf

Alberta Health Services. (2017). *2017–2020 health plan and business plan: Year 3*. Retrieved from https://www.albertahealthservices.ca/about /Page13365.aspx

Alberta Health Services. (2018a). *Alberta long-term care quality indicators, 2016– 2017*. Retrieved from https://www.albertahealthservices.ca/assets /about/publications/2017-18-annual-report-web-version.pdf

Alberta Health Services. (2018b). *Annual Report 2017–2018*. Retrieved from https://www.albertahealthservices.ca/assets/about/data/ahs-data-rai -qis-2016-17.pdf

Alberta Health Services. (2018c). Monitoring measures. Retrieved from https://www.albertahealthservices.ca/about/Page12640.aspx

Alberta Health Services. (2018d). Organizational structure. Retrieved from https://www.albertahealthservices.ca/assets/about/org/ahs-org-orgchart.pdf

Alberta Health Services. (2019a). *Annual report 2018–2019*. Retrieved from https://www.albertahealthservices.ca/assets/about/publications/2018-19 -annual-report-web-version.pdf

Alberta Health Services. (2019b). Meet Alberta's strategic clinical networks. Retrieved from https://albertahealthservices.ca/assets/about/scn/ahs-scn -quick-facts.pdf

Alberta Health Services. (2020). *Annual report 2019–2020*. Retrieved from https://www.albertahealthservices.ca/assets/about/publications/2019-20 -annual-report-web-version.pdf

Alberta Health Services. (2021a). Community engagement and communications. Retrieved from https://www.albertahealthservices.ca/about/Page12822.aspx

Alberta Health Services. (2021b). Glenrose Rehabilitation Hospital quick facts. Retrieved from http://www.albertahealthservices.ca/assets/hospitals/grh /grh-home-quick-facts.pdf

Alberta Health Services. (2021c). Patient experiences. Retrieved from https:// albertahealthservices.ca/info/Page15876.aspx

Alberta Health Services. (2021d). Performance measures. Retrieved from https://www.albertahealthservices.ca/about/performance.aspx

Alberta Innovates. (2017). *Annual report 2016-17*. Retrieved from https:// albertainnovates.ca/wp-content/uploads/2016/10/AI-AR-2017_Web.pdf

Alberta Labour and Immigration. (2018). Workplace injury, disease and fatality statistics: Provincial summary, 2018. Retrieved from https://open.alberta .ca/publications/workplace-injury-disease-and-fatality-statistics-provincial -summary

Alberta Medical Association. (n.d.). PCN governance framework. Retrieved from https://www.albertadoctors.org/services/physicians/our-agreements /pcn-governance

Alberta Medical Association. (2016). A short summary: Tentative AMA amendment agreement package. https://www.albertadoctors.org /Member%20Services/AMA_AGREEMENT_PKG_SUMMARY_3.pdf

Alberta Medical Association. (2018a). Clinical alternative relationship plan. Retrieved from https://www.albertadoctors.org/539.aspx

Alberta Medical Association. (2020). [website]. Retrieved from https://www .albertadoctors.org/

Alberta Municipal Affairs. (2019). Alberta's municipal population total from 1960 to 2019. Retrieved from https://open.alberta.ca/publications/alberta -municipal-population-total

Alberta Netcare. (2018). Alberta Netcare EHR: Information included in the EHR. Retrieved from https://www.albertanetcare.ca/HealthInformation.htm

Alberta Netcare Learning Centre. (2018). Community information integration. Retrieved from http://www.albertanetcare.ca/learningcentre/CII.htm

Alberta Treasury Board and Finance. (2015). *Budget 2015: Fiscal plan.* Retrieved from https://open.alberta.ca/dataset/bb4b0922-f7c6-4099-953e -8913472a47ef/resource/57c66e37-e136-4eac-9d31-c19d136652ac /download/fiscal-plan-complete.pdf

Alberta Treasury Board and Finance. (2017, 9 February). *2016 Census of Canada: Population and dwelling release.* Retrieved from https://open .alberta.ca/dataset/7d02c106-a55a-4f88-8253-4b4c81168e9f/resource /e435dd59-2dbd-4bf2-b5b6-3173d9bd6c39/download/2016-census -population-and-dwelling-counts.pdf

Altus Group. (2018). *Canadian construction cost guide.* Retrieved from https:// creston.ca/DocumentCenter/View/1957/Altus-2018-Construction -Cost-Guide-web-1

Anderson, D. (2019, 11 December). Alberta's energy "war room" launches in Calgary. *CBC News.* Retrieved from https://www.cbc.ca/news/canada /calgary/alberta-war-room-launch-calgary-1.5392371

Armstrong, W. (2002). *Eldercare – On the auction block.* Edmonton, AB: Consumers' Association of Canada, Alberta Chapter.

Aucoin P. (2012). New political governance in Westminster systems: Impartial public administration and management performance at risk. *Governance,* 25(2), 177–99. https://doi.org/10.1111/j.1468-0491.2012.01569.x

Babych, S. (2019, 11 December). Province turns to private sector for help reducing surgery wait times. *Calgary Herald.* Retrieved from https:// calgaryherald.com/news/local-news/province-turns-to-private-sector-for-help -reducing-surgery-wait-times

Bahler, B. (2018, February). Clarity from chaos: Multiple initiatives, one goal. Paper presented at the Primary Care Network (PCN) Strategic Leadership

Forum, Edmonton, AB. Retrieved from https://actt.albertadoctors.org/events /2018%20Spring%20PCN%20Forum/2%20-%20ClarityFromChaos.pdf

Baker, G.R., Norton, P.G., Flintoft, V., Blais, R., Brown, A. Cox J., ... Tamblyn, R. (2004). The Canadian Adverse Events Study: The incidence of adverse events among hospital patients in Canada. *CMAJ, 170*(11), 1678–86. https://doi .org/10.1503/cmaj.1040498

Bakx, K. (2016, 28 October). Alberta government urged to explain why it rejects public-private partnerships. Retrieved from https://www.cbc.ca /news/canada/calgary/p3s-alberta-ndp-construction-1.3823010

Barker, P., & Church, J. (2017). Revisiting health regionalization in Canada: More bark than bite? *International Journal of Health Services, 47*(2), 333–51. https://doi.org/10.1177/0020731416681229

Barrie, D. (2004). Ralph Klein, 1992–. In B.J. Rennie (Ed.), *Alberta premiers of the twentieth century* (pp. 255–79). Regina, SK: University of Regina, Canadian Plains Research Centre.

Barua, B. (2017). *Waiting your turn: Wait times for health care in Canada, 2017 report.* Retrieved from https://www.fraserinstitute.org/sites/default/files /waiting-your-turn-2017.pdf

Barua, B., & Ren, F. (2016). *Waiting your turn: Wait times for health care in Canada, 2016 Report.* Retrieved from https://www.fraserinstitute.org/sites /default/files/waiting-your-turn-wait-times-for-health-care-in-canada-2016.pdf

Beesoon, S., Robert, J. & White, J. (2019). Surgical Strategic Clinical Network: Improving quality, safety and access to surgical care in Alberta. *CMAJ, 191*(Suppl. 1), S27–9. https://doi.org/10.1503/cmaj.190590

Bell, E. (2004). Ernest C. Manning, 1943–1968. In B.J. Rennie (Ed.), *Alberta premiers of the twentieth century* (pp. 107–24). Regina, SK: University of Regina, Canadian Plains Research Centre.

Bellefontaine, M. (2019, 28 October). Alberta government plans sweeping changes through 2 omnibus bills. *CBC News.* Retrieved from https://www .cbc.ca/news/canada/edmonton/alberta-omnibus-bills-1.5338632

Bellefontaine, M. (2020, 20 April) Alberta mask issues a matter of personal preference, official says. *CBC News.* Retrieved from https://www.cbc.ca /news/canada/edmonton/alberta-procedural-masks-health-care-1.5539134

Bengoechea, E.G., Pasco, A.C., Thiem, A., & Langhout, N. (2004). *An environmental scan of workplace wellness programs in Alberta.* Edmonton, AB: Alberta Centre for Active Living.

Bennett, D. (2020, 9 January). Alberta doctors not ruling out court challenge in response to billing changes. *Canadian Press.* Retrieved from https:// globalnews.ca/news/6389774/alberta-doctors-billing-changes-court -challenge/

Berta, W., Laporte, A., Zarnett, D., Valdmanis, V., & Anderson, G. (2006). A pan-Canadian perspective on institutional long-term care. *Health Policy, 79,* 175–94. https://doi.org/10.1016/j.healthpol.2005.12.006

Birch, S., Goldsmith, L., & Mäkelä, M. (1994). *Paying the piper and calling the tune: Principles and prospects for reforming physician payment methods in Canada.* Hamilton, ON: McMaster University, McMaster University Centre for Health Economics and Policy Analysis.

Blomqvist, Å., & Busby, C. (2015). *Rethinking Canada's unbalanced mix of public and private healthcare: Insights from abroad.* Commentary No. 420. Toronto, ON: C.D. Howe Institute.

Boothe, P., & Johnson, B. (1993). *Stealing the emperor's clothes: Deficit offloading and national standards in health care.* Commentary No. 41. Toronto, ON: C.D. Howe Institute.

Born, K., Huynh, T., & Levinson, W. (2019). Reflecting on Choosing Wisely Canada at five years: Accomplishments, challenges and opportunities for reducing overuse and improving quality. *HealthcarePapers,* 18(1), 9–17.

Borsellino, M. (1993, 20 July). Another con? Gov't med school cuts go deeper than 10%. *Medical Post.*

Boschma, G. (2011). Deinstitutionalization reconsidered: Geographic and demographic changes in mental health care in British Columbia and Alberta, 1950–1980. *Social history, 44*(88), 223–56. https://doi.org/10.1353/his .2011.0020

Bourne, J., & Merrill, P. (2011). Rat control in Alberta. *The Canadian Encyclopedia.* Retrieved from https://www.thecanadianencyclopedia.ca/en /article/rat-control-in-alberta/

Bow, M.R., & Cook, F.T. (1935). The history of the Department of Public Health of Alberta. *Canadian Public Health Journal, 26*(8), 384–96. https:// www.jstor.org/stable/41979367

Boychuk, G.W. (2008). *The regulation of private health funding and insurance in Alberta under the Canada Health Act: A comparative cross-provincial perspective.* Calgary: The School of Policy Studies, University of Calgary. Retrieved from https://journalhosting.ucalgary.ca/index.php/sppp/article /view/42306/30198

Boychuk, T. (1999). *The making and meaning of hospital policy in the United States and Canada.* Ann Arbor, MI: University of Michigan Press

Boyle McCauley Health Centre. (2018). About us. Retrieved from https://www .bmhc.net/about-us.html

Bright, D. (2000, 1 May). Alberta's hostility towards labour. Alberta Views. Retrieved from https://albertaviews.ca/albertas-hostility-towards-labour/

Brownsey, K. (2005). Ralph Klein and the hollowing of Alberta. In T. Harrison (Ed.), *The return of the Trojan horse: Alberta and the new world (dis)order* (pp. 23–36). Montreal: Black Rose Books

Burke, A. (2016, 13 June). Veterans long-term care wings face "expiry date." *CBC News.* Retrieved from https://www.cbc.ca/news/canada/ottawa/veterans-long-term-care-wings-face-expiry-date-1.3624150

Busby, C., Jacobs, A., & Muthukumaran, R. (2017). *In need of a booster: How to improve childhood vaccination coverage in Canada.* Commentary No. 477. Ottawa ON: C. D. Howe Institute.

Campanella, D., & Flanagan, G. (2012). *Impaired judgement: The economic and social consequences of liquor privatization in Western Canada.* Edmonton, AB: Parkland Institute/Canadian Centre for Policy Alternatives.

Campbell, D., Manns, B.J., Soril, L., & Clement, F. (2017). Comparison of Canadian public medication insurance plans and the impact on out-of-pocket costs. *CMAJ Open, 5*(4): E808–13. https://doi.org/10.9778/cmajo.20170065

Canada. (2007). Health Transition Fund. Retrieved from https://www.canada.ca/en/health-canada/services/health-care-system/ehealth/canada-health-infostructure/health-canada-funding-programs/health-transition-fund.html

Canada. (2016). Canada's health care system. Retrieved from https://www.canada.ca/en/health-canada/services/canada-health-care-system.html

Canada. (2017). Canadian Tobacco Alcohol and Drugs (CTADS): 2015 summary. Retrieved from https://www.canada.ca/en/health-canada/services/canadian-tobacco-alcohol-drugs-survey/2015-summary.html

Canada. (2020). Major federal transfers: Federal support to Alberta. Retrieved from https://www.canada.ca/en/department-finance/programs/federal-transfers/major-federal-transfers.html#Alberta

Canada. (2021). *Canada Health Act annual report 2019–20.* Retrieved from https://www.canada.ca/en/health-canada/services/publications/health-system-services/canada-health-act-annual-report-2019-2020.html

Canada, Department of Finance. (2021). Federal transfers to provinces and territories. Retrieved from https://www.canada.ca/en/department-finance/programs/federal-transfers.html

Canada Health Infoway. (2017). Use of electronic medical records among Canadian physicians: 2017 update. Retrieved from https://www.infoway-inforoute.ca/en/component/edocman/resources/reports/benefits-evaluation/3362-2017-cma-workforce-survey-digital-health-results

Canadian Academy of Health Sciences. (2014). *Improving access to oral health care for vulnerable people living in Canada.* Retrieved from https://cahs-acss.ca/wp-content/uploads/2015/07/Access_to_Oral_Care_FINAL_REPORT_EN.pdf

Canadian Agency for Drugs and Technologies in Health (CADTH). (2017). Medical imaging in Canada 2017: Provincial summary for Alberta. Retrieved from https://www.cadth.ca/sites/default/files/pdf/Provincial%20Summaries /cmii_2017_provincial_summary_alberta.pdf

Canadian Association of Optometrists. (2015, 26 June). Alberta government formally approves optometry scope expansion. News release. Retrieved from https://opto .ca/news/alberta-government-formally-approves-optometry-scope-expansion

Canadian Dental Association. (2020). *The state of oral health in Canada.* Retrieved from https://www.cda-adc.ca/stateoforalhealth/

Canadian Federation of Nurses Unions. (2020). *Nursing contracts in Canada.* Retrieved from https://nursesunions.ca/wp-content/uploads/2021/01/2020 _nurse_contracts_EN.pdf

Canadian Healthcare Association. (2009). *New directions for facility-based long term care.* Ottawa, ON: Author.

Canadian Institute for Health Information. (2007). *Medical imaging in Canada.* Retrieved from https://secure.cihi.ca/free_products/MIT_2007_e.pdf

Canadian Institute for Health Information. (2013). *Drug expenditure in Canada, 1985–2012.* Retrieved from http://publications.gc.ca/collections /collection_2013/icis-cihi/H115-27-2012-eng.pdf

Canadian Institute for Health Information. (2015). *How Canada compares: Results from the Commonwealth Fund 2014.* Ottawa, ON: Author.

Canadian Institute for Health Information. (2016a). Commonwealth Fund survey, 2016. Retrieved from https://www.cihi.ca/en/commonwealth-fund-survey-2016

Canadian Institute for Health Information. (2016b). *Regulated nurses, 2015.* Retrieved from https://secure.cihi.ca/free_products/Nursing_Report_2015 _en.pdf

Canadian Institute of Health Information. (2016c). Supply, distribution and migration of Canadian physicians 2015. Alberta Profile. Retrieved from https://secure.cihi.ca/estore/productSeries.htm?pc=PCC34

Canadian Institute for Health Information. (2017a). *Community mental health and addiction information: A snapshot of data collection and reporting in Canada.* Retrieved from https://secure.cihi.ca/free_products/CIHI-comm -mental-health-en-web.pdf

Canadian Institute for Health Information. (2017b). *NACRS emergency department visits and length of stay by province/territory, 2017–2018.* Retrieved from https://www.cihi.ca/en/nacrs-emergency-department-visits-and-length -of-stay-2017-2018

Canadian Institute for Health Information. (2017c). *Regulated nurses, 2016: RN/NP data tables.* Retrieved from https://www.cihi.ca/sites/default/files /document/rn-np-2016-data-tables-en-web.xlsx

Canadian Institute for Health Information. (2017d). *Seniors in transition: Exploring pathways across the care continuum.* Retrieved from https://www .cihi.ca/sites/default/files/document/seniors-in-transition-report-2017-en .pdf

Canadian Institute for Health Information. (2017e). *Wait times for priority procedures in Canada, 2017.* Retrieved from https://secure.cihi.ca/free _products/wait-times-report-2017_en.pdf

Canadian Institute for Health Information. (2018a). Canada, Jurisdiction Profile, SMDB Data Tables. https://www.cihi.ca/en/scotts-medical-database -metadata

Canadian Institute for Health Information. (2018b) Canada's health care providers: Provincial profiles, 2008 to 2017 – Data table 1. Retrieved from https://www.cihi.ca/sites/default/files/document/hcp-2017-data-tables-en -web.xlsx

Canadian Institute for Health Information. (2018c). Canada's health care providers: Provincial profiles 2008–2017, data tables. Retrieved from https:// www.cihi.ca/sites/default/files/document/hcp-2017-data-tables-en-web.xlsx

Canadian Institute for Health Information. (2018d). Licensed practical nurses. Retrieved from https://www.cihi.ca/en/licensed-practical-nurses

Canadian Institute for Health Information. (2018e). OECD interactive tool: International comparisons: Patient safety. Retrieved from https://www.cihi .ca/en/oecd-interactive-tool-international-comparisons-patient-safety

Canadian Institute for Health Information. (2019). *Physicians in Canada, 2018.* Retrieved from https://secure.cihi.ca/free_products/physicians-in-canada -2018.pdf

Canadian Institute for Health Information. (2020a). National health expenditure trends: data tables. Retrieved from https://www.cihi.ca/en/national-health -expenditure-trends

Canadian Institute for Health Information. (2020b). National physician database – Utilization data, 2018–2019. Retrieved from https://secure.cihi .ca/estore/productSeries.htm?pc=PCC476

Canadian Institute for Health Information. (2020c). Nursing in Canada, 2019. Retrieved from https://www.cihi.ca/en/nursing-in-canada-2019

Canadian Institute for Health Information. (2020d). Your health system: Avoidable deaths from preventable causes details for Alberta. Retrieved from https://yourhealthsystem.cihi.ca/hsp/indepth?lang=en#/indicator/037/2 /C20018/

Canadian Institute for Health Information. (2020e). Your health system: Avoidable deaths from treatable causes details for Alberta. Retrieved from

https://yourhealthsystem.cihi.ca/hsp/indepth?lang=en#/indicator/038/2
/C20018/

Canadian Institute for Health Information. (2021a). Health indicators
interactive tool. Retrieved from https://yourhealthsystem.cihi.ca/epub
/search.jspa

Canadian Institute for Health Information. (2021b). Hospital stays in Canada.
Retrieved from https://www.cihi.ca/en/hospital-stays-in-canada

Canadian Institute for Health Information. (2021c). Your health system:
Ambulatory care sensitive conditions details for Alberta. Retrieved from
https://yourhealthsystem.cihi.ca/hsp/indepth?lang=en#/indicator/019/2
/C20018/

Canadian Institute for Health Information. (2021d). Your health system:
Cost of a standard hospital stay details for Alberta. Retrieved from https://
yourhealthsystem.cihi.ca/hsp/indepth?lang=en#/indicator/015/2/C20018/

Canadian Institute for Health Information. (2021e). Your health system:
Hospital deaths (HSMR) details for Alberta. Retrieved from https://
yourhealthsystem.cihi.ca/hsp/indepth?lang=en#/indicator/005/2/C20018/

Canadian Institute for Health Information. (2021f). Your health system: Repeat
hospital stays for mental illness details for Alberta. Retrieved from https://
yourhealthsystem.cihi.ca/hsp/indepth?lang=en#/indicator/007/2/C20018/

Canadian Institute for Health Information & Choosing Wisely Canada. (2017).
Unnecessary care in Canada. Retrieved from https://www.cihi.ca/sites/default
/files/document/choosing-wisely-baseline-report-en-web.pdf

Canadian Institutes of Health Research. (2018). CIHR in numbers, 2017–18.
Retrieved from https://cihr-irsc.gc.ca/e/50218.html

Canadian Life and Health Insurance Association. (2020). *Canadian life and
health insurance facts: 2020 edition.* Retrieved from http://clhia.uberflip.com
/i/1287746-canadian-life-and-health-insurance-facts-2020/0?

Canadian Medical Association. (2016). *The state of seniors health care in Canada.*
Retrieved from https://www.cma.ca/sites/default/files/2018-11/the-state-of
-seniors-health-care-in-canada-september-2016.pdf

Canadian Medical Association. (2019). Number of physicians by province/
territory and by specialty, Canada, 2019. Retrieved from https://www.cma.ca
/sites/default/files/2019-11/2019-01-spec-prov.pdf

Canadian Mental Health Association, Alberta Division. (n.d.) Mental illness in
Canada. Retrieved from https://alberta.cmha.ca/mental-illness-in-canada/

Canadian Museum of History. (n.d.). Making Medicare: The history of health
care in Canada, 1914–2007. Retrieved from https://www.historymuseum.ca
/cmc/exhibitions/hist/medicare/medic00e.html

Carey, G., Crammond, B., & Keast, R. (2014). Creating change in government to address the social determinants of health: How can efforts be improved? *BMC Public Health, 14*, 1087. https://doi.org/10.1186/1471-2458-14-1087

CBC News. (2009, 27 April). Alberta gambling revenue expected to outstrip oilsands royalties. *CBC News.* Retrieved from https://www.cbc.ca/news /canada/calgary/alberta-gambling-revenue-expected-to-outstrip-oilsands -royalties-1.779547

CBC News. (2009, 7 October). Alberta hires cheaper nurses to tackle shortage. *CBC News.* Retrieved from https://www.cbc.ca/news/canada/edmonton /alberta-hires-cheaper-nurses-to-tackle-shortage-1.777016

CBC News. (2012, 2 April). Alberta Tories promise 140 family clinics. *CBC News.* Retrieved from https://www.cbc.ca/news/canada/manitoba/alberta -tories-promise-140-family-clinics-1.1206863

CBC News. (2021). Tracking the coronavirus. *CBC News.* Retrieved from https://newsinteractives.cbc.ca/coronavirustracker/

Chen, P. (2013, 27 June). The gulf between doctors and nurse practitioners. *New York Times.* Retrieved from https://well.blogs.nytimes.com/2013/06/27 /the-gulf-between-doctors-and-nurse-practitioners/

Church, J., & Barker, P. (1998). Regionalization of health services in Canada: A critical perspective. *International Journal of Health Services, 28*(3), 467–86. https://doi.org/10.2190/UFPT-7XPW-794C-VJ52

Church, J., & Noseworthy, T. (1999). Health care reform in Alberta: Market rhetoric and reality. In T. Sullivan & D. Drache (Eds.), *Globalization and health reform: Public success, private failure* (pp. 186–203). London, UK: Routledge.

Church, J., Skrypnek, R., & Smith. N. (2018). Improving physician accountability through primary care reform in Alberta. *Healthcare Papers, 17*(4), 48–55. https://doi.org/10.12927/hcpap.2018.25576

Church, J., & Smith, N. (2006). Health reform and privatization in Alberta. *Canadian Public Administration, 49*(4), 486–505. https://doi.org/10.1111 /j.1754-7121.2006.tb01995.x

Church, J., & Smith, N. (2008). Health reform in Alberta: The introduction of health regions. *Canadian Public Administration, 51*(2), 217–38. https://doi .org/10.1111/j.1754-7121.2008.00016.x

Church, J., & Smith, N. (2009). Health reform and wait times policy in Alberta under the Klein government. *Canadian Political Science Review, 3*(4), 63–84.

Church, J., & Smith, N. (2013a). Health reform in Alberta: Fiscal crisis, political leadership and institutional change within a single-party democratic state. In H. Lazar, P.-G. Forest, J.N. Lavis, & J. Church (Eds.), *Paradigm freeze: Why it is so hard to reform health care in Canada* (pp. 35–63). Montreal, PQ/Kingston, ON: McGill-Queen's University Press. Retrieved from https://www.queensu

.ca/iigr/sites/webpublish.queensu.ca.iigrwww/files/files/pub/archive
/books/ParadigmFreezeLockedLowRes.pdf

Church, J., & Smith. N. (2013b). *The introduction of APPs in Alberta*. Retrieved
from http://www.queensu.ca/iigr/sites/webpublish.queensu.ca.iigrwww
/files/files/Res/crossprov/Church-AlbertaAPP.pdf

Citizen Watch. (n.d.). Continuing care in Alberta. Retrieved from http://www
.continuingcarewatch.com/profit_motive.php

Climenhaga, D. (2020, 28 May). Jason Kenney offers medical equipment
to Ontario, Quebec, and B.C.; Pitches national solidarity on resource
development. *Alberta Politics.Blog*. Retrieved from https://albertapolitics
.ca/2020/04/jason-kenney-offers-medical-equipment-to-ontario-quebec-and
-b-c-pitches-national-solidarity-on-resource-development/

COACH: Canada's Health Informatics Association. (2013). *2013 Canadian
telehealth report*. Toronto, ON. Retrieved from https://www.synaptek.ca/wp
-content/uploads/2017/10/TeleHealth-Public-FINAL-web-062713-secured
.pdf

Cohen, M., McGregor, M., Ivanova, I., & Kinkaid, C. (2012). *Beyond the hospital
walls: Activity based funding versus integrated health care reform*. Vancouver BC:
Canadian Centre for Policy Alternatives.

Cole, L.W., & Foster, S.R. (2001). *From the ground up: Environmental racism and
the rise of the environmental justice movement*. New York, NY: New York University
Press.

College and Association of Registered Nurses of Alberta. (2020). [Home page].
Retrieved from https://www.nurses.ab.ca/

College of Dieticians of Alberta. (2020). Role of the college. Retrieved from
http://www.collegeofdietitians.ab.ca/

College of Family Physicians of Canada, Prison Health Program Committee.
(2016, 14 July). Position statement on health care delivery. Retrieved from
https://portal.cfpc.ca/resourcesdocs/uploadedFiles/Directories
/Committees_List/Health%20Care%20Delivery_EN_Prison%20Health.pdf

College of Licensed Practical Nurses of Alberta. (2018). Welcome to CLPNA
[Home page]. Retrieved from https://www.clpna.com/

College of Opticians of Alberta. (2016). *2015 annual report*. Retrieved from
https://acao.wpengine.com/wp-content/uploads/PDFs/2015-annual-report
-website.pdf

College of Opticians of Alberta. (2018). [Home page]. Retrieved from https://
acao.ca/

College of Physicians and Surgeons of Alberta. (n.d.-a). Diagnostic imaging.
Retrieved from https://cpsa.ca/facilities-clinics/accreditation/diagnostic
-imaging/

College of Physicians and Surgeons of Alberta. (n.d.-b). Physician Achievement Review (PAR) program. Retrieved from http://www.cpsa.ca/par-program/

College of Registered Psychiatric Nurses of Alberta. (2018). Welcome to the College of Registered Psychiatric Nurses of Alberta [Home page]. Retrieved from https://www.crpna.ab.ca/

Commonwealth Fund. (2016). Commonwealth Fund's international health policy survey of adults, 2016 data tables. Retrieved from https://www.cihi.ca/en/commonwealth-fund-survey-2016

Conference Board of Canada. (2016). Income per capita. Retrieved from https://www.conferenceboard.ca/hcp/provincial/economy/income-per-capita.aspx

Crichton, A., Hsu, D., & Tsang, S. (1990). *Canada's health care system: Its funding and organization.* Ottawa, ON: Canadian Hospital Association Press.

CTV News. (2015, 28 May). With only one clinic in Canada, wait for transgender surgery often months long. *CTV News.ca.* Retrieved from https://www.ctvnews.ca/health/with-only-one-clinic-in-canada-wait-for-transgender-surgery-often-months-long-1.2396678

Daly, T. (2015). Dancing the two-step in Ontario's long-term care sector: Deterrence, regulation, consolidation. *Studies in Political Economy, 95,* 29–58. https://doi.org/10.1080/19187033.2015.11674945

Dawson, T. (2019, 4 July). Alberta announces public inquiry into "shadowy" foreign funding of environmental groups. *Canada.com.* Retrieved from https://o.canada.com/news/politics/alberta-announces-public-inquiry-into-shadowy-foreign-funding-of-environmental-groups/wcm/462050a2-2baa-4a5b-a9a6-7364fbd1a64b

Decilia, B. (2014, 7 August). Alberta nurses agree on new contract with province. *CBC News.* Retrieved from https://www.cbc.ca/news/canada/calgary/alberta-nurses-agree-on-new-contract-with-province-1.2730803

Denis, J.-L., & Forest, P.G. (2012). Real reform begins within: An organizational approach to health care reform. *Journal of Health Politics, Policy and Law, 37*(4), 633–45. https://doi.org/10.1215/03616878-1597457

Doty, M.M., Tikkanen, R., Shah, A., & Schneider, E.C. (2019). Primary care physicians' role in coordinating medical and health-related social needs in eleven countries. *Health Affairs, 39*(1), 115–23. https://doi.org/10.1377/hlthaff.2019.01088

Downar, J., & Francescutti, L. (2017). Medical assistance in dying: Time for physicians to step up to protect themselves and patients. *CMAJ, 26*(189), E849–50. https://doi.org/10.1503/cmaj.170462

Drees, L.M. (2010). The Nanaimo and Charles Camsell Indian Hospitals: First Nations' narratives of health care, 1945 to 1965. *Social History, 43*(85), 165–91. https://doi.org/10.1353/his.2010.0002

Dryden, J. (2020, 25 April). With $20B Alberta deficit possible, Kenney warns province won't be able to "insulate everyone." *CBC News*. Retrieved from https://www.cbc.ca/news/canada/calgary/alberta-jason-kenney-covid-19 -coronavirus-trevor-tombe-1.5544476

Duckett, S. (2010). Second wave reform in Alberta. *Healthcare Management Forum, 23*(4), 156–8. https://doi.org/10.1016/j.hcmf.2010.08.006

Duckett, S. (2011). Getting the foundations right: Alberta's approach to healthcare reform. *Health Policy, 6*(3):22–6. https://doi.org/10.12927/hcpol.2013.22176

Duckett, S. (2015). Alberta: Health spending in the land of plenty. In G.P. Marchildon and L. Di Matteo (Eds.), *Bending the cost curve in health care* (pp. 297–326). Toronto, ON: University of Toronto Press.

Duckett, S., Bloom, J., & Robertson, A. (2012). Planning to meet the care need challenge in Alberta, Canada. *International Journal of Health Planning and Management, 27*(3), e186–96. https://doi.org/10.1002/hpm.2112

Duckett, S., & Peetoom, A. (2013). *Canadian Medicare: We need it and we can keep it*. Montreal, PQ/Kingston, ON: McGill-Queen's University Press.

Emery, H., & Kneebone, R. (2013). *Three strikes and you're out*. In D.L. Ryan (Ed.), *Boom and bust again: Policy challenges for a commodity-based economy* (pp. 39–58). Edmonton: University of Alberta Press.

Esmail, N. (2017). *Complementary and alternative medicine: Use and public attitudes, 1997, 2006, and 2016*. Vancouver, BC: Fraser Institute.

Estabrooks, C.A., Squires, J.E., Carleton, H.L., Cummings, G.G., & Norton P.G. (2015). Who is looking after mom and dad? Unregulated workers in Canadian long-term care homes. *Canadian Journal on Aging, 34*(1), 47–59. https://doi.org/10.1017/S0714980814000506

Evans, R.G. (2016). Hang together or hang separately: The viability of a universal health care system in an aging society. In M.L. Barer, G.L. Stoddart, K.M. McGrail, & C.B. McLeod (Eds.), *An undisciplined economist: Robert G. Evans on health economics, health care policy and population health* (pp. 127–53). Montreal, PQ/Kingston, ON: McGill-Queen's University Press.

Evans, R.G., & McGrail K.M. (2008). Richard III, Barer-Stoddart and the Daughter of Time. *Healthcare Policy, 3*(3), 18–28.

Federation of Canadian Municipalities. (2016). *Canadian infrastructure report card: Informing the future: Key messages*. Retrieved from http:// canadianinfrastructure.ca/downloads/Canadian_Infrastructure_Report _Card_Key_Messages_2016.pdf

Ferede, E. (2013). *The response of tax bases to the business cycle: The case of Alberta*. Edmonton, AB: Institute for Public Economics Policy Series, Department of Economics, University of Alberta. Retrieved from https://era .library.ualberta.ca/items/e2b596e8-89ea-4e85-a4e2-3026e44d7547

Ferguson, A. (2007, 26 August). Cocaine easier to buy than pizza. *Edmonton Journal*, A1. Retrieved from https://www.pressreader.com/canada /edmonton-journal/20070826/281487861961695

Findlay, S.S., Eastabrooks, S.A., Cohn, D., & Pollock, C. (2002). Nursing human resource planning in Alberta: What went wrong? *Policy Politics and Nursing Practice*, *3*(4), 348–57. https://doi.org/10.1177/1527154022374

Finkel, A. (2012). The boomers become the workers: Alberta, 1960–1980. In A. Finkel (Ed.), *Working people in Alberta: A history* (pp. 141–72). Edmonton, AB: Athabasca University Press.

Flood, C.M., & Archibald, T. (2001). The illegality of private health care in Canada. *CMAJ*, *164*(6), 825–30.

Flood, C.M., & May, K. (2012). A patient charter of rights: How to avoid a toothless tiger and achieve system improvement. *CMAJ*, *184*(14), 1583–7. https://doi.org/10.1503/cmaj.111050

Franks, C.E.S. (1987). *The Parliament of Canada*. Toronto: University of Toronto Press.

French, J. (2019, 17 September). New nurse practitioners coming to Alberta communities. *Edmonton Journal*. Retrieved from https://edmontonjournal .com/news/local-news/new-nurse-practitioners-coming-to-alberta-communities

French, J. (2020, 30 March). Here's what powers the Alberta government has during states of emergency. *CBC News*. Retrieved from https://www.cbc .ca/news/canada/edmonton/alberta-government-pandemic-statement-of -emergency-1.5513122

Fries, C.J. (2008). Classification of complementary and alternative medical practices: Family physicians' ratings of effectiveness. *Canadian Family Physician*, *54*(11), 1570–1

Gallichan-Lowe, S. (2018, 6 March). Alberta government losing billions of dollars in oil revenue annually: report. *Global News*, 6 March 2018. Retrieved from https://globalnews.ca/news/4065021/alberta-losing-billions-oil-revenue/

Gamble, J.-M., Eurich, D.T., & Johnson, J.A. (2010). A comparison of drug coverage in Alberta before and after the introduction of the National Common Drug Review Process. *Healthcare Policy*, *6*(2), e117–44. https://doi .org/10.12927/hcpol.2010.22037

Geddes, G. (2017). *Medicine unbundled: A journey through the minefields of Indigenous health care*. Vancouver, BC: Heritage House.

Gerein, K. (2014, 2 December). Alberta hospitals crumbling, rural facilities underused and system manipulated by politics. *Edmonton Journal*. Retrieved from https://edmontonjournal.com/news/local-news/alberta-hospitals -crumbling-rural-facilities-underused-and-system-manipulated-by-politics-with -video

Gerein, K. (2015a, 6 September). Money for midwives: Alberta promises $1.8 million. *Calgary Herald.* Retrieved from https://www.pressreader.com /canada/calgary-herald/20150916/281745563175650

Gerein, K. (2015b, 1 November). The dire state of hospitals: A political fiasco. *Alberta Views.* Retrieved from https://albertaviews.ca/dire-state-hospitals/

Gerein, K. (2016a, 12 March). Alberta physicians still failing on after-hours care, regulator finds. *Edmonton Journal.* Retrieved from https:// edmontonjournal.com/news/local-news/alberta-physicians-still-failing-on -after-hours-care-regulator-finds

Gerein, K. (2016b, 15 August) Alberta health advocate remains a work in progress two years after creation. *Edmonton Journal.* Retrieved from https:// edmontonjournal.com/news/politics/alberta-health-advocate-remains-a -work-in-progress-two-years-after-creation/

Gerein, K. (2016c, 24 August). Alberta doctors claim top spot as nation's highest earners. *Edmonton Journal.* Retrieved from https://edmontonjournal .com/news/local-news/alberta-doctors-claim-top-spot-as-nations-highest -earners

Gerein, K. (2017a, 21 March). Alberta health minister hopes to transform system with big investment in home care. *Edmonton Sun.* Retrieved from https://www.edmontonsun.com/2017/03/20/alberta-health-minister-hopes -to-transform-system-with-big-investment-in-home-care

Gerein, K. (2017b, 29 September). Alberta Health Services signs $459-million deal for massive new technology system. *Edmonton Journal.* Retrieved from https://edmontonjournal.com/news/local-news/alberta-health-services -signs-459-million-deal-for-massive-new-technology-system

Gerein, K. (2018, 2 July). New Alberta health advocate appointee to work double duty. *Edmonton Journal.* Retrieved from https://edmontonjournal .com/news/politics/new-alberta-health-advocate-appointee-to-work-double -duty

Gereluk, W. (2012). Alberta labour in the 1980s. In A. Finkel (Ed.), *Working people in Alberta: A history* (pp. 173–204). Edmonton, AB: Athabasca University Press.

Gillespie, C. (2010). *Living in hope: A response to 2009–2010 bed closure process at the Alberta Hospital.* Edmonton, AB: Parkland Institute. Retrieved from https://www.parklandinstitute.ca/living_in_hope

Giovannetti, J. (2019, 3 February) Alberta opioid overdose fatalities hit record levels last year, data show. *Globe and Mail.* Retrieved from https://www .theglobeandmail.com/canada/article-alberta-opioid-overdose-fatalities-hit -record-levels-last-year-data/

Giovannetti, J., Pereira, M., & Wolfe, J. (2017, 19 June). What happened to Alberta's cash stash: The life and death of the province's rainy-day fund. *Globe*

and Mail. Retrieved from https://www.theglobeandmail.com/news
/alberta/what-happened-to-albertas-cash-stash/article24191018/

Givetash, L. (2015, 17 June). Canada needs to invest in new hospitals, says
health care association. *Globe and Mail.* Retrieved from https://www
.theglobeandmail.com/life/health-and-fitness/health/canada-needs-to
-invest-in-new-hospitals-says-health-care-association/article25002235/

Global News. (2020, 8 April). Kenney says Alberta "definitely" has enough
personal protective equipment to last until June. *Global News.* Retrieved from
https://globalnews.ca/video/6797465/kenney-says-alberta-definitely
-has-enough-personal-protective-equipment-to-last-until-june

Goodkey, R. (2001). The Alberta perspective. In L. Bernier & E.H. Potter
(Eds.), *Business planning in Canadian public administration* (pp. 69–79).
Toronto, ON: Institute of Public Administration of Canada.

Graff-McRae, R. (2021). Time to care: Staffing and workload in Alberta's long-
ter care facilities. Edmonton, AB: Parkland Institute. Retrieved from https://
www.parklandinstitute.ca/time_to_care

Graham, K.E.R., Chorzempa, H.L., Valentine, P.A., & Magnan, J. (2012).
Evaluation health research impact: Development and implementation of
Alberta Innovates – Health Solutions impact framework. *Research Evaluation,*
21(5), 354–67. https://doi.org/10.1093/reseval/rvs027

Green, R. (1990). Physicians, entrepreneurism, and the problem of conflict of
interest. *Theoretical Medicine, 11,* 287–300. https://doi.org/10.1007
/BF00489819

Hale, G. (2013). Emergency management in Alberta: A study in multilevel
governance. In D. Henstra (Ed.), *Multilevel governance and emergency*
management in Canadian municipalities (pp. 134–89). Toronto, ON: University
of Toronto Press.

Hall, E. (1964). *Royal Commission on Health Services: Vol. 1. 1964.* Ottawa, ON:
Queen's Printer.

Hancock, T. (1993). The evolution, impact and significance of the Healthy
Cities/Healthy Communities movement. *Journal of Public Health Policy, 14*(1),
5–18. https://doi.org/10.2307/3342823

Hanrahan, H., Mackenzie, B., Orridge, C., Saunders, J., Worthington, K., &
Deber, R.B. (1992). Heritage, votes, money and medicine: Rural health
care in Alberta. In R. Deber (Ed.), *Case studies in Canadian health policy and*
management, vol. 1 (pp. 143–54). Ottawa, ON: Canadian Hospital Association
Press.

Hardcastle, L., & Ogbogu, U. (2021, 31 March). Compensation agreement
rejected by Alberta doctors was flawed. *CBC News.* Retrieved from https://

www.cbc.ca/news/canada/calgary/road-ahead-alberta-medical-association
-doctors-agreement-rejected-1.5971133

Harrison, A., Pablo, A., & Verhoef, M. (1999). The consumer's role in
co-ordination: Making sense of transitions in health care. In A. Mark & S.
Dobson (Eds.), *Organizational behaviour in health care: The research agenda*
(pp. 47–62). London, UK: Macmillan Press.

Hastings, J.E.F., & Mosley, L. (1980). Introduction: The evolution of organized
community health services in Canada. In C.A. Meilicke & J.L. Storch (Eds.),
*Perspectives on Canadian health and social services policy: History and emerging
trends* (pp. 145–55). Ann Arbor, MI: Health Administration Press.

Health Canada. (2011). *Canadian Alcohol and Drug Use Monitoring Survey.*
Retrieved from https://www.canada.ca/en/health-canada/services/health
-concerns/drug-prevention-treatment/drug-alcohol-use-statistics/canadian
-alcohol-drug-use-monitoring-survey-tables-2011.html

Health Council of Canada. (2013). *Progress report 2013: Health care renewal
in Canada.* Retrieved from https://healthcouncilcanada.ca/files
/ProgressReport2013_EN.pdf

Health Quality Council of Alberta. (2004). *Annual review 2003–2004: A catalyst
for positive change.* Retrieved from https://hqca.ca/about/annual-reports/

Health Quality Council of Alberta. (2005). *Alberta quality matrix for health.*
Retrieved from https://d10k7k7mywg42z.cloudfront.net/assets
/56a00bd2d4c9612e3610b6ce/HQCA_11x8_5_Matrix.pdf

Health Quality Council of Alberta. (2010). *Patient safety framework for Albertans.*
Retrieved from https://hqca.ca/wp-content/uploads/2018/05
/HQCA_Patient_Safety_Framework_081010.pdf

Health Quality Council of Alberta. (2013). *Continuity of Patient Care Study.*
Retrieved from https://d10k7k7mywg42z.cloudfront.net/assets
/53275975f002ff4d14000011/Dec19_ContinuityofPatientCareStudy.pdf

Health Quality Council of Alberta. (2014a). *Review of Alberta Health Services'
continuing care wait list: First available appropriate living option policy.* Retrieved
from https://d10k7k7mywg42z.cloudfront.net/assets
/538f4ef14f720a2000000016/FAALO_FINAL_Report.pdf

Health Quality Council of Alberta. (2014b). *Review of quality assurance in
continuing care health services in Alberta.* Calgary, AB: Author.

Health Quality Council of Alberta. (2014c). *Satisfaction and experience with
healthcare services: A survey of Albertans.* Retrieved from https://hqca.ca
/surveys/satisfaction-experience-with-healthcare-services/

Health Quality Council of Alberta. (2016a). *Improving continuity of care: Key
opportunities and a status report on recommendations from the 2013 Continuity of Patient*

Care Study. Retrieved from https://d10k7k7mywg42z.cloudfront.net
/assets/57867c01d4c961047f0c5e8b/Continuity_of_Care_2016_FINAL.pdf

Health Quality Council of Alberta. (2016b). *Understanding patient and provider experiences with relationship, information, and management continuity.* Retrieved from https://d10k7k7mywg42z.cloudfront.net/assets
/57b633e8a0b5dd12760bf7b8/Relationship_Information_Management
_Continuity_Aug2016.pdf

Health Quality Council of Alberta. (2017). *Provincial plan for integrated laboratory services in Alberta.* Retrieved from https://www.hqca.ca/wp
-content/uploads/2018/05/Provincial_Plan_for_Integrated_Laboratory
_Services_in_Alberta_FINAL_.pdf

Health Quality Council of Alberta. (2018). Fact sheet: 2017 long-term care family experience survey. Retrieved from https://hqca.ca/wp-content
/uploads/2018/05/HQCA_2017_LTC_Fact_Sheet.pdf

Health Quality Ontario. (2018). *Measuring Up 2018.* Retrieved from https://
hqontario.ca/Portals/0/Documents/pr/measuring-up-2018-en.pdf

Health Sciences Association of Alberta. (n.d.). Our history. Retrieved from
https://hsaa.ca/about-us/our-history/

Hooker, R.S., & Everett, C.M. (2012). The contributions of physician assistants in primary care systems. *Health and Social Care in the Community, 20*(1), 20–31. https://doi.org/10.1111/j.1365-2524.2011.01021.x

Hoskins, R. (2017, 1 April). Holy healthcare: Our religious hospitals problem. *Alberta Views.* Retrieved from https://albertaviews.ca/holy-healthcare/

Humbert, G.J. (2004). *A compendium of the Catholic Health Association of Canada: Appendix 3. Catholic hospitals in Canada.* Retrieved from http://www.chac.ca
/about/history/docs/compendium_hospitals.pdf

Hunt, S. (2020, 20 April) Additional measures to ease COVID-19 pressures at Alberta. *CTV News.* Retrieved from https://calgary.ctvnews.ca/additional
-measures-to-ease-covid-19-pressures-at-alberta-continuing-care-facilities
-1.4904339

Hurley, J., & Guindon, G.E. (2008). *Private health insurance in Canada.* Retrieved from https://macsphere.mcmaster.ca/bitstream/11375/16729/1/252967.pdf

Institute of Fiscal Studies and Democracy. (2017). *Past, present, future: Health care costs in Alberta.* Ottawa, ON: Author.

Institute of Medicine (US), Committee on the Use of Complementary and Alternative Medicine by the American Public. (2005). Introduction. In *Complementary and alternative medicine in the United States* (pp. 13–33). Washington, DC: National Academies Press. Retrieved from https://www
.ncbi.nlm.nih.gov/books/NBK83799/pdf/Bookshelf_NBK83799.pdf

Jackson, A. (2004). The unhealthy Canadian workplace. In D. Raphael (Ed.), *Social determinants of health: Canadian perspectives* (pp. 79–94). Toronto, ON: Canadian Scholars' Press.

Jin, M., Naumann, T., Regier, L., Bugden, S., Allen, M., Salach, L., ... Dolovich, L. (2012). A brief overview of academic detailing in Canada: Another role for pharmacists. *Canadian Pharmacy Journal, 154*(3), 142–6. https://doi.org/10.3821/145.3.cpj142

Kenney, J. (2020, 18 April). Happy to report. *Twitter.* Retrieved from https://twitter.com/jkenney/status/1251654816243183617

Khaliq, A., Walston, S.L., & Thompson, D.M. (2005). *The impact of hospital CEO turnover in U.S. hospitals: Final report prepared for the American College of Healthcare Executives.* Retrieved from http://citeseerx.ist.psu.edu/viewdoc/download?doi=10.1.1.619.9124&rep=rep1&type=pdf

Kotani, N., & Goldblatt, A. (1994). Alberta: A haven for health promotion. In A. Pederson, M. O'Neill, & I. Rootman (Eds.), *Health promotion in Canada: Provincial, national and international perspectives* (pp. 166–77). Toronto, ON: WB Saunders Canada.

Kury de Castillo, C. (2017, 5 June). Supervised opioid consumption site planned for Calgary, 4 applications in Edmonton. *Global News,* 5 June 2017. Retrieved from, https://globalnews.ca/news/3504532/supervised-opioid-consumption-site-planned-for-calgary-4-applications-in-edmonton/

Laframboise, H.L. (1971). Administrative reform in the federal public service: Signs of a saturation psychosis. *Canadian Public Administration, 14*(3), 303–25. https://doi.org/10.1111/j.1754-7121.1971.tb00283.x

LaJeunesse, R.A. (2002). *Political asylums.* Edmonton, AB: Muttart Foundation.

Lampard, S. (2012). The Hoadley Commission (1932–34) and health insurance in Alberta. In G.P. Marchildon (Ed.), *Making Medicare: New perspectives on the history of Medicare in Canada* (pp. 183–206). Toronto, ON: University of Toronto Press.

Landon, S., & Smith, C. (2013). Government revenue volatility in Alberta. In D.L. Ryan (Ed.), *Boom and bust again: Policy challenges for a commodity-based economy* (pp. 225–66). Edmonton, AB: University of Alberta Press.

Lawson, J. (2012). *Options for laboratory transformation.* Retrieved from https://www.health.gov.bc.ca/library/publications/year/2012/options-for-laboratory-transformation.pdf

Lee, J. (2017, 31 July). Number of Alberta doctors prescribing medical marijuana jumps 50 per cent in 4 months. *CBC News,* 31 July 2017. Retrieved from https://www.cbc.ca/news/canada/calgary/calgary-doctors-medical-marijuana-1.4227022

Lee, J. (2020, 7 May) Calgary woman moves dad from long-term care home amid calls to stop the deaths. *CBC News*. Retrieved from https://www.msn.com/en-ca/news/canada/advocates-demand-more-oversight-in-albertas-long-term-care-homes/ar-BB13Jvm5

Leonard, P., & Sweetman, A. (2015). Paying the health workforce. In G.P. Marchildon & L. Di Matteo (Eds.), *Bending the cost curve in health care: Canada's provinces in international perspective* (pp. 139–68). Toronto, ON: University of Toronto Press.

Lesage, E. (2006). *An administrative history of the government of Alberta, 1905–2005*. Edmonton, AB: Provincial Archives of Alberta.

Levinson, D.R. (2010). *Adverse events in hospitals: National incidence among Medicare beneficiaries*. Department of Health and Human Services, Office of the Inspector General. Retrieved from https://oig.hhs.gov/oei/reports/oei-06-09-00090.pdf

Lewandowski, R., & Sułkowski, Ł. (2018). New public management and hybridity in healthcare: The solution or the problem? In A.B. Savignon, L. Gnan, A. Hinna, and F. Monteduro (Eds.), *Hybridity in the governance and delivery of public services* (pp. 141–66). Bingley, UK: Emerald Publishing.

Lewis, S., & Kouri, D. (2004). Regionalization: Making sense of the Canadian experience. *Healthcare Papers, 5*(1), 12–31. https://doi.org/10.12927/hcpap.2004.16847

Liepert, R. (2009). *Changes to provincial health structures in Alberta*. Retrieved from https://www.healthinnovationforum.org/article/recent-changes-to-provincial-health-structures-in-alberta/

Ludwick, D.A., & Doucette, J. (2009). The implementation of operational processes for the Alberta electronic health record: Lessons for electronic medical record adoption in primary care. *Electronic Healthcare, 7*(4), 107–11.

Lux, M. (2016). *Separate beds: A history of Indian hospitals in Canada, 1920s–1980s*. Toronto, ON: University of Toronto Press.

Macfarlane, D., & Durbin, J. (2005). *Mental health and addiction services in regionalized health governance structures: A review: Final report*. Toronto, ON: Centre for Addiction and Mental Health.

Maclaren, V.V. (2016). Video lottery is the most harmful form of gambling in Canada. *Journal of Gambling Studies, 32*, 459–85. https://doi.org/10.1007/s10899-015-9560-z

Macpherson, C.B. (2013). *Democracy in Alberta: Social Credit and the party system*. Foreword by Nelson Wiseman. Toronto, ON: University of Toronto Press.

Macrotrends. (2020). Crude oil prices – 70 year historical chart. Retrieved from https://www.macrotrends.net/1369/crude-oil-price-history-chart

Mahaffey, C. (2013, 1 November). Home as hospital: How seniors' health care ends up costing families. *Alberta Views*. Retrieved from https://albertaviews .ca/home-as-hospital/

Mandel, C. (1998, 1 April). Who wins? Government and citizens clash over VLTs. *Alberta Views*. Retrieved from https://albertaviews.ca/who-wins/

Marchildon G. P. (2008). Reforming health management in Canada. *Health Law in Canada, 29*(2), 9–15.

Marchildon, G.P. (2013). *Health systems in transition* (2nd ed.). Toronto, ON: University of Toronto Press.

Marchildon, G.P. (2015). The crisis of regionalization. *Healthcare Management Forum, 28*(6), 236–8. https://doi.org/10.1177/0840470415599115

Marchildon, G.P. (2016). Douglas versus Manning: The ideological battle over Medicare in postwar Canada. *Journal of Canadian Studies, 50*(1), 129–49. https://doi.org/10.3138/jcs.2016.50.1.129

Marchildon, G.P., & Allin, S. (2012). Responsibility and accountability in Canadian healthcare. In B. Rosen, A. Israel, & S. Shortell (Eds.), *Responsibility and accountability in health care: Addressing an emerging global challenge* (pp. 221–6). Singapore: World Scientific.

Marchildon, G.P., Allin, S., & Merkur, S. (2020). *Canada health system review 2020.* Vol. 22, no. 3 of *Health systems in transition.* Copenhagen, DK: World Health Organization, Regional Office for Europe. https://apps.who.int/iris /handle/10665/336311

Marchildon, G.P., & Di Matteo, L. (2015). Introduction and overview. In G.P. Marchildon & L. Di Matteo (Eds.), *Bending the cost curve in health care: Canada's provinces in international perspective* (pp. xv-xxxvi). Toronto: University of Toronto Press.

Marchildon, G.P., & Lockhart, W. (2012). Common trends in public stewardship of health care. In B. Rosen, A. Israel, & S. Shortell (Eds.), *Responsibility and accountability in health care: Addressing an emerging global challenge* (pp. 255–69). Singapore: World Scientific.

McGregor, M., & Ronald, L. (2011). Residential long-term care for Canadian seniors: Non-profit, for-profit, or does it matter? IRPP Study #14. Retrieved from http://irpp.org/wp-content/uploads/2011/01/study-no14.pdf

McIntosh, A. (2020). Privatization pressures in Alberta heath care: Laboratory services, home care, and telehealth under austerity. Edmonton AB: Parkland Institute. Retrieved from https://www.parklandinstitute.ca/privatization _pressures_in_alberta_health_care

McIntosh, T. (2018). From autonomous gatekeepers to system stewards: Can the Alberta Agreement change the role of physicians in Canadian Medicare?

HealthcarePapers, 17(4), 56–62. https://doi.org/10.12927/hcpap .2018.25575

McLaren, L., Patterson, S., Thawer, S., Faris, P., McNeil, D., Potestio, M., & Shwart, L. (2016). Measuring the short-term impact of fluoridation cessation on dental caries in Grade 2 children using tooth surface indices. *Community Dentistry and Oral Epidemiology, 44*(3), 274–82. https://doi.org/10.1111 /cdoe.12215

Mertz, E. (2013, 14 November). NDP says Alberta government plans to cut nursing positions. *Global News.* Retrieved from https://globalnews.ca /news/967562/ndp-says-alberta-government-plans-to-cut-nursing-positions/

Mertz, E. (2019, 22 April). Alberta government halts construction work on superlab site in Edmonton. *Global News.* Retrieved from https://globalnews .ca/news/5191127/alberta-ucp-kenney-edmonton-superlab-health/

Morgan, S.G., Martin, D., Gagnon, M.A., Mintzes, B., Daw, J.R., & Lexchin, J. (2015). *Pharmacare 2020: The future of drug coverage in Canada.* Vancouver, BC: University of British Columbia Pharmaceutical Policy Research Collaboration.

Mossialos, E., Wenzel, M., Osborne, R., & Anderson, C. (2015). *International profiles of health care systems.* New York, NY: Commonwealth Fund.

Naugler, C., & Wyonch, R. (2019). *What the doctor ordered: Improving the use and value of laboratory testing.* Commentary No. 533. Toronto, ON: C.D. Howe Institute.

Naylor, C.D. (1986). *Private practice, public payment: Canadian medicine and the state 1911–1966.* Montreal, PQ/Kingston, ON: McGill-Queen's University Press.

NCCAM (National Center for Complementary and Alternative Medicine). (2000). *Expanding horizons of healthcare: Five-year strategic plan 2001–2005.* NIH publication, no. 01-5001. Washington DC: U.S. Department of Health and Human Services, Public Health Services, National Institutes of Health. Retrieved from https://files.nccih.nih.gov/expanding-horizons-of -healthcare-five-year-strategic-plan-2001-2005.pdf

Neilsen, L., & Sweetman, A. (2018). Measuring physicians' incomes with a focus on Canadian-controlled private corporations. *Healthcare Papers, 17*(4), 77–86. https://doi.org/10.12927/hcpap.2018.25572

Neufeld, L. (2019). "Alarming rates" of syphilis and gonorrhea continue in Alberta. *CBC News,* 3 May 2019. Retrieved from https://www.cbc.ca/news /canada/edmonton/gonorrhea-syphilis-alberta-rates-increase-strong -1.5122463

O'Brien, B., Harvey, S., Sommerfeldt, S., Beischel, S., Newburn-Cook, C., & Schopflocher, D. (2010). Comparison of costs and associated outcomes between women choosing newly integrated autonomous midwifery care and matched controls: A pilot study. *Journal of Obstetrics and Gynaecology Canada, 32*(7), 650–8. https://doi.org/10.1016/S1701 -2163(16)34568-6

O'Brien Institute of Public Health. (n.d.). Alberta fact sheet. Retrieved from https://obrieniph.ucalgary.ca/files/iph/alberta-fact-sheet.pdf

OECD (Organisation for Economic Co-operation and Development). (2010). *OECD health policy studies: Improving health sector efficiency: The role of information and communication technologies.* Retrieved from https://ec.europa.eu/health /sites/health/files/eu_world/docs/oecd_ict_en.pdf

Office of the Auditor General of Alberta. (2012). *Report of the Auditor General of Alberta, July 2012.* Retrieved from https://www.oag.ab.ca/wp -content/uploads/2020/05/2012_-_Report_of_the_Auditor_General_of _Alberta_-July_2012.pdf

Office of the Auditor General of Alberta. (2014a, September). *Report on chronic disease management.* Retrieved from https://www.oag.ab.ca /reports/oag-health-report-chronic-disease-management-sept-2014/

Office of the Auditor General of Alberta. (2014b, October). *Report of the Auditor General of Alberta.* Retrieved from https://www.oag.ab.ca/wp -content/uploads/2020/05/2014_-_Report_of_the_Auditor_General_of _Alberta_-_October_2014.pdf

Office of the Auditor General of Alberta. (2017, May). *Better healthcare for Albertans: A report by the Office of the Auditor General of Alberta.* Retrieved from https://www.oag.ab.ca/reports/bhc-report-may-2017

Office of the Child and Youth Advocate Alberta. (2018). *Summary report: Five years of investigations: April 1, 2012–March 31, 2017.* Retrieved from https:// www.ocya.alberta.ca/wp-content/uploads/2014/08/OCYARpt_2018 _Investigations_FiveYearSummary.pdf

Office of the Information and Privacy Commissioner of Alberta. (2018). About the OIPC. Retrieved from https://www.oipc.ab.ca/about-us/about-the-oipc .aspx

Onestopmap. (n.d.). Map of Alberta defined. Retrieved from https://www .onestopmap.com/alberta/alberta-705/

Ontario Health Coalition. (2020). Release & Analysis: COVID-19 death rates in Ontario long-term care homes significantly higher and increasing in for-profit homes vs. nonprofit and publicly owned homes. Retrieved from https://www.ontariohealthcoalition.ca/index.php/death-rates-in-long-term -care-by-ownership-release/

Osborne, D.E., & Gaebler, T. (1992). *Re-inventing government: How the entrepreneurial spirit is transforming the public sector.* New York, NY: Plume.

Pal, L. (1992). The political executive and political leadership in Alberta. In A. Tupper & R. Gibbons (Eds.), *Government and politics in Alberta* (pp. 31–66). Edmonton, AB: University of Alberta Press.

Palley, H.A. (2013). Long-term care service policies in three Canadian provinces: Alberta, Quebec and Ontario – Examining the national and subnational contexts. *International Journal of Canadian Studies, 47*, 57–85. https://doi.org/10.3138/ijcs.47.57

Paramedic Association of Canada. (2011). National occupational competency profile for paramedics. Retrieved from https://www.paramedic.ca/uploaded /web/documents/2011-10-31-Approved-NOCP-English-Master.pdf

Parsons, V. (2002). *Bad blood: The tragedy of the Canadian tainted blood scandal.* Toronto, ON: Lester & Orpen Dennys.

Patients Collaborating with Teams (PaCT): Patient representative goals and role. (2017). Retrieved from https://actt.albertadoctors.org/file/patient -representative-goals—role.pdf

Patten, S. (2015). The politics of Alberta's one-party state. In B.M. Evans & C.W. Smith (Eds.), *Transforming provincial politics: The political economy of Canada's provinces and territories in the neoliberal era* (pp. 255–83). Toronto, ON: University of Toronto Press.

Peach, I. (2004). *Managing complexity: The lessons of horizontal policy-making in the provinces.* The Scholar Series. Regina, SK: Saskatchewan Institute of Public Policy.

Peckham, A., Sara, K., Church, J., Chatwood, S., & Marchildon, G. (2018). *Primary care reforms in Ontario, Manitoba, Alberta, and the Northwest Territories: A rapid review prepared for the Canadian Foundation for Healthcare Improvement.* Rapid Review No. 2. Toronto, ON: North American Observatory on Health Systems and Policies. Retrieved from https://ihpme.utoronto.ca/wp-content/uploads/2018/09/NAO-Rapid -Review-2-_EN.pdf

Physician Resource Planning Committee. (2006). *Predicting physician supply and future need: 2006 update report to the Minister of Alberta Health and Wellness.* Retrieved from https://open.alberta.ca/publications/predicting -physician-supply-and-future-need

Physiotherapy Alberta – College and Association. (n.d.). [Home page]. Retrieved from https://www.physiotherapyalberta.ca/

Picard, A. (2006, 27 July). Alberta's new Lego Hospital definitely not just for kids. *Globe and Mail.* Retrieved from https://www.theglobeandmail.com /life/health-and-fitness/albertas-new-lego-hospital-definitely-not-just-for -kids/article730995/

Pike, S. (2019, 10 December). Health care coalition concerned about potential privatization in Alberta. *City News.* Retrieved from https://edmonton .citynews.ca/2019/12/10/health-care-coalition-concerned-privatization -alberta/

Plain, R.H.M. (1995). *The role played by health reform in the re-inventing of government within Alberta.* Ottawa, ON: Health Canada.

Plain, R.H.M. (1997). *Working together: The reform of regional health authority within Alberta: A report presented to the MLA Committee on the Review of Health Region Boundaries.* Edmonton, AB: MLA Committee on the Review of Health Region Boundaries.

Points West Living. (n.d.). Welcome to Points West Living [Home page]. Retrieved from http://www.pointswestliving.com

Poland, B.D., Green, L.W., & Rootman, I. (2000). *Settings for health promotion: Linking theory and practice.* Thousand Oaks, CA: Sage.

Polanyi, M. (2004). Understanding and improving the health of work. In D Raphael (Ed.), *Social determinants of health: Canadian perspectives* (pp. 95–105). Toronto, ON: Canadian Scholars' Press.

Pratt, S. (2015, 10 February). Alberta short more than 3,300 hospital beds: Study. *Edmonton Journal.* Retrieved from https://edmontonjournal.com /news/local-news/alberta-short-more-than-3300-hospital-beds-study

Provincial and Territorial Ministers of Health. (2000). *Understanding Canada's health care costs: Interim report.* Retrieved from https://www.gov.nl.ca /publicat/hreport.pdf

Public Health Agency of Canada. (n.d.). *Maternal mortality in Canada.* Retrieved from http://publications.gc.ca/site/eng/9.507441/publication.html

Quinonez, C. (2020). *Dentistry in Alberta: Time for a checkup?* Edmonton AB: The Parkland Institute. Retrieved from https://www.parklandinstitute.ca /dentistry_in_alberta

Reid, J.L., Hammond, D., Tariq, U., Burkhalter, R., Rynard, V.L., & Douglas, O. (2019). *Tobacco use in Canada: Patterns and trends, 2019 edition.* Waterloo, ON: Propel Centre for Population Health Impact, University of Waterloo.

Rennie, B.J. (2004a). *Alberta premiers of the twentieth century.* Regina, SK: University of Regina, Canadian Plains Research Centre.

Rennie, B.J. (2004b). Richard Reid, 1934–1935. In B.J. Rennie (Ed.), *Alberta premiers of the twentieth century* (pp. 107–24). Regina, SK: University of Regina, Canadian Plains Research Centre.

Ries, N., & Fisher, K. (2013). The increasing involvement of physicians in complementary and alternative medicine: Considerations of professional regulation and patient safety. *Queens Law Journal, 39*(1), 273–99.

Rose, R., & Davies, P.L. (1994). *Inheritance in public policy: Change without choice in Britain*. New Haven, CT: Yale University Press.

Rowand, R.S. (2002). Planning for Canada's health workforce: Past, present and present. *Healthcare Papers*, *3*(2), 28–32. https://doi.org/10.12927/hcpap..17147

Royal Bank of Canada. (2021). Provincial fiscal tables. September. Retrieved from http://www.rbc.com/economics/economic-reports/pdf/canadian-fiscal/prov_fiscal.pdf

Rusnell, C., & Russell, J. (2013, 20 June). Legal experts contradict Horne on Alberta Health Services executive bonuses. *CBC News*. Retrieved from https://www.cbc.ca/news/canada/edmonton/legal-experts-contradict-horne-on-Alberta Health Services-executive-bonuses-1.1317826

Ruttan, S. (2009, 1 November). Supersized: Forged in secrecy, Alberta's new health superboard continues the dismantling of public healthcare. *Alberta Views*. Retrieved from https://albertaviews.ca/supersized/

Saltman, R.B. (2008). Decentralization, re-centralization and future European health policy. *European Journal of Public Health*, *18*(2), 104–6. https://doi.org/10.1093/eurpub/ckn013

Saltman, R.B., & Ferroussier-Davis, O. (2000). The concept of stewardship in health policy. *Bulletin of the World Health Organization*, *78*(6): 732–9.

Sanofi Canada. (2020). *The 2020 Sanofi Canada Health Care Survey: Future forward*. Retrieved from https://www.sanofi.ca/-/media/Project/One-Sanofi-Web/Websites/North-America/Sanofi-CA/Home/en/Products-and-Resources/sanofi-canada-health-survey/sanofi-canada-healthcare-survey-2020-EN.pdf

Schiebelbein, J. (2012).Women, labour, and the labour movement. In A. Finkel (Ed.), *Working people in Alberta: A history* (pp. 243–65). Edmonton, AB: Athabasca University Press.

Schwartz, B., & Brent, R. (Eds). (1999). *Aging, autonomy and architecture: Advances in assisted living*. Baltimore, MD: Johns Hopkins University Press.

Sherwood, D. (2002). The state of the Healthy Communities movement in Canada. *Plan Canada*, *42*(4), 11–12. https://doi.org/10.25316/IR-489

Shortt, S.E.D., & Macdonald, J.K. (2002). Toward an accountability framework for Canadian healthcare. *Healthcare Management Forum*, *15*(2), 24–32. https://doi.org/10.1016/S0840-4704(10)60577-7

Simons, P. (2016, 13 February). Paula Simons: If Covenant Health won't obey law, it shouldn't get public funds to run public hospitals. *Edmonton Journal*. Retrieved from https://edmontonjournal.com/opinion/columnists/paula-simons-if-covenant-health-wont-obey-law-it-shouldnt-get-public-funds-to-run-public-hospitals

Simpson, J.E. (2003). Utilization patterns and trends. *Health Policy Research Bulletin*, 7, 9–13. https://doi.org/10.1016/S1464-2859(03)00035-X

Singh, A.E., & Romanowski, B. (2019). The return of syphilis in Canada: A failed plan to eliminate this infection. *Journal of the Association of Medical Microbiology and Infectious Disease Canada (JAMMI)*, 4(4), 215–17. https://doi.org/10.3138/jammi.2019-08-22

Sinnema, J. (2011, 25 July). Licensed practical nurses to step into bigger role. *Edmonton Journal*. Retrieved from https://www.pressreader.com/canada/edmonton-journal/20110725/282458525621264

Sinnema, J. (2016, 4 February). Electronic health record system will cost hundreds of millions, but is vital, government official says. *Edmonton Journal*. Retrieved from https://edmontonjournal.com/news/politics/electronic-health-record-system-will-cost-hundreds-of-million-but-is-vital-government-official-says

Smart, A. (2019, 18 December). Indigenous opposition to pipeline shouldn't outweigh others: Provinces. *Canadian Press*. Retrieved from https://www.ctvnews.ca/politics/indigenous-opposition-to-pipeline-shouldn-t-outweigh-others-provinces-1.4735682

Smith, H. (2010, 1 November). No place to age: The costs and indignities of long-term care in Alberta. *Alberta Views*. Retrieved from https://albertaviews.ca/no-place-age/

Speers, K. (2005). Performance measurement in the government of Alberta. *Governance*, 2(1), 58–76. https://doi.org/10.7202/1039148ar

Spenceley, S.M., Andres, C., Lapins, J., Wedel, R., Gelber, T., & Halma, L.M. (2013). *Accountability by design: Moving primary care reform ahead in Alberta*. Retrieved from https://www.policyschool.ca/wp-content/uploads/2016/03/s-spenceley-care-reform.pdf

Stabile, M., Thomson, S., Allin, S., Boyle, S., Busse, R., Chevreul, K., ... Mossialos, E. (2013). Health care cost containment strategies used in four other high-income countries hold lessons for the United States. *Health Affairs*, 32(4): 643–52. https://doi.org/10.1377/hlthaff.2012.1252

Staples, D. (2020, 11 April). David Staples: Masterminds behind Alberta's medical supplies surge to meet COVID-19 crisis. *Edmonton Journal*. Retrieved from https://edmontonjournal.com/opinion/columnists/david-staples-masterminds-behind-albertas-medical-supplies-surge-to-meet-covid-19-crisis/

Stark, E. (2016, 10 March). Albertans have highest debt load in Canada, Equifax says. *CBC News*. Retrieved from https://www.cbc.ca/news/canada/calgary/alberta-calgary-consumer-debt-equifax-1.3484940

Starr, P. (1982). *The social transformation of American medicine.* New York, NY: Basic Books.

STARS. (2021). Mission record. Retrieved from https://stars.ca/helicopter-air -ambulance/mission-record/ab/

Statistics Canada. (2008). Table 1. Health regions reference maps. Retrieved from https://www150.statcan.gc.ca/n1/pub/82-583-x/2010001/article /11229-eng.pdf

Statistics Canada. (2011). Focus on geography series, 2011 census: Province of Alberta. Retrieved from https://www12.statcan.gc.ca/census -recensement/2011/as-sa/fogs-spg/Facts-pr-eng.cfm?Lang=eng&GC=48

Statistics Canada. (2012). Table 2.1: Population estimates, age distribution and median age as of July 1, 2012, Canada, provinces and territories. Retrieved from https://www.statcan.gc.ca/pub/91-215-x/2012000/t583-eng.htm

Statistics Canada. (2016a). Population projections for Canada (2013 to 2063), provinces and territories (2013–2038): Section 3: Results at the provincial and territorial levels, 2013–2038. Retrieved from https://www.statcan.gc.ca /pub/91-520-x/2014001/section03-eng.htm#a11

Statistics Canada. (2016b). Table 15.7: Land and freshwater area, by province and territory. Retrieved from https://www150.statcan.gc.ca/n1/pub/11 -402-x/2010000/chap/geo/tbl/tbl07-eng.htm

Statistics Canada. (2017a). Health at a glance. Retrieved from https://www150 .statcan.gc.ca/n1/pub/82-624-x/2012001/article/11696-eng.htm

Statistics Canada. (2017b). Health Indicators, 2017. Retrieved from https:// www150.statcan.gc.ca/n1/pub/82-221-x/82-221-x2013001-eng.htm

Statistics Canada. (2018a). Table 13-10-0710-01: Deaths and mortality rates, by age group. Retrieved from https://www150.statcan.gc.ca/t1/tbl1/en /tv.action?pid=1310071001

Statistics Canada. (2018b). Table 13-10-0371-01: Life expectancy at birth and at age 65. Retrieved from https://www150.statcan.gc.ca/t1/tbl1/en /tv.action?pid=1310037101

Statistics Canada. (2018c). Table 13-10-0743-01: Premature and potentially avoidable mortality, three-year average, Canada, provinces, territories, health regions and peer groups. Retrieved from https://www150.statcan.gc.ca/t1 /tbl1/en/tv.action?pid=1310074301

Statistics Canada. (2019). Table 17-10-0009-01: Population estimates, quarterly. Retrieved from https://www150.statcan.gc.ca/t1/tbl1/en /tv.action?pid=1710000901

Statistics Canada. (2020) Table: 13-10-0096-01 (formerly CANSIM 105): Health characteristics, annual estimates. Retrieved from https://www150.statcan .gc.ca/t1/tbl1/en/cv.action?pid=1310009601

Stefanick, L. (2013, June). *Transparency, accountability and good governance: Is Alberta cursed?* Paper presented at the conference of the Canadian Association of Political Science, Victoria, BC. Retrieved from https://auspace.athabascau. ca/bitstream/handle/2149/3372/Stefanick%2C%20Lorna_CPSA.2013.pdf

Stewart, D.K., & Archer, K. (2001). *Quasi-democracy? Parties and leadership selection in Alberta.* Vancouver, BC: UBC Press.

Stoddart, G.L., & Barer, M.L. (1992). Toward integrated medical resource policies for Canada: 6. Remuneration of physicians and global expenditure policy. *CMAJ, 147*(1), 33–8.

Sutherland, J.M., & Crump, R.T. (2013). Alternative level of care: Canada's hospital beds, the evidence and options. *Healthcare Policy, 9*(1), 26–34. https://doi.org/10.12927/hcpol.2013.23480

Sutherland, J.M., Repin, N., & Crump, R.T. (2012). *Reviewing the potential roles of financial incentives for funding healthcare in Canada.* Ottawa, ON: Canadian Foundation for Healthcare Improvement.

Sutherland, J.M., Repin, N., & Crump, R.T. (2013). *The Alberta Health Services patient/care based funding model for long term care: A review and analysis.* Vancouver, BC: University of British Columbia, Centre for Health Services and Policy Research.

Sutherland, R. (2011). *False positive: Private profit in Canada's medical laboratories.* Halifax, NS: Fernwood.

Sutherland, R. (2012). The effect of for-profit laboratories on the accountability, integration, and cost of Canadian health care services. *Open Medicine, 6*(4), e166-70.

Sutherland, R.W., & Fulton, M.J. (1992). *Health care in Canada: A description and analysis of Canadian health services.* Ottawa, ON: The Health Group.

Taft, K., & Steward, G. (2000). *Clear answers: The economics and politics of for-profit medicine.* Edmonton, AB: University of Alberta Press.

Tait, C.L., Butt, P., Henry, R., & Bland, R. (2017). "Our next generation": Moving towards a surveillance and prevention framework for youth suicide in Saskatchewan First Nations and Métis population. *Canadian Journal of Community Mental Health, 36*(1), 55–65. https://doi.org/10.7870/cjcmh-2017-004

Taylor, M.G. (1987). *Health insurance and Canadian public policy: The seven decisions that created the Canadian health care system* (2nd ed.). Montreal, PQ/ Kingston, ON: McGill-Queen's University Press.

Theman, T. (2016, 2 August). *Trevor's take on: Alberta Health review of PCNs. The Messenger.* Retrieved from http://www.cpsa.ca/trevors-take-on-alberta -health-review-of-pcns/

Tombe, T. (2020, 28 April). For Alberta, the day of fiscal reckoning has arrived. *CBC News.* Retrieved from https://www.cbc.ca/news/canada

/calgary/road-ahead-opinion-trevor-tombe-alberta-fiscal-reckoning-1
.5546481

Tully, P., & Saint-Pierre, E. (1997). Downsizing Canada's hospitals, 1986/87 to
1994/95. *Health Reports, 8*(4), 33–9.

Tupper, A. (2004). Peter Lougheed, 1971–1985. In B.J. Rennie (Ed.), *Alberta
premiers of the twentieth century* (pp. 203–28). Regina, SK: University of Regina,
Canadian Plains Research Centre.

Tupper, A., & Doern, G.B. (1990). Alberta budgeting in the Lougheed era. In
A.M. Maslove (Ed.), *Budgeting in the provinces: Leadership and the premiers* (pp.
121–41). Toronto, ON: Institute of Public Administration of Canada.

Tupper, A., Pratt, L., & Urquhart, I. (1992). The role of government.
In A. Tupper & R. Gibbons (Eds.), *Government and politics in Alberta* (pp. 31–
66). Edmonton, AB: University of Alberta Press.

United Nurses of Alberta. (2002). *The first 25 years, 1977–2002: Strength in unity.*
Retrieved from https://www.una.ca/files/uploads/2013/8/1977-2002
_UNA_History_Document.pdf

United Nurses of Alberta. (2018). [Home page]. Retrieved from https://www
.una.ab.ca/

University of Alberta. (n.d.-a). Faculty of Medicine and Dentistry: Our faculty.
Retrieved from https://www.ualberta.ca/medicine/about/whyfomd
/ourfaculty/index.html

University of Alberta. (n.d.-b). Faculty of Nursing: Program description.
Retrieved from https://www.ualberta.ca/nursing/programs/graduate
-programs-and-admissions/master-of-nursing-program/program-description
.html

University of Calgary. (2015). *Cumming School of Medicine strategic plan 2015–
2020.* Retrieved from https://issuu.com/ucalgarymedicine/docs
/csmstrategicplan2015web

Urquhart, I. (2010, 1 October). Petrostate: When an overdeveloped sense
of prosperity causes an underdeveloped sense of democracy. *Alberta Views.*
Retrieved from https://albertaviews.ca/petrostate/

Vayda, E., & Deber, R.B. (1992). The Canadian health-care system: A
developmental overview. In C.D. Naylor (Ed.), *Canadian health care and the
state: A century of evolution* (pp. 125–40). Montreal, PQ/Kingston, ON: McGill-
Queen's University Press.

Walker, R. (1993, 19 January). Alberta to cut medical enrollment by 10%.
Medical Post.

Wang, C.H., & Kuo, N.W. (2006). Zeitgeists and development trends in long-
term care facility design. *Journal of Nursing Research, 14*(2), 123–32. https://
doi.org/10.1097/01.JNR.0000387570.43727.12

Wang, F.-L., & Twilley, L. (2006). *Predictors of multiple births and infant deaths in Alberta.* Edmonton, AB: Alberta Health and Wellness.

Wasylenko, E. (2013). Jugglers, tightrope walkers, and ringmasters: Priority setting, allocation and reducing moral burden. *Healthcare Management Forum, 26*(2), 77–81. https://doi.org/10.1016/j.hcmf.2013.04.006

Welds, K. (2017, 21 March). Drug plan trends report: Alarm about costs sparks "monumental shift." *Benefits Canada.* Retrieved from https://www.benefitscanada.com/news/drug-plan-trends-report-alarm-about-costs-sparks-monumental-shift-95051

Wellesley Institute. (2015). *Low earnings, unfilled prescriptions: Employer-provided health benefit coverage in Canada.* Retrieved from http://www.wellesleyinstitute.com/wp-content/uploads/2015/07/Low-Earnings-Unfilled-Prescriptions-2015.pdf

Wherry, A. (2020, 25 April). Can this pandemic be the crisis that finally forces us to fix long-term care? *CBC News.* Retrieved from https://www.cbc.ca/news/politics/covid-pandemic-coronavirus-long-term-care-1.5544722

Whiteside, H. (2015). *Purchase for profit: Public-private partnerships and Canada's public health care system.* Toronto, ON: University of Toronto Press.

Wild, C., Wolfe, J., Wang, J., & Ohinmaa, A. (2014). *Gap analysis of public mental health and addiction programs (GAP-MAP): Final report.* Edmonton, AB: University of Alberta, School of Public Health. Retrieved from https://open.alberta.ca/publications/gap-analysis-of-public-mental-health-and-addictions-programs-gap-map-final-report

Williams, R.J., Belanger, R.D., & Arthur, J.N. (2011). *Gambling in Alberta: History, current status, and socioeconomic impacts. Final report to the Alberta Gaming Research Institute.* Retrieved from https://prism.ucalgary.ca/handle/1880/48495

Wilson, D.R., Woodhead-Lyons, S.C., & Moores, D.G. (1998). Alberta's Rural Physician Action Plan: An integrated approach to education, recruitment and retention. *CMAJ, 158*(3), 351–4.

Wood, J. (2015, 9 May). NDP will scrap health care levy, some fee increases. *Calgary Herald.* Retrieved from https://calgaryherald.com/news/politics/ndp-will-scrap-health-care-levy-some-fee-increases

Wright, S. (2013, 21 July). The home care consolidation debacle: Fred Horne's mission impossible. *Susan on the Soap Box* (blog). Retrieved from https://susanonthesoapbox.com/2013/07/21/the-home-care-consolidation-debacle-fred-hornes-mission-impossible/

Yourex-West, H. (2015, 11 June). New rules say Alberta doctors must provide after-hours care. *Edmonton Journal.* Retrieved from https://globalnews.ca/news/2050461/new-rules-say-alberta-doctors-must-provide-after-hours-care/

Yun, T. (2021, 3 May). "It'll crash tremendously": Alberta now leads Canada and U.S. in per capita COVID-19 cases. *CTV News*. Retrieved from https://www.ctvnews.ca/health/coronavirus/it-ll-crash-tremendously-alberta-now-leads-canada-and-u-s-in-per-capita-covid-19-cases-1.5412090

Zelmer, J., & Leeb, K. (2004). CIHI survey: Challenges for providing maternity services: The impact of changing birthing practices. *Healthcare Quarterly*, 7(3), 21–3. https://doi.org/10.12927/hcq.2004.16459

Zwicker, J., & Emery, H. (2015). *How is funding medical research better for patients? Valuing the impact of Alberta's health research*. Retrieved from https://www.policyschool.ca/wp-content/uploads/2016/03/funding-medical-research-zwicker-emery.pdf

Index

Printed and bound by CPI Group (UK) Ltd, Croydon, CR0 4YY

13/04/2025

14656517-0003